|  |  |  |
|---|---|---|
|  |  |  |
|  |  |  |
|  |  |  |
|  |  |  |
|  |  |  |

# THE LIFE AND LYRICS OF ANDREW MARVELL

# The Life and Lyrics of
# Andrew Marvell

## Michael Craze

*First published 1979 by*
**THE MACMILLAN PRESS LTD**
*London and Basingstoke*
*Associated companies in Delhi*
*Dublin Hong Kong Johannesburg Lagos*
*Melbourne New York Singapore Tokyo*

*Printed in Great Britain by*
*Billings and Sons Ltd*
*Guildford, London and Worcester*

---

**British Library Cataloguing in Publication Data**

Craze, Michael
 The life and lyrics of Andrew Marvell
 1. Marvell, Andrew – Criticism and interpretation
 I. Title II. Marvell, Andrew
 821'.4        PR3546

 ISBN 0–333–26250–6

---

To my wife Carol and our family

# Contents

## Contents

# Preface

Marvell's fame as a lyrical poet may have been 'slower than empires' to grow, but it is now worldwide. Every American and Commonwealth university's English faculty gives lectures on Marvell. Every final examination on seventeenth-century literature asks a question on him. His extra-mural admirers are legion. More and more teenagers in schools are studying him. The one pity at present is that so many see so few of his poems or, worse, see only excerpts.

In this book all the lyrics are printed in full, in the order in which I suggest they were written. Each has its own chapter. Where relevant, I translate Marvell's Latin. 'He was a great master of the Latin tongue', wrote John Aubrey in the 1680s. 'An excellent poet in Latin or English: for Latin verse there was no man could come into competition with him.' In 'The Garden' (26) I have translated 'Hortus', his Latin poem on the same theme. In 'On a Drop of Dew' (33) I have translated its Latin twin, 'Ros'. I have summarised the Latin lines on Oliver St John's 'Embassy' (19) and translated the Latin 'Epigramma in Duos Montes' ('Epigram on Two Mounts') (20); half of it covers the same ground as 'Upon the Hill and Grove at Bill-borow' (21).

In my commentaries I have sought to bridge the gap of three centuries between his day and ours. He knew all his Bible, in the Authorised Version of 1611. His readers did too. We do not. He had Greek and Latin literature and mythology at his finger tips. Many of his readers had too. We have not.

In the actual arrangement of a chapter I have followed no set routine. Sometimes I print the whole lyric and then add my comment. Most often I divide the lyric into appropriate sections and comment on one at a time.

I have printed no separate notes, but I am always concerned with the sense. Marvell knew what he meant and it ought to be possible to roll the years back and stand where he stood. I frequently disagree with the usual explanations. My own are sometimes novel, sometimes revolutionary; they are never made without thought.

Except where specifically stated, my text is substantially that of
H. M. Margoliouth in Volume I of *The Poems and Letters of Andrew
Marvell*, second edition (Oxford University Press, 1952), as modified
by P. Legouis and E. E. Duncan-Jones in the third edition (1971). But I
have also taken full account of Bodleian MS. Eng. poet. d. 49, which I
read at Oxford in 1958 and which has been so much more accessible
since 1969 when The Scolar Press Limited, Menston, Yorkshire,
England, published the pages of inked corrections in their facsimile of
Marvell's *Miscellaneous Poems 1681*. I have not accepted half the
corrections that E. S. Donno did in her *Andrew Marvell: The Complete
Poems* (Penguin Books, 1972), but I accept many more than Legouis
and Duncan-Jones.

I began researching 'The Life' in 1955. In the 23 years since then
many persistent enquirers have uncovered many new facts. We know
much more now about the 1640s, the ten years that took the poet
from age 19 to age 29, a key decade in anyone's life. I write rather
more than is usual about the poet's father, who in my view was not a
Puritan, but an orthodox Anglican priest until Archbishop Laud
altered orthodoxy. I give my authorities in my notes at the end of
'The Life'.

In conclusion, I wish to thank my son Peter, an English specialist,
for kindly reading my original typescript and making many helpful
suggestions. And I should like to thank my friend Mrs Judith
Lavalette for typing the whole book twice.

*24 September 1978*                                      *Michael Craze*

# THE LIFE

The Marvells were South Cambridgeshire farmers. They were living in Meldreth and Shepreth for 300 years before their first scholar was born. His school is not known, but he was christened Andrew at Shepreth on 12 April 1580 and he entered Emmanuel College, Cambridge in 1601. He stayed there the full seven years for his Master's degree and then worked in the East Riding of Yorkshire for thirty-three years as a priest.

Andrew Marvell the poet was this priest's son. He was born on 31 March 1621 in the rectory of Winestead near Hull, the fourth child and first son of Anne Marvell (née Pease). Her fifth and last child, John, died aged one year, and Andrew therefore grew up as an only son with three elder sisters, Anne, Mary, Elizabeth.

He grew up in Hull. From 1624 on, Mr Marvell served the Corporation there as Master of the Charterhouse and Lecturer in Holy Trinity Church. He lived in the Charterhouse, an almshouse that flourishes still, and saw to the almsfolk and chapel. He preached in the mayoral church. Though Hull was a city and county, it did not become a parish until 1661;[1] Holy Trinity Church was a chapel-of-ease in the parish of Hessle, whose vicar preached there.

Mr Marvell redressed this imbalance. Such indeed was his ultimate fame that Thomas Fuller's *The Worthies of England* (1662) included him in the two dozen Worthies of Cambridgeshire. Fuller paid him this tribute:

> . . . he was well-beloved; most *facetious* in his discourse, yet *grave* in his *carriage*; a most excellent preacher who like a good husband never *broached* what he had new brewed, but preached what he had pre-studied some competent time before; insomuch that he was wont to say that he would cross the common proverb which called *Saturday* the working day and *Munday* the holy day of preachers.

Fuller ended: 'His excellent comment upon Saint Peter is daily desired and expected, if the envy and covetousness of private persons, for their own use, deprive not the public of the benefit thereof.' Of this commentary there is no sign, but a sermon of his entitled 'Israel and England parallel'd' is in the Inner Temple Library. He preached it in October 1626, wrote it out fair on 28 April 1627 and sent it to Mrs Anne Sadleir, a daughter of the great lawyer Sir Edward Coke, with an epistle dedicatory which calls her 'one who hath bene a constant benefactresse to me and my family'. Other sermons and writings of his fill an octavo MS. volume in Hull Central Library. In the early eighteenth century it belonged to John Warburton, Somerset Herald, who wrote in it: 'Mr Andrew Marvell of Kingston Super Hull was the writer of the within Sermons etc. He was a Presbitrion Minister there and Father of A. Marvell the Poet.' A careful reading of the volume, however, shows the writer to have been no Presbyterian, but an orthodox Anglican divine, faithful to his ordination vows and the prayer book and loyal to the Crown. His death in January 1641 saved him from the dilemmas of the Civil Wars and the onset of Presbyterianism. As his son wrote of him thirty years later: 'He dyed before ever the War broke out, having lived with some measure of reputation, both for Piety and Learning: and he was moreover a Conformist to the established Rites of the Church of England, though I confess none of the most over-running or eager in them.'[2] He was no Laudian high church man, but he observed all the saints' days and wore a surplice in church.

The family's move from Winestead to Hull when the child Andrew was three and a half solved the problem of his schooling. Hull had a first-class Grammar School with strong Cambridge connections. Its one hundred boys ranged in age from four to eighteen and were taught by two clerics. James Burney was Master until he became vicar of Beverley in 1632 and then Anthony Stephenson the Usher took over. Both men were graduates of Trinity College, Cambridge and it must have been on their recommendation that Andrew Marvell went to Trinity, and went when he did.

The College's extant Admission Books do not begin until 1635, but the boy signed the Cambridge University roll (matriculated) as of Trinity College on 14 December 1633, aged twelve years and eight months. Since the university term ran from 10 October to 16 December, he must have gone up when just twelve and a half. Thirteen was not an uncommon age of entry for a clever boy, but the last twelve-year-old to matriculate from Trinity had been Francis Bacon sixty years before.

Only a few facts are certain about Andrew Marvell's Cambridge career.[3] The first is that a Latin poem and a Greek poem of his were printed in *Musarum Cantabrigiensium Concentus et Congratulatio*, the volume with which the University complimented the King and Queen on the birth of Princess Anne on 17 March 1637. Some 120 of the 2500 men in residence contributed, from the Vice-Chancellor down. A mere handful, headed by the Professor, contributed Greek. The fifteen-year-old Marvell wrote a fifty-two-line updated version of Horace's 'Ode to Octavian on the Victory of Actium' and a ten-line Greek epigram based on the new baby's being the fifth child, an unlucky number because of the Gowrie Conspiracy on 5 August 1600 and the Gunpowder Plot on 5 November 1605, but now lucky at last. Both poems were manifestly 'pre-studied'. Neither pretended to know the sex of the babe. Other future national poets to contribute were Joseph Beaumont, Richard Crashaw and Abraham Cowley. Edward King, soon to be the Lycidas of John Milton, was also there.

Trinity College made Marvell a Scholar on 13 April 1638. On 28 April his mother was buried at Hull. On 27 November of the same year his father re-married. The new Mrs Marvell had been born Lucy Alured and had lived in the Charterhouse at Hull when her father was Master. She married, first, Francis Darley in 1612 and their daughter, Edith Darley, was now Mrs Robert Moore of Hull and had a one-year-old son. Widowed, she married a Mr Harris. Then she was widowed again. As the second Mrs Marvell, she returned to her childhood home. In March 1639 her stepson Andrew Marvell took his B.A. degree. Later in the year her daughter died, leaving a motherless grandson.

On 23 January 1641 worse befell. Mr Marvell was being ferried home from Barton-on-Humber when the boat capsized on a sandbank and he was drowned. This, at any rate, was what Fuller wrote after he had consulted the family some fifteen years later. He added a marginal note that the drowned man was 'with Mrs Skinner (daughter of Sir Ed. Coke) a very religious Gentlewoman'. Certainly Mrs Bridget Skinner, widow, was all those things: she was also, like her sister Mrs Sadleir above, an old family friend of the Marvells. She lived at Thornton Curtis, Lincolnshire, five miles from Barton, and one can believe that Mr Marvell was returning from there. But Mrs Skinner herself was not drowned. She made her last will seven years later and in 1653 it was proved by Cyriack Skinner, her son and executor.

Mr Marvell's body was never found. There was therefore no inquest or funeral. Andrew was still at Cambridge, working for his M.A. Presumably he hurried home on receipt of the news, and apparently he did not return to his studies. In September the College, because of his absence, formally gave him three months' notice. He never proceeded with his M.A. At Hull he had two married sisters: Anne was Mrs James Blaydes and Mary Mrs Edmond Popple; Elizabeth was twenty-two and unmarried. The Corporation let her and her stepmother stay on in the Charterhouse. It gave William

Styles £150 a year to be non-resident Master of the Charterhouse and Lecturer in Holy Trinity Church. It is from his 1643 Charterhouse Accounts that we know Mrs Marvell stayed on, for one item reads: 'paid for worke done about Mrs Marvile's house 16s. 9d.'.

Elizabeth had a husband by then. She had married the widower Robert Moore and had taken charge of his son, her stepmother's grandson.

As for Andrew, the story persisted in Hull that he was at one time a clerk there. In 1829 an old house in High Street was taken down and two objects were made from the timber. John Stone made a circular box which he inscribed: 'In memory of Andrew Marvell, the celebrated patriot, of Kingston-upon-Hull, this box is formed from oak out of a building where he served his clerkship'. A metal plate on an armchair in the White Hart in 1864 recorded that its oak came 'from the building in High Street where it is said the celebrated and patriotic Andrew Marvell served his clerkship'. If the story is true, he is most likely to have been a clerk in 1641. Nothing else is known of his activities in that year.

On 22 April 1642 the Governor of Hull obeyed the Parliament and denied entrance to the King. It has always been thought unlikely that Marvell was there and now it is known for certain that on 17 February 1642 he was resident in London. On that day he took the new statutory oath of Protestant Allegiance before Robert List, Constable of St Sepulchre's parish, who entered him as dwelling on the north side of Cowcross.[4] It is also known that on 8, 10 and 21 February he 'witnessed' three Savile family deeds.[5] Presumably that was in London: the two witnesses who signed above him were both London lawyers.

On 31 March 1642 Andrew Marvell came of age. By then the Hull lawyers had had fourteen months to deal with his father's affairs. No will has survived, but the only son probably inherited some money as well as some books. One thing is certain. He inherited his grandfather's Meldreth estate. The old man had been buried at Hull on 13 April 1628 ('Andrew Marvell yeoman', the register said) and two faded deeds have survived which relate to the poet's sale of the property.[6]

The main deed was signed by the poet on 12 November 1647. It conveyed from 'Andrew Marvell of Kingston super Hull gentleman' to 'John Stacey of Orwell in the County of Cambridge gentleman', in return for a certain (but unstated) sum of English money to be paid at and upon the sealing and delivery of these presents,

All that messuage or tenement with a croft to the same adjoining and one close of land containing by estimation three acres and a half be it more or less situate lying and being in Meldreth in the county of Cambridge aforesaid between the lands late of the said Andrew Marvell now John Stacey on both sides the east end abutting on the King's highway called the south end street And the west end upon a certain water course called Fullbrook.

The deed goes on to grant powers of attorney to Henry Gosling and Robert Ashhust to give seisin of the property to John Stacey on Marvell's behalf. But on 23 December 1647 the deed was endorsed:

Sealed and delivered was this present deed and also possession state and seisin of the within mentioned messuage or tenement was properly and peaceably taken and delivered by the within named Andrew Marvell to the within named John Stacey according to the effect and true meaning of this deed notwithstanding the letter of attorney within inserted.

The one clue to the selling price is a separate small bond, dated also 12 November 1647, binding Andrew Marvell in the sum of £80 to carry out his side of the bargain. It is in Latin with an English explanation beneath.

The least that the sale brought Marvell would be £40, half the penal £80. The most would be the full £80. But two facts to note are: first, that the poet was thus personally engaged on 12 November and 23 December 1647; second, that he had already in a separate earlier transaction sold to the same John Stacey lands to the north and south of this three-and-a-half-acre meadow and bordering the full length of both sides.

These new facts have to be fitted in with an old one, namely that at some stage in the 1640s Marvell was on the Continent for four years. When John Milton introduced him by a dictated letter dated 21 February 1653 to Lord President Bradshaw, he said: 'His father was the Minister of Hull, and he hath spent four years abroad in Holland, France, Italy, and Spaine, to very good purpose, as I believe, and the gaineing of these four languages'.[7] The problem is to place those four years.

We can safely assume that he learnt his Dutch, French, Italian and Spanish in that order and gave roughly one year to each. The fixing of any year would thus tend to fix all. Fortunately one year can be fixed.

There are two ways of arriving at the Italian year and they coincide. There is, first, his Horatian satire 'Fleckno, an English Priest at Rome', based on an acquaintance with this Londoner in Rome one Lent. Now Richard Flecknoe, a Catholic priest, left England in 1640 for Ghent, went on to Brussels in 1642 and Paris in 1644. From Paris he was sent to Rome with a commission to secure from the Vatican the legalisation of the marriage of Beatrix de Cusance, Duchess of Lorrain, to King Charles IV and he had funds for that purpose. He was in Rome all 1645 and most of 1646.[8] Marvell caricatured him as a bad poet and worse musician living in an attic no bigger than a coffin and so poverty-stricken as to be not so much fasting as living on air. This points to Lent 1646.

There is, secondly, the fact that in the autumn of 1645 the seventeen-year-old Duke of Buckingham and sixteen-year-old Lord Francis Villiers, his brother, arrived in Rome with their tutor and a large retinue and rented a house on the Trinità del Monte until 21 May 1646 when they left for home.[9] Two years later Francis was killed and Marvell wrote 'An Elegy upon the Death of my Lord Francis Villiers'. That adjective 'my' and every line of the elegy attest a friendship that can only have been sealed in Rome. And there was the Spanish year still to come.

Our conclusion is that Marvell left London in the spring of 1643 for Holland and sailed back to London or Hull at the end of the 1647 summer. He then set about replenishing his purse by negotiating the final Meldreth property sale. He would have wasted no time before putting this in hand and collecting four years' rent.

His travels were not a grand tour. He was grafting four modern languages on to his Latin and Greek. He was, in the long term, preparing for a public career. The situation was the same then as thirty years later when in 1676 Samuel Pepys wrote to Peter Skinner in Holland:

> . . . wishing only that since you are abroad you could find yourself in a condition of passing so much time there and in France as might suffice for the making you master of the French and Dutch languages, which are with more facility to be obtained abroad, and without which no man under any public character can, as the world goes, support himself in any public charge, either here or in any foreign court.

As the world went in 1646, the Italian and Spanish languages were equally marketable.

It is time to discard the idea that he travelled abroad as a tutor at some unidentified nobleman's expense. He needed to be independent. He was not without means. To what moneys he could put together in Hull from his father's estate and from friends and relations, he was able to add the proceeds of his first Meldreth land sales to John Stacey. They may have been large. He could still afford not to sell at that stage his grandfather's house and home meadow, which instead he presumably let. No parent would in any case have entrusted a son to the care of such an untravelled novice.

One has only to look at the miniature portrait of Marvell, supposedly painted by Franz Cleyn (Francis Clein of Mortlake), in the Duke of Buccleuch's Collection. Legouis has dubbed it 'the dreamy young man, gazing queerly'.[10] 'Young man' he certainly is, not the returned traveller aged twenty-six or more.

Cleyn's 'pencil', however, has brought out the poet in Marvell, not 'dreaming' so much as listening with pleasure to other men's words. We know that he left behind him in England one poem of lyrical merit, the original draft of 'A Dialogue between Thyrsis and Dorinda' in the 1681 Folio. In 1952 J. P. Cutts found it in the British Museum in the writing of William Lawes, set to his music but with no poet's name.[11] Since the Royalist Lawes lost his life in the Rowton Heath engagement near Chester in September 1645, the music was earlier than that and the poem earlier still. There is no gainsaying this.

Nor is it surprising. Lawes was in Richard Lovelace's Royalist circle[12] and Marvell and Lovelace were friends from their Cambridge days. They may have met again in London after Lovelace's release from prison in June 1642 and for most of 1643–46 Lovelace was in Holland and France. He came back to London late in 1646. When Marvell came back a year later, the first poem that he wrote for publication was entitled 'To his Noble Friend Mr Richard Lovelace upon his Poems'. It can be confidently dated in, or very soon after, December 1647. Lines 21–4 explicitly say that Lovelace's manuscript book had just gone to the Licensers:

> The barbed Censurers begin to looke
> Like the grim consistory on thy Booke;
> And on each line cast a reforming eye,
> Severer then the yong Presbytery.

Parliament had reformed the Church of England in 1645 by forcing the parishes into the Scottish Presbyterian mould, with every ten or twelve grouped into one Presbytery or Class and a Synod overseeing the Classes. The Royalists hated the change. In 1644 Parliament had passed the 'Ordinance for Printing', under which all manuscripts had to be licensed by the appropriate Committee before any printer could touch them. How long the licensing took one cannot say, but Lovelace was highly suspect and his 'Poems called Lucasta or Epodes, Odes, Sonnetts, songs' was licensed on 4 February 1648. It was not published until fifteen months later on 14 May 1649, but for ten of those months Lovelace was back in prison.

The Licensers cannot have seen Marvell's poem. It was slipped in. Among sixteen commendatory poems it came tenth, signed 'Andr. Marvell'.

Neither did the Licensers see 'An Elegy upon the Death of my Lord Francis Villiers', which was privately printed without any author's name or date. The author, however, was Marvell and 1648 was the date. His friend Lord Francis took part in a minor Royalist rising and was killed on 7 July 1648 at Kingston-upon-Thames, two miles from the seat of his sister, Mary Duchess of Richmond and Lennox. Marvell brought her into the poem as if he knew her. He had certainly known her husband's brothers, Lord John and Lord Bernard Stuart; they were at Trinity with him and their work also appeared in ' *Musarum Cantabrigiensium Concentus*' in 1637; both had already been killed fighting for the King. It is likely, then, that Marvell took his Villiers Elegy to the Richmonds at Richmond and that they had it printed. The dead man's mother and brother were abroad. No-one in 1648 would have cared to submit to the Parliamentary Licensers a poem whose opening apostrophe to Fame included:

> Much rather thou I know expectst to tell
> How heavy Cromwell gnasht the earth and fell.
> Or how slow Death farre from the sight of day
> The long-deceived Fairfax bore away.
>
> (ll. 13 – 16)

Marvell's next elegy was printed over his name a year later and more dispassionately entitled 'Upon the Death of Lord Hastings'. The circumstances were ironic but uncontroversial. Henry Lord Hastings died of smallpox on 24 June 1649, aged nineteen, on the eve of his intended marriage with Elizabeth, daughter of the great Court physician Sir Theodore Mayerne, who could not save him. Henry Lord Hastings was the only son and heir of the Earl and Countess of Huntingdon and in their grief they commissioned the unemployed playwright Richard Brome to edit a memorial volume *Lachrymae Musarum, The Tears of the Muses*. A note in the 1649 edition explained that seventy-five pages had been printed when Marvell's poem and some others arrived and these were appended as 'Postcript Elegies'. In the 1650 edition, however, Marvell's was moved up to page 43.

He wrote two poems in 1650 which can be dated to the month, 'An Horatian Ode upon Cromwell's Return from Ireland' in July and 'Tom May's Death' in December. Neither was printed. Both have a London background. The first is so good that it destroys the case of those critics who seek to postpone the best lyrics to a year when Marvell could be considered mature. In his thirtieth year, when he wrote this, he was mature.

The conclusion, then, is that in the three years 1648−50 he was living in London on his £40 or £80, working at his own poems and poetry in general and cultivating the society of current poets and artists. For instance, he watched the painter Peter Lely at work. It is equally clear that, until the regicides executed Charles I on 30 January 1649, Marvell was a loyal subject who kept Royalist company and shared his companions' distrust of Cromwell and Fairfax. Eighteen months later the whole climate had changed. When Cromwell rode into London as the conqueror of Ireland, Marvell admired the new leader and drew parallels with Republican Rome and held out patriotic hopes of an English resurgence in Europe under him:

> A Caesar he ere long to Gaul,
> To Italy an Hannibal,
>     And to all States not free
>     Shall Clymaterick be.

Four months later, however, when Thomas May died in the night, Marvell ridiculed the Royalist turncoat in a stinging satire. Critics have puzzled over the paradox here, that an apparent conversion to Cromwell in July should in November be followed by an attack on the Parliamentary secretary and historian. But this can be explained. The *animus* against May was long-standing. He stood for the Laureateship after Ben Jonson's death in 1637 and lost it to Davenant. Like a bad loser, he had then taken the Parliament's side early on in the

1640s and been execrated by Royalists even before Marvell and
Lovelace went abroad. The returning Royalists execrated him even
more; he had prospered. Marvell was only expressing their long-felt
disgust. When May died of suffocation after heavy drinking in
November 1650, Marvell wrote for his friends' amusement what he
might have written in the same circumstances at any time in the
previous three years. He had enjoyed satirising Flecknoe in 1646 and
he enjoyed this. But the 'Horatian Ode' in July 1650 had been a
responsible, objective reappraisal of the republican scene in national
terms; it looked forward more than it looked back. For all Marvell
knew in 1650, there would never be a king of England again.

With the disappearance of the Court, and the Puritan triumph, the
climate of poetry in London was changing. In January 1651 Marvell
left London and began a new life. It is reasonable, therefore, to ascribe
to the pre-1651 period his more traditional and Cavalier lyrics: 'The
Fair Singer', 'Young Love', 'Daphnis and Chloe', 'The Match', 'The
Definition of Love', 'The Nymph complaining for the death of her
Faun', 'The unfortunate Lover', 'The Gallery', and 'To his Coy
Mistress' (first version). How much he later altered the others, we are
not yet able to tell. Manuscripts may yet turn up.

Marvell's whole situation now changed. He accepted a salaried
post in the Yorkshire household of General Lord Fairfax as modern
languages instructor to his only child Mary, aged twelve. He was
teaching her French and Italian when he wrote English and Latin
Commendatory Poems for his Hull friend Dr Witty's 'Popular
Errors in Medicine' very early in 1651. He had just finished teaching
her when John Milton wrote to Lord President Bradshaw about him
on 21 February 1653 and said amongst other things: 'he now comes
lately out of the house of Lord Fairfax, who was General, where he
was intrusted to give some instruction in the languages to the Lady,
his daughter'.[13] So it looks as if, in keeping with the universal
grammar school calendar, he began in mid-January 1651 and finished
a week before Christmas 1652.

In those two well-regulated years he wrote three poems at least for
Lord Fairfax, 'Upon the Hill and Grove at Bill-borow' and 'Upon
Appleton House' in English and '*Epigramma in Duos montes Amo-
sclivum et Bilboreum*' in Latin. He wrote his verses for Dr Witty in
February 1651, having seen him and his book in the New Year at
Hull. He evidently began his Latin poem '*Hortus*' that spring, for it
spoke of his finding innocence and quiet in the garden after years of
vain search in cities, and of his being weary and thirsty for a better life.

Afterwards, or at the same time, he wrote the expanded English version, 'The Garden'. He wrote the last three of the four 'Mower' poems and the eclogue 'Ametas and Thestylis making Hay-Ropes'; and he wrote 'Musicks Empire', or so we believe.

At the beginning of 1653 he was introduced to John Milton with a view to enlisting his help in acquiring some public employment. Since 1649 Milton had been Secretary for Foreign Affairs to the Commonwealth Council of State. Since March 1652 he had been totally blind. From March to December Georg Rudolph Weckherlin had come back from retirement and helped him, but Weckherlin died. On 21 February 1653 Milton dictated the tactful letter to John Bradshaw, Lord President of the Council, telling him: 'that there will be with you to-morrow upon some occasion of business a gentleman whose name is Mr Marvile; a man whom both by report and the converse I have had with him I judge to be of singular desert for the State to make use of; who also offers himself, if there be any employment for him'. There followed the rough *curriculum vitae* quoted already above, and then the letter went on:

> If upon the death of Mr Wakerley the Councell shall think that I shall need any assistance in the performance of my place (though for my part I find no encumbrance of that which belongs to me, except it be in attendance at Conference with Ambassadors, which I must confess in my condition I am not fit for) it would be hard for them to find a man so fit every way for that purpose as this gentleman: one who, I believe, in a short time would be able to do them as good service as Mr Ascan. [14]

'Mr Ascan' was Anthony Ascham, a Cambridge graduate. Appointed by Parliament in 1646 to tutor James Duke of York, he was the Parliament agent in Hamburg in 1649 and next year went to Madrid as ambassador, only to be assassinated by English Royalists on arrival. In resurrecting his name, Milton was proposing a parallel career abroad, if not at home, for the similarly qualified Mr Marvell.

The letter evidently went before the Council, because it is preserved in the Public Record Office, but Cromwell dissolved Parliament and wound up the Council in April and for the next three months ruled as Dictator. Instead of a public appointment he gave Marvell a private one, as tutor at Eton College to a new boy, William Dutton, in whom he was interested. Under the Eton system, the lessons from the two masters in school could be supplemented by individual tuition from a tutor provided by the parents. Only in this way would a boy learn a modern language. So Dutton and Marvell lived together in the Windsor house of John Oxenbridge, Fellow of Eton, and Cromwell paid the bills.

William Dutton was heir to his dead father's Gloucestershire estate and he had for guardian John Dutton, MP, a wealthy uncle. There was an understanding between this uncle and Cromwell that the boy should ultimately marry Frances Cromwell. John Dutton's will, dated 14 January 1656, gave Cromwell the guardianship of the boy and of an estate settled on him by deed, and it named this hoped-for marriage 'in order to my former desires and according to the discourse that hath passed between us'.[15] John Dutton died in 1657. Andrew Marvell knew at Eton that he was tutoring Cromwell's future son-in-law and that his own career depended on the great man's good opinion. His first report in a letter 'For his Excellence, the Lord General Cromwell', dated 28 July 1653, is extant and its fine penmanship and deferential eloquence make it a landmark.[16] No other reports have survived.

A letter from Marvell to Milton 'at his house in Petty France, Westminster' dated 2 June 1654 from 'Eaton' has also survived.[17] It ends: 'am exceeding glad to thinke that Mr Skyner is got near you, the Happinesse which I at the same Time congratulate to him and envie'. This is the Cyriack Skinner to whom Milton that year addressed Sonnet XXI, 'Cyriack, whose Grandsire on the Royal Bench of British Themis', and the following year addressed Sonnet XXII 'Upon his Blindness'. His grandfather was Sir Edward Coke, the great lawyer, and he himself had been a boy in Milton's private school. He is the obvious link between Milton and Marvell for, as we have seen, Mrs Bridget Skinner (née Coke) of Thornton Curtis near Barton-on-Humber was a close friend of Marvell's father, and she was the mother of Cyriack. The second generation of Skinners and Marvells were equally friendly. Witness Marvell's poem 'The Picture of little T.C. in a Prospect of Flowers', which is best dated 1653. It is highly probable that 'little T.C.' was Theophila Cornewall, baptised in September 1644, the daughter of Theophila Cornewall (née Skinner), Cyriack's sister, then living at Thornton Curtis; she would be 'big T.C.'. Marvell continued all his life to be a friend of both Skinner and Milton.

John Oxenbridge was in his first year as Fellow of Eton and Vicar of New Windsor. In 1634 he had been deprived of a Fellowship at Magdalen Hall, Oxford, by Archbishop Laud and in 1635–41 he had

had two long spells in Bermuda. In the second, a Newcastle merchant's daughter, Jane Butler, sailed out to him and married him there. They came back when the Laudian tyranny was overturned and he had since ministered to many Independent Congregations, including that in Hull from 1644 to 1648; Marvell may well have known that. They and their children lived in Windsor until Oxenbridge leased a house in Eton from the College on 3 August 1654; Marvell signed the deed as a witness.[18]

At some stage in the half-year between Appleton and Eton he had written his third satire, 'The Character of Holland'. In ridiculing a country with which England was by then at war, he drew heavily on his more amusing observations in 1643—44. Not until the 1681 Folio appeared was the poem printed entire, but lines 1—100 were twice printed anonymously, in 1665 and 1672, each time when anti-Dutch feeling ran high. Lines 101—52 were then left out because of references to the Common Wealth in lines 118 and 132 and the mention of Dean, Monck and Blake in line 150; these were the Generals at sea from 26 November 1652 to 3 June 1653, on which day Dean was killed.

Eton in the 1650s was very close to the centre of national affairs. Cromwell's Hampton Court Palace was no distance away. John Bradshaw lived at Eton. The Provost of Eton, Francis Rous, was a veteran Cornish MP and in July 1653 became Speaker of the House of Commons and a member of the new Council of State. The 'ever memorable' Anglican scholar John Hales, though ejected from his Fellowship in 1649, still lived near Eton. Marvell came to know him well. But his first Eton friend outside the Oxenbridge household was Nathaniel Ingelo, a Fellow since 1651. In November 1653 this talented man sailed for Sweden in the embassy of Bulstrode Whitelocke, MP, as his chaplain and master of music.[19] In February 1654 Marvell sent to him in Sweden the sixty-seven Latin elegiac couplets which in the 1681 Folio bore the long title 'A Letter to Doctor Ingelo, then with my Lord Whitlock, Ambassador from the Protector to the Queen of Sweden'. And after the Anglo-Swedish Treaty for amity, commerce and free navigation was signed in Uppsala on 28 April 1654, two Latin epigrams by Marvell accompanied the portrait of the Protector that was sent to the Queen. Cromwell was using the tutor at Eton: Marvell was in demand at Hampton Court.

Marvell's own Latin verses at this time probably included '*Ros*', the vivid set of twenty-three elegiac couplets that complemented his English lyric 'On a Drop of Dew'. The influence of the Oxenbridge household's piety and the effect of his own responsible charge, together with the new fervour of the 1650s, changed his choice of themes and redirected his art. To Cromwell he had written at the outset, in that letter of 28 July 1653:

> The Care which your Excellence is pleas'd to take of him (i.e. William Dutton) is no small incouragement and shall be so represented to him. But above all I shall labour to make him sensible of his Duty to God. For then we begin to serve faithfully when we consider that he is our Master. And in this both he and I ow infinitely to your Lordship, for having placed us in so godly a family as that of Mr Oxenbridge whose Doctrine and Example are like a Book and a Map, not onely instructing the Eare but demonstrating to the Ey which way we ought to travell.[20]

At Eton, then, one can believe that he wrote not only 'Bermudas', which in the 1681 Folio stood sixth, but the five poems before it and the two after it: 'A Dialogue, between the Resolved Soul, and Created Pleasure'; 'On a Drop of Dew'; '*Ros*'; 'The Coronet'; 'Eyes and Tears' (with one verse done also in Latin); 'Clorinda and Damon'; and 'A Dialogue between the Soul and Body' (which may be incomplete).

He certainly wrote at Eton his state poem 'The First Anniversary of the Government under O.C.'. This anniversary fell on 16 December 1654 and these 402 lines were a personal offering to Cromwell which the great man saw fit to publish. The official weekly *Mercurius Politicus* of Marchamont Needham gave notice of the forthcoming publication in the issue of 11–18 January 1655 and the government printer Thomas Newcomb printed it without naming the author. But Cromwell knew that Marvell had written it; of that we can be sure. In estimating how long it took to write, one should note that lines 159–66 refer to the death of Cromwell's mother at a great age and she, in fact, died on 16 November 1654, aged 93.

> And thou, great Cromwell, for whose happy birth
> A Mold was chosen out of better Earth;
> Whose Saint-like Mother we did lately see
> Live out an Age, long as a Pedigree . . .

The poem is a personal tribute to the Protector, but it is also a patriotic eulogy of England's new-found international strength. In eight places it draws on the Bible, in three places on poems by Milton. But at no point does it deserve to be called 'lyrical'.

After two years at Eton, William Dutton and Marvell spent one year in France. Three separate documents prove the pair to have been at Saumur in Touraine in January, March and August 1656. Alexander Callandar wrote from Paris on 26 January to 'Monsieur Williamson, Gentilhomme Anglois à Saumur' and added the postcript: 'Si vous visitez Mr Dutton et Monsieur Merville son Gouverneur je vous supplie de leur faire mes très-humbles baisemains (compliments).'[21] Now Callandar, an ex-London-schoolmaster, was living with his wife and children at Saumur and was only breaking his journey in Paris on the way back to England on business. And Mr Williamson was the Sir Joseph (1633–1701) of future fame; with two young men under him he had just gone to Saumur. Evidently Dutton and Marvell had already been there long enough for Callandar to know them and esteem them at their true worth. At the other end on 15 August J. Scudamore, writing from Saumur to the Royalist councillor Sir Richard Browne in Paris, reported the presence of many English in Saumur but none of note save Lord Paget's son and 'Mr Dutton, called by the French *Le Genre du Protecteur* whose Governour is one Mervill, a notable English Italo-Machavillian'.[22] So the story had spread in Saumur that Dutton was as good as married to Frances Cromwell, and Scudamore knew that this Marvell had been a Royalist and was now Cromwell's man. Ironically enough it was to a Scudamore that Dutton was eventually married. How much longer he stayed in France, one cannot say. William's uncle John died in January 1657, a year after making his last will, and presumably the young man was back at Sherborne by then. How old was he? His own first child was christened John at Sherborne on 24 August 1664. If he was not younger than Frances Cromwell, he was at least fifteen when a new boy at Eton.

At Saumur Marvell read the French verse translation of Lucan by Georges de Brebeuf which had come out in 1655. The four French lines that represented lines 220–1 of *Pharsalia*, Book III, Marvell turned back into three Latin hexameter lines; a small matter, but Corneille later expressed envy of Brebeuf for having composed those four lines. Marvell's judgement in picking them out was apparently sound.

The year 1657 was Marvell's *annus mirabilis*, a wonderful year. In June he wrote for Oliver Cromwell the Blake Victory poem which the 1681 Folio editors entitled 'On the Victory obtained by Blake over the Spaniards, in the Bay of Santacruze, in the Island of Teneriff'. By that bold naval incursion into a strongly fortified harbour Admiral Blake destroyed all sixteen Spanish treasure ships without losing a single ship of his own. The day was 20 April, but the news did not reach London until 28 May and a public thanksgiving was held there on 3 June. The same emotion impelled Marvell to poetry that had driven him to the 'Horatian Ode' seven years before. That was a lyrical poem; this he cast in the mould of 'The First Anniversary', addressing it to Cromwell again. It was first published by William Crook in 1674 in *A New Collection of Poems and Songs* and then re-published by H. Rogers in 1678, with only a change of title to 'Melpomene: Or the Muses Delight'. No hint of authorship appeared and the 'you' and 'your' that had greeted Cromwell were changed to 'we' and 'our' or 'England' or 'English'. Lines 39–52 were altogether cut out:

> Your worth to all these Isles, a just right brings,
> The best of Lands should have the best of Kings.                40
> And these want nothing Heaven can afford,
> Unless it be, the having you their Lord;
> But this great want, will not a long one prove,
> Your Conquering Sword will soon that want remove.
> For *Spain* had better, Shee'l ere long confess,                45
> Have broken all her Swords, then this one Peace;
> Casting that League off, which she held so long,
> She cast off that which only made her strong.
> Forces and art, she soon will feel, are vain,
> Peace, against you, was the sole strength of *Spain*.           50
> By that alone those Islands she secures,
> Peace made them hers, but War will make them yours.

Line 40 voices the hopes of those who wanted Cromwell to make himself King and did not accept his refusal as final, any more than the Romans did Caesar's. Lines 45–52 refer to the peace between Spain and England that lasted from 1630 to 1656, when Spain declared war.

On 2 September 1657 Marvell was at last appointed Latin Secretary to the Council. The so-called 'Second Protectorate' had been set up on 26 June and the new Privy Council of Nine on 13 July. Thurloe was Secretary and Marvell became his Assistant with a salary of £200 a year, paid quarterly. He did not attend the Council and he did not partner Milton in any way. He was deputed by Thurloe to meet ambassadors or write letters abroad. Milton was a law to himself and state papers were sent to his home.

At Whitehall on 11 November 1657 Frances Cromwell, aged nineteen, was married to the Earl of Warwick's grandson Robert Riche, aged twenty-three. On 19 November 1657, at Hampton Court this time, her elder sister Mary, aged twenty-one, was married to Thomas Bellasis, Viscount Fauconberg or Falconbridge, aged thirty. For this wedding Marvell wrote two pastorals which, one supposes, were set to music and performed. In the 1681 Folio they were called 'Two Songs'. Lord Fauconberg was a cousin of the Fairfaxes of Nun Appleton and his family had connections with Hull. This may explain Marvell's interest, if the initiative was his; but if it was Cromwell's, it is one of many signs that the Protector was happy about Mary's wedding and not about the wedding of Frances.

In 1658 there were no Cromwell wedding bells. On 16 February Frances's husband Robert Riche died of consumption. On 6 August the Protector's second daughter Elizabeth Claypole died after a long illness, aged twenty-nine. He struggled to the funeral in Westminster Abbey on 10 August. On Friday, 3 September he himself died. His body, embalmed, lay in open state at Somerset House, where Marvell viewed it. In lines 247–56 of 'A Poem Upon the Death of O.C.' he wrote:

> I saw him dead, a leaden slumber lyes,
> And mortal sleep over those wakefull eyes:
> Those gentle rays under the lids were fled,
> Which through his looks that piercing sweetnesse shed;
> That port which so majestique was and strong,
> Loose and depriv'd of vigour, stretch'd along:
> All wither'd, all discolour'd, pale and wan,
> How much another thing, no more that man?
> Oh! humane glory, vaine, oh! death, oh! wings,
> Oh! worthlesse world! oh transitory things!

He ended the poem with a hopeful salute to Richard Cromwell, the new Protector, in lines 305–24, which concluded thus:

> Cease now our griefs, calme peace succeeds a war,
> Rainbows to storms, Richard to Oliver.
> Tempt not his clemency to try his pow'r,
> He threats no deluge, yet foretells a showre.

On 6 December the new Privy Council decided to call a new Parliament for 27 January 1659, using the old constituency basis. This meant two Members for Hull and the Corporation nominated John Ramsden and Andrew Marvell as candidates. Sir Henry Vane, the surviving Long Parliament Member, stood for re-election, but he had offended Oliver Cromwell and was still *persona non grata* at Court. Knowing that the Court Party meant to mobilise the magistrates against his election, he stood also at Bristol and at Whitchurch in Hampshire. The Mayor of Hull was William Ramsden, the Sheriff Edmond Popple, Marvell's brother-in-law. John Ramsden and Marvell were duly elected. Defeated at Bristol and Hull, Vane was elected at Whitchurch.

Undoubtedly the Protector's Court backed Marvell, just as it backed the Secretary of the Council, John Thurloe (elected for Cambridge University), and the Chief Clerk of the Council, William Jessop (elected at Stafford). The Court needed all the support it could manage for the Cromwell Dynasty. In Hull Marvell's main backer was Edmond Popple, who was not only Sheriff that year but was also an Elder Brother of Trinity House. Thus we find Popple a fortnight before the election telling the Benchers of Hull Corporation that 'his brother in law Mr Andrew Marvell' was desirous of being made a Free Burgess, 'which the Bench taking into consideration and accompting the good service he hath allready done for this Town, they are pleased to grant him his freedome'. It seems, then, that as Latin Secretary to the Council Marvell had been able to help the Corporation of Hull.

In the event, however, Richard Cromwell's Parliament lasted only three months. He was forced to dissolve it on 25 April 1659 and to recall the Rump on 7 May. Automatically Sir Henry Vane came back as MP for Hull, and Ramsden and Marvell went out. Then Cromwell abdicated on 25 May and the Dynasty came to a halt. In Parliament the Rumpers carried on until dismissed by the Army on 13 October. On 26 December, however, the Army brought them back and on 21 February 1660 the secluded Members of the Long Parliament were brought back as well. On 16 March the House was dissolved and writs for a new Election were issued.

On 2 April Hull again returned John Ramsden (227 votes) and Andrew Marvell (141). The Parliament met on 25 April. Charles Stuart was proclaimed King on 8 May in London and on 29 May he arrived there amid wild scenes of rejoicing.

Through all those changes of fortune, and the power struggles convulsing the realm, Marvell continued in his salaried employment as Latin Secretary. Milton, however, was discharged from office in April 1660 and Thurloe in May; in June both were pursued by the law. Marvell, a comparatively new state servant, went unmolested. He was even able to save Milton from trial in a court of law and to champion him in the Commons.

On 29 December 1660 the King dissolved the 'Convention Parliament' in order to have one of his own. On 1 April 1661 Hull elected Colonel Anthony Gilby (294 votes) and Andrew Marvell (240); John Ramsden sank to fourth place. This 'Cavalier Parliament' lasted until January 1679. It outlasted Marvell by five months.

Hull paid its Members 6s. 8d. for every day that Parliament sat and in return the Corporation expected to receive Parliamentary news post-haste. Marvell's extant letters to the Mayor and Corporation number 295 and cover the period from 17 November 1660 to 6 July 1678; when the House was adjourned or prorogued, there were, of course, gaps.

He was also abroad twice in 1662–65. For ten months from mid-May 1662 he was in Holland on state business at the behest of a Privy Councillor, the Earl of Carlisle. Only in the last two of the months did Parliament sit, but in Hull they frowned at his missing even that much and there were plans to replace him. From July 1663 to January 1665 he was abroad again, as Secretary to the Earl of Carlisle on Special Embassies to Russia, Sweden, and Denmark. This time he took care to obtain formal leave of absence from the Commons and from Hull. He never lacked caution.

The Carlisle Mission spent five months in Moscow, having journeyed there by barge and sledge from the port of Archangel. Negotiations for a trade treaty proved futile and the disappointed Mission travelled south to Riga and went by ship to Stockholm. They spent six weeks there, and then seven in Copenhagen. Secretary Marvell wrote all the Ambassador's addresses and letters in English or Latin and made all the local arrangements. From Hamburg they came overland to Calais, crossed the Channel and coasted to Westminster. An Account of the Mission was printed in 1669.[23]

By then Marvell was back at his poetry; but his new work was all satire. In July 1667 he had written 'Clarindon's House-Warming'; it was anonymously printed that year, bound up with 'Directions to a Painter' 'by Sir John Denham' (a false attribution). In the rest of 1667 he wrote the 990 lines of 'The last Instructions to a Painter', not printed until 1689 and named then 'Esquire Marvel's'. He completed

'The Kings Vowes' early in 1670 and 'Further Advice to a Painter' early in 1671. And after Colonel Blood failed narrowly to steal the Crown Jewels on 9 May 1671, Marvell wrote the Latin epigram '*Bludius et Corona*' and inserted an English version in 'The Loyall Scot', a satire written in spasms between 1667 and 1673.

Parliament stood adjourned or prorogued from April 1671 to February 1673 and in the second half of that long interval Marvell entered the arena of religious prose controversy and revealed a new talent. He set out to combat three publications of 1670–2 by the thirty-year-old Samuel Parker, Archdeacon of Canterbury, the latest pet of Archbishop Sheldon. Like most of the Cavalier Parliament, Parker was *for* the Authority of the State over the Conscience of Subjects in the Matter of External Religion and *against* Toleration of Dissenters. Marvell was *against* Papists in England, but he was *for* Freedom of Worship for Dissenters and in 1668 had spoken strongly in the Commons against the renewal of the expired 'Conventicles Act'. The House nevertheless passed it by 144 votes to 78, whereupon the King, who favoured Toleration, prevented its becoming law by adjourning Parliament before the Lords could vote. This weapon of adjournment he came to use more and more. And in March 1672 he issued 'The Declaration of Indulgence', suspending all penal laws against Dissenters and Catholics and Jews.

This was the position when Marvell wrote *The Rehearsal Transpros'd* and had it printed anonymously without licence and without being registered by the Stationers' Company. It was a memorable and a topical title. The Duke of Buckingham's farce 'The Rehearsal' was the latest stage success, not least for the fun it made of Dryden, Poet Laureate since 1670, in the character of 'Mr Bayes'; it projected him as a secondhand writer transmuting other men's prose into verse and their verse into prose and it dubbed this 'transversing' and 'transprosing'. Marvell's pamphlet called Parker 'Mr Bayes' throughout. It analysed the three publications in turn and ridiculed every argument. The delighted King promptly arranged for a second impression to be licensed and so made legal. Thousands read it and laughed.

No fewer than six replies were published in the first half of 1673, including 'The Transproser Rehearsed' (anonymous, but by Richard Leigh) and 'A Reproof to the Rehearsal Transprosed' (528 pages long) by Parker himself. Both these assumed Milton and Marvell to be joint authors of *The Rehearsal Transpros'd* and proceeded to vilify the pair. Leigh even coined the epigram:

O Marvellous fate! O fate full of marvel!
That *Nol's Latin pay* two *clerks* should desarve ill!
Hiring a *Gelding*, and Milton the *Stallion*;
His *Latin* was gelt and turn'd pure *Italian*.

The last lines exploited the fact that Marvell was a childless bachelor
and Milton had married three times.

Marvell read Parker's 'Reproof' in manuscript at the printer's and
he wrote to his Commons ally, Sir Edward Harley, on 3 May 1673:

Dr Parker will be out the next weeke. I have seen of it already 330
pages and it will be much more. I perceive by what I have read that
it is the rudest book that ever was publisht (I may say), since the first
invention of printing. Although it handles me so roughly yet I am
not at all amated by it. But I must desire the advice of some few
friends to tell me whether it will be proper for me and in what way
to answer it . . . I am (if I may say it with reverence) drawn in, I
hope by a good Providence, to intermeddle in a noble and high
argument which therefore by how much it is above my capacity I
shall use the more industry not to disparage it.[24]

In December he published *The Rehearsal Transpros'd: The Second
Part* 'by Andrew Marvel'. This time he printed his name, the better to
exonerate Milton. The result was that everyone knew whom to
applaud for their light entertainment. He was famous and Parker was
silenced.

Religion in Marvell's view was personal and spiritual, not worldly,
not external. As a boy, he had been brought up in the Anglicanism of
his father. He had later been deeply impressed by the Puritanism of
Milton and the Oxenbridges and Cromwell. Like them, he was a
regular reader of the Bible. He was now again a conforming member
of the Church of England. But he admired the fervour of Owen and
Baxter and could not bear to see such men of God abused by the fat
young pluralist Archdeacon Parker, whom before the Restoration he
had once met in Milton's house.

As Marvell told his readers in *The Second Part*, he had deliberately
not communicated with Milton at all when working on *The
Rehearsal Transpros'd* in 1672, 'lest I should in any way involve him in
my consequences', and 'by chance' he had not visited him in the two
years before that. Late in 1673, however, he found him busy with a
second edition of *Paradise Lost*. This came out in 1674, prefaced by

two sets of commendatory verses, by 'S.B., *M.D.*' (Samuel Barrow, *Medicinae Doctor*) in Latin and by 'A.M.' (Andrew Marvell) in English. It was Milton's last book. He died on 8 November 1674 and was buried according to the rites of the Church of England in the chancel of his parish church, St Giles, Cripplegate, next to his father. 'All his learned and great Friends in London', Toland wrote, 'accompanied his Body'.[25] In that case, Marvell was there.

Marvell was now writing verse satire again. 'The Statue in Stocks-Market' (1674), 'The Statue at Charing-Cross' (1675) and 'A Dialogue between the Two Horses' (1675) used the same metre and sniped at the two King Charleses. Yet Charles II was delighted with the 'Two Horses' and knew much of the poem by heart, according to Defoe. To the same period belongs 'Upon his Majesties being made free of the City' (1674–75). All four had to wait to be posthumously printed, but in manuscript they were thoroughly well aired at the time. Marvell, however, was far from acknowledging his offspring, especially in London. 'The times are something criticall', he wrote on 21 October 1675 to Mayor Shires in Hull, 'beside that I am naturally and now more by my Age inclined to keep my thoughts private'.[26] This was a new Mayor who had unwisely passed on part of a previous letter to a third party in London. Marvell objected.

He needed to be cautious, for he had written in the previous spring an audacious parody of the expected King's Speech from the Throne at the opening of the thirteenth session of the Cavalier Parliament on 13 April 1675. To Mayor Hoare and the Hull Corporation he sent a summary of the actual speech, clause by clause. The King said, for instance, 'That for his part he should always maintaine the Religion and the Church of England as now established and be all his life constant in that profession'. These were, of course, mere words. The King's tenderness to 'Italian Catholics' was as well known as the people's aversion to 'Popery'.

In his parody Marvell made the King say:

'For your Religion, my late Proclamation (for Indulgence) is a true Picture of my Mind: he that can't as in a Glass see my Zeal for the Church of England, doth not deserve any further satisfaction, for I declare him Willful, Abominable and not Good. Some may perhaps be startled and crye — how comes this sudden Change? To which I answer, I am a Changeling. I think that is a full Answre. But to convince Men that I mean as I say there are three Arguments. First, I tell You so, and you know I never broke my

word. Secondly, my Lord Treasurer says so, and he never told a
Lye. Thirdly, my Lord Lauderdale will undertake for me, and I
should be loath by any Act of mine to forfeit the Credit he hath
with you.

If you desire more instances of my Zeal, I have them for you. For
Example, I have converted all my Natural sons from Popery and
may say without Vanity, it was my owne Worke, and so much the
more peculiar than the begetting of them. It would do Your Heart
good to hear how prettily little George can read in the Psalter.

They are all fine Children, God bless 'em and so like me in their
Understandings'.

In 1676 he published his third pamphlet in support of toleration,
naming his new opponent 'Mr Smirke' after a vacuous character in
Etherege's latest comedy *The Man of Mode, or Sir Fopling Flutter*. It
was a case of Marvell 'intermeddling' again. An anonymous
pamphlet, *The Naked Truth*, had been printed in 1675; its author,
Herbert Croft, Bishop of Hereford, drew on the Councils of the
Primitive Church to argue for Toleration. In 1676 it was anonymously attacked by Francis Turner, Master of St John's College,
Cambridge and Chaplain to the Duke of York, in a pamphlet entitled
*Animadversions upon a late Pamphlet entitled the Naked Truth*. At this
point Marvell stepped in to support the one bishop who favoured
toleration and in April or May 1676 he published *Mr Smirke; or, The
Divine in Mode: being Certain Annotations, upon the Animadversions on
the Naked Truth. Together with a Short Historical Essay, concerning
General Councils, Creeds, and Impositions, in Matters of Religion*. He
gave the author's name as 'ANDREAS RIVETUS, Junior, an anagram
of RES NUDA VERITAS'. Behind this, it should not have been difficult
to see 'ANDREAS MARVELL, Junior', but in law that would not have
sufficed as proof. Nor would the style, though it too gave the author
away. Sir Christopher Hatton seized on one weakness when he wrote
to his brother on 23 May 1676: 'I hope Andrew Marvel will . . . be
made an example for his insolence in calling Dr Turner, Chaplain to
His Royal Highness, "Chaplain to Sir Fobling Busy", as he terms him
in his scurrilous satyrical answer to his "Animadversions on Naked
Truth".' But nothing happened to Marvell, except that he was aware
of being watched. Nathaniel Ponder, however, his Chancery Lane
bookseller–publisher, was gaoled on 10 May for unlicensed printing.
In spite of the Bishop of London's rage at the Essay, it went
unpunished and in the next thirty years was reprinted four times.

Marvell's grasp of early Church History was remarkable for a layman. And in 1678 he published (with a licence) 'Remarks Upon a Late Disingenuous Discourse, Writ by one T.D.', in which he defended Cromwell's old Presbyterian chaplain John Howe against the Calvinist Thomas Danson on the subject of Predestination. He amused himself and his readers by taking 'T.D.' to mean 'The Discourse' and referring to Howe's opponent only as 'It'.

But his weightiest pamphlet was political. In the last week of 1677 he published *An Account of the Growth of Popery and Arbitrary Government in England. More Particularly from the Long Prorogation of November 1675. Ending the 15th of February 1677, till the Last Meeting of Parliament, the 16th of July 1677. Printed at Amsterdam and recommended for the reading of all English Protestants*. It was, of course, printed in London and he extended it at the eleventh hour to include the further meeting and adjournment of 3 December.

The leaders of the Court Party were stung into advertising, in the *London Gazette* of 21–25 March 1678, large rewards for information against the author and the printer. Of several replies to the pamphlet one was 'A Letter from Amsterdam, to a Friend in England', dated 18 April 1678, which named 'Andrew' as 'a shrewd man against Popery'. Another was 'The Growth of Knavery', written by the Chief Licenser himself, Sir Roger L'Estrange.

On 10 June 1678 we find Marvell giving hooded news of his pamphlet in a letter to Will Popple, his nephew at Bordeaux:

> There came out, about Christmass last, here a large Book concerning 'the Growth of Popery and Arbitrary Government'. There have been great Rewards offered in private, and considerable in the Gazette, to any who could inform of the Author or Printer, but not yet discovered. Three or four printed Books since have described, as near as it was proper to go, the Man being a Member of Parliament, Mr *Marvell* to have been the Author; but if he had, surely he should not have escaped being questioned in Parliament, or some other Place. [27]

He took care not to sign this letter.

*The Growth of Popery* was a grave, pessimistic review of England's position and the Government's behaviour since 1667. It attacked the pro-French crypto-Catholics in England. It attacked Louis XIV and all the architects of the Third Dutch War of 1672–74. It recommended the Protestant Dutch as the natural allies of Protestant

England. It condemned the Government's arbitrary interference with the House of Commons, 'kickt from Adjournment to Adjournment, as from one stair down to another, and when they were at the bottom kickt up again, having no mind yet to *Go out of Doors*'. It dwelt at length on the corruption of the House, then in its seventeenth year. Two-thirds of the Members were in Government offices or anxious to be so. Most of the other third were so deep in debt that 'if they be not in Parliament, they must be in Prison'. It continued:

> But notwithstanding these there is an hanfull [handful] of *Salt*, a sparkle of *Soul*, that hath hitherto preserved this grosse Body from Putrefaction, some *Gentlemen* that are constant, invariable, indeed *English* men, such as are above *hopes*, or *fears*, or *dissimulation*, that can neither flatter, nor betray their King, or Country: But being conscious of their own Loyalty, and Integrity, proceed throw [through] good and bad report, to acquit themselves in their Duty to God, their Prince, and their Nation.

High in this noble category the Whigs of the next few decades placed Andrew Marvell himself. He had formulated their articles of faith. He grew to be their exemplar.

On 16 August 1678 Andrew Marvell died of malaria ('a tertian ague') in Great Russell Street, London, in a house he had rented the previous year to shelter two bankrupt Hull men fleeing from the law. On 18 August he was buried inside the church of St Giles in the Fields, but not the present church. He left no will.

In 1681 a printer, Roger Boulter, published *Miscellaneous Poems* 'by Andrew Marvell, Esq;, Late Member of the Honourable House of Commons' and, to authenticate the contents of the Folio, he included a Certificate, signed by 'Mary Marvell', that 'all these Poems . . . are printed according to the exact Copies of my late dear Husband, under his own Hand-Writing, being found since his Death among his other Papers'. She signed this on 15 October 1680.

She was Mary Palmer, his Great Russell Street housekeeper; no lady, and not his wife.[28] But she and her fellows who did this for their gain, may well have saved his lyrics from extinction. Had the poet died after a long illness, he might in the course of it have arranged the preservation and publication himself. He had preserved his manuscripts and there were still thirteen years to go before he should arrive at threescore and ten. Our thanks, then, should go to 'Mary Marvell'. Bad deeds can have good results.

## NOTES

1 By Act of Parliament. See *The Poems and Letters of Andrew Marvell* (Oxford University Press, 1971), II, 359.

2 D. I. B. Smith (ed.), *Andrew Marvell. The Rehearsal Transpros'd and The Rehearsal Transpros'd, The Second Part* (Oxford University Press, 1971) 'The Second Part', pp.203–4.

3 Thomas Cooke (1726) first told the story of the Jesuits seducing the boy from Cambridge to London and Roman Catholicism and of his father's rescuing him 'after several months'. I omit it as far too uncertain. Cooke dated it soon after 1633.

4 House of Lords Record Office, Protestation Returns for Middlesex, Ossulton Division.

5 Humberside County Record Office. Sotheron-Estcourt MSS., Yorkshire Estates, DDSE(2) 16/62 and 16/146. And see Pauline Burdon, 'Marvell after Cambridge', *The British Library Journal*, Spring 1978, pp.42–8.

6 In 1933 Reginald L. Hine, F.S.A., of Hertfordshire sold them to Hull Central Library on the strength of the clear Marvell signature.

7 Public Record Office, SP 18/33, No. 75.

8 Richard Flecknoe, *A Relation of Ten Years' Travels in Europe, Asia, Affrique and America* (1656).

9 J. W. Stoye, *English Travellers Abroad 1604–67* (Jonathan Cape, 1952), pp.302–4.

10 P. Legouis, *Andrew Marvell* (Oxford University Press, 1965), p.240.

11 Letter in the *Times Literary Supplement*, 8 August 1952.

12 Murray Lefkowitz, *William Lawes* (Routledge & Kegan Paul, 1960), pp.19–21.

13 Public Record Office, SP 18/33, No. 75.

14 Ibid.

15 *Notes and Queries*, CLXX (1936), p.411.

16 Facsimile and transcript in *The Poems and Letters of Andrew Marvell*, II, 304–5.

17 Ibid., II, 305–6.

18 Letter from Noel Blakiston in the *Times Literary Supplement*, 8 February 1952.

19 Ruth Spalding, *The Improbable Puritan* (Faber, 1975), p.144.

20 *The Poems and Letters of Andrew Marvell*, II, 304–5.

21 Letter from E. E. Duncan-Jones in the *Times Literary Supplement*, 20 June 1958.

22 Letter in the *Times Literary Supplement*, 2 December 1949.

23 G. de Miège, *A Relation of Three Embassies* (1669); M. C. Bradbrook and M. G. Lloyd Thomas, *Andrew Marvell* (Cambridge University Press, 1940), Appendix B.

24 *The Poems and Letters of Andrew Marvell*, II, 328.

25 John Toland's 'Life of John Milton' (1698) in Helen Darbishire's *The Early Lives of Milton* (Constable, 1932), p.193.

26 *The Poems and Letters of Andrew Marvell* (Oxford University Press, 1971), II, 166.

27 Ibid., II, 357.

28 F. S. Tupper, *Proceedings of the Modern Language Association of America*, June 1938.

# THE LYRICS

# 1 'A Dialogue between Thyrsis and Dorinda' (the early version)

The argument for Marvell's authorship of this dialogue is based on its presence (in a later version) in the 1681 Folio of his works, with its second half largely re-written.

The words of this early version come from the British Museum Additional MS. 31432, which comprises sixty-one musical settings in the autograph of William Lawes (1602−45). He was killed in action, fighting on the Royalist side at the Battle of Rowton Heath near Chester on 24 September 1645, when Marvell was in his third year abroad. Since it is unthinkable that Marvell sent Lawes a poem from abroad, one can safely conclude that this was written before 1643 in England and is Marvell's first known pastoral.

These are the British Museum MS. words, but extra punctuation has had to be supplied, there being little in the musical score. The title is taken from there.

## DIALOGUE. THIRSIS: DORINDA

| | | |
|---|---|---|
| Dorinda: | When Death shall Snatch us from these kidds, | |
| | And shutt up our devided lidds, | |
| | Thirsis, O Tell mee, prithy doe, | |
| | Wither thou and I shall goe. | |
| Thirsis: | To Elizium. | |
| Dorinda: | But wher is't? | 5 |
| Thirsis: | A Chast Soule can never miss't. | |
| Dorinda: | I know now way but to my home. | |
| | Is our cell Elizium? | |
| Thirsis: | Cast thy face to yonder sky, | |
| | Wher the Milky path doth lye. | 10 |
| Both: | 'Tis a straight and Easye way | |
| | That leads to everlasting day. | |

31

Dorinda:    Ther birds may pearch, but how can I,
            That have noe wings and canott fly?
Thirsis:    O doe not sigh, deare Nimph, for fyre          15
            That hath noe wings still doth aspire,
            Untill it knock against the Pole.
            Heaven is the centre of the soule.
Dorinda:    But in Elizium how doe they
            Passe Eternity away?                           20
Thirsis:    They know not what it is to feare,
            Free from the Wolf and Horrid Beare.
            Ther their Lambs are alwayes full,
            Grasse more softer then our Wooll.
            A fix't spring. A Constant Sun.               25
            A day that Ever is begun.
            Oaten Pipes like Gold that play
            A never ceasing Rowndelay,
            A never ceasing Rowndelay.
            Perpetuall Rivers ther doe flow.              30
            Flowers live and Garlands Grow.
            Shepherds ther beare Equall sway.
            Everie Nimph is Queene of May,
            Everie Nimph, everie Nimph is Queene of May.
            Why then should we heere make delay,          35
            Since we may bee as free as they?

# 2     'To his Noble Friend Mr Richard Lovelace, upon his POEMS'

SIR,

Our times are much degenerate from those
Which your sweet Muse, which your fair Fortune chose,
And as complexions alter with the Climes,
Our wits have drawne th'infection of our times.
That candid Age no other way could tell                   5
To be ingenious, but by speaking well.

Who best could prayse, had then the greatest prayse,
'Twas more esteem'd to give, then weare the Bayes:
Modest ambition studi'd only then,
To honour not her selfe, but worthy men.                    10
These vertues now are banisht out of Towne,
Our Civill Wars have lost the Civicke crowne.
He highest builds, who with most Art destroys,
And against others Fame his owne employs.
I see the envious Caterpillar sit                           15
On the faire blossome of each growing wit.
    The Ayre's already tainted with the swarms
Of Insects which against you rise in arms.
Word-peckers, Paper-rats, Book-scorpions,
Of wit corrupted, the unfashion'd Sons.                     20
The barbed Censurers begin to looke
Like the grim cónsistóry on thy Booke;
And on each line cast a reforming eye,
Severer then the yong Presbýterý.
Till when in vaine they have thee all perus'd,              25
You shall for being faultlesse be accus'd.
Some reading your *Lucasta*, will alledge
You wrong'd in her the Houses Priviledge.
Some that you under sequestration are,
Because you write when going to the Warre,                  30
And one the Book prohibits, because *Kent*
Their first Petition by the Authour sent.
    But when the beauteous Ladies came to know
That their deare *Lovelace* was endanger'd so:
*Lovelace* that thaw'd the most congealed brest,            35
He who lov'd best, and them defended best,
Whose hand so rudely grasps the steely brand,
Whose hand so gently melts the Ladies hand,
They all in mutiny though yet undrest
Sally'd, and would in his defence contest.                  40
And one the loveliest that was yet e're seen,
Thinking that I too of the rout had been,
Mine eyes invaded with a female spight,
(She knew what pain 'twould be to lose that sight.)
O no, mistake not, I reply'd, for I                         45
In your defence, or in his cause would dy.
But he secure of glory and of time

Above their envy, or mine aid doth clime.
Him, valianst men, and fairest Nýmphs approve,
His Booke in them finds Judgement, with you Love.      50

Andr. Marvell.


Lovelace's *Lucasta* was entered in the Stationers' Register on 14 May
1649 and was on sale at sixpence soon after. Of the fourteen sets of
Commendatory Verses Marvell's came ninth to begin with. Later, by
a rearrangement of pages, it was moved up to first place.

It was written eighteen months earlier in December 1647, when
the text of the book had just gone to the Licensers in manuscript. That
is what lines 21 – 3 mean by saying:

The barbed Censurers begin to looke
Like the grim consistory on thy Booke.


A Royalist with Lovelace's record was bound to be treated with
suspicion by any Parliamentary committee. Its members cannot have
hurried or scamped their work. Yet they licensed *Lucasta* on 4
February 1648. The subsequent delay in its printing must have been
due to the author's imprisonment from 9 June 1648 to 10 April 1949.
For one thing it slowed down the assembly of Commendatory
Verses. John Pinchbacke, for instance, in his lines wrote of 'our seven
years paines in the past wars'; since the Civil Wars only began in July
1642, he clearly wrote this well on in 1649. And, in fact, three of the
thirty surviving copies of *Lucasta* were bound first without the
Commendatory Verses and then re-bound with them.

In short, Marvell's poem appeared many months later than he
expected and in the meantime it had become slightly dated. He wrote
it in the metre he had used for the 170 lines of 'Fleckno, an English
Priest at Rome' twenty months earlier. He arranged it in the form of a
letter, with (1) superscription, (2) Sir, (3) text, and (4) signature. He
seems to have envisaged three paragraphs of sixteen lines and one final
couplet. This plan did not quite work out. At line 45 he embarked on
direct speech to the militant lady and could not escape from the
second person (though it is plural in lines 46 and 50). The last six lines
are therefore continuous.

In his superscription he addressed Lovelace correctly from his point
of view as Mr (not Colonel), because he was an Oxford M.A. (1636)
incorporated at Cambridge (1637); it was at Cambridge that they

must have first met. Lovelace was then a brilliant young man of
twenty, the absolute owner of Kentish estates. He went on to sparkle
at Court and do well overseas as a soldier. The ladies all loved him. He
wrote the words of their favourite songs. He had beautiful looks.
These points are dwelt on in Marvell's poem.

Lovelace had come back from three years in Holland and France in
the autumn of 1646. Marvell came back from over four years in
Holland, France, Italy and Spain a year later. His first paragraph
naturally compares the London of 1647 with the London of 1639–
42. He begins with the simile of a continental traveller, 'as
complexions alter with the Climes'. He finishes with a choice couplet:

> I see the envious Caterpillar sit
> On the faire blossome of each growing wit.

The second paragraph relies on their common pro-Royalist, anti-
Parliamentarian sentiments. Since their last London meeting,
Parliament had passed the Printing Ordinance and imposed
Presbyterianism, 'the Presbytery', on the Church of England.
Marvell disliked both changes. In lines 27–30 he alludes to the two
lyrics that opened *Lucasta*; so he had certainly read the manuscript.
The first bore the title 'Song TO LUCASTA, Going beyond the Seas'
and had this final verse:

> So then we doe anticipate
>> Our after-fate,
> And are alive i' th' skies,
>> If thus our lips and eyes
> Can speak like spirits unconfin'd
> In Heav'n, their earthy bodies left behind.

Marvell's lines 27–8 suggest that the Parliamentary privilege of free
speech is infringed by 'unconfined spirits' speaking freely in Heaven.

The second bore the title 'Song. TO LUCASTA, Going to the
Warres'. They were Dutch wars, not the Civil Wars, but hostile
Licensers may have taken them as Civil and applied the standard
penalty of 'sequestering' the author's estates.

The remaining couplet touches lightly on the weightiest reason for
distrusting Lovelace:

*confisticated, seized*

And one the Book prohibits because *Kent*
Their first Petition by the Authour sent.

For the Long Parliament had clapped Lovelace in prison on 30 April
1642 and kept him there till 21 June, when they gave him conditional
freedom on two sureties totalling £10,000. His crime was to dare to
bring to the Bar of the House a copy of the same pro-Royalist
petition from gentlemen in Kent that had been burnt by the common
hangman on the House's orders the day before. The Commons
welcomed anti-Royalist petitions, but the Kent one sought curbs on
the militia and demanded the restoration of the Book of Common
Prayer.

In the more Cavalier third paragraph the ladies come in at the door
and irony and satire fly out of the window. The tone changes. The
portrayal of Lovelace accords better with the gallantry of his poems.
It places him not merely in the Philip Sidney chivalric tradition, but
the older Arthurian. One remembers the end of Sir Ector's Dirge
over Sir Lancelot in *Morte D'Arthur*: 'And thou was the mekest man
and the Gentyllest that ever ete in hall amonge ladyes; and thou were
the sternest knyght to thy mortall foo that ever put spere in the
breste'. The English has advanced as a literary language from Malory
to Marvell, but the chivalric tests are the same. There is a touch of
Lancelot in Lovelace:

> Whose hand so rudely grasps the steely brand,
> Whose hand so gently melts the Lady's hand.

The internal rhymes ('hand', 'brand', 'hand', 'hand') and the
scrupulous balance help to highlight the couplet. The fine blend of
grimness and dalliance is helped by the siege metaphors surrounding
the ladies who ran to the rescue of Lovelace and 'in mutiny though yet
undrest' (minus armour) 'sally'd' (made a sortie). It would become
mock-heroic if it went on much longer like that, but Marvell's reply
in lines 45–6, and the last six lines as a whole, restore seriousness and
he ends on the appropriate note of encomium.

*A speech or piece of writing that praises someone or something highly*

# 3  'Daphnis and Chloe'

Marvell took his title from the Greek prose romance 'Daphnis and Chloe', written by the otherwise unknown Longus in the third century A.D. He took his stanza form from Shakespeare's 'The Phoenix and the Turtle', the first verse of which goes:

> Let the bird of loudest lay
> On the sole Arabian tree,
> Herald sad and trumpet be,
> To whose sound chaste wings obey.

It is true that Thomas Carew chose this same metre for 'The Separation of Lovers' (1640), but he indented his two middle lines, whereas Shakespeare and Marvell did not. Nevertheless the first twenty-five of Marvell's trochaic quatrains deal with 'the separation' of Daphnis from Chloe. The last two quatrains bring about an extraordinary end, an intellectual peripeteia which springs a surprise, but destroys all our sympathy for Daphnis. Like so much Cavalier poetry, 'Daphnis and Chloe' expresses a male hedonist point of view. Its moral is immoral. Therein lies its wit.

### I

> *Daphnis* must from *Chloe* part:
> Now is come the dismal Hour
> That must all his Hopes devour,
> All his Labour, all his Art.

### II

> Nature, her own Sexes foe,                    5
> Long had taught her to be coy:
> But she neither knew t'enjoy,
> Nor yet let her Lover go.

### III

> But, with this sad News surpriz'd,
> Soon she let that Niceness fall;               10
> And would gladly yield to all,
> So it had his stay compriz'd.

### IV

Nature so her self does use
To lay by her wonted State,
Lest the World should separate.      15
Sudden Parting closer glews.

### V

He, well read in all the wayes
By which men their Siege maintain,
Knew not that the Fort to gain
Better 'twas the Siege to raise.      20

### VI

But he came so full possest
With the Grief of Parting thence,
That he had not so much Sence
As to see he might be blest.

### VII

Till Love in her Language breath'd      25
Words she never spake before;
But then Legacies no more
To a dying Man bequeath'd.

### VIII

For, Alas, the time was spent,
Now the latest minut's run      30
When poor *Daphnis* is undone,
Between Joy and Sorrow rent.

### IX

At that *Why*, that *Stay my Dear*,
His disorder'd Locks he tare;
And with rouling Eyes did glare,      35
And his cruel Fate forswear.

### X

As the Soul of one scarce dead,
With the shrieks of Friends aghast,
Looks distracted back in hast,
And then streight again is fled.                    40

### XI

So did wretched *Daphnis* look,
Frighting her he loved most.
At the last this Lovers Ghost
Thus his Leave resolved took.

### XII

Are my Hell and Heaven Joyn'd                    45
More to torture him that dies?
Could departure not suffice,
But that you must then grow kind?

### XIII

Ah my *Chloe* how have I
Such a wretched minute found,                    50
When thy Favours should me wound
More than all thy Cruelty?

### XIV

So to the condemned Wight
The delicious Cup we fill;
And allow him all he will,                    55
For his last and short Delight.

### XV

But I will not now begin
Such a Debt unto my Foe;
Nor to my Departure owe
What my Presence could not win.                    60

## XVI

Absence is too much alone:
Better 'tis to go in peace,
Than my Losses to increase
By a late Fruition.

## XVII

Why should I enrich my Fate?                65
'Tis a Vanity to wear,
For my Executioner,
Jewels of so high a rate.

## XVIII

Rather I away will pine
In a manly stubborness                       70
Than be fatted up express
For the *Canibal* to dine.

## XIX

Whilst this grief does thee disarm,
All th'Enjoyment of our Love
But the ravishment would prove               75
Of a Body dead while warm.

## XX

And I parting should appear
Like the Gourmand *Hebrew* dead,
While with Quailes and *Manna* fed,
He does through the Desert err.               80

## XXI

Or the Witch that midnight wakes
For the Fern, whose magick Weed
In one minute casts the Seed,
And invisible him makes.

## XXII

Gentler times for Love are ment.    85
Who for parting pleasure strain
Gather Roses in the rain,
Wet themselves and spoil their Scent.

## XXIII

Farewel therefore all the fruit
Which I could from Love receive:    90
Joy will not with Sorrow weave,
Nor will I this Grief pollute.

## XXIV

Fate I come, as dark, as sad,
As thy Malice could desire;
Yet bring with me all the Fire    95
That Love in his Torches had.

## XXV

At these words away he broke;
As who long has praying ly'n,
To his Heads-man makes the Sign,
And receives the parting stroke.    100

## XXVI

But hence Virgins all beware.
Last night he with *Phlogis* slept;
This night for *Dorinda* kept;
And but rid to take the Air.

## XXVII

Yet he does himself excuse;    105
Nor indeed without a Cause.
For, according to the Lawes,
Why did *Chloe* once refuse?

Having spent twenty-five stanzas building a castle, Marvell takes two
to knock it down. 'No virgin in future must trust a man.' 'Daphnis
had only ridden to Chloe for the sake of the outing.' The talk about
'parting' was all a lie. But Daphnis can justify his conduct:

> For, according to the Lawes,
> Why did Chloe once refuse?

Now 'the Lawes' are not what E. S. Donno suggests in her *Andrew
Marvell* (Penguin, 1972), 'the laws of Nature'; Nature had taught
Chloe to be coy. They might be the Cavalier conventions, which
expected an unattached lady to yield to any gallant not of inferior
birth. But L. N. Wall has pointed to a tract dated 16 April 1647 in the
Thomason Collection and entitled *A Parliament of Ladies: with their
Lawes newly enacted*. It may well be that Marvell is alluding to these
ladies' less-than-virtuous 'Lawes'. He liked ending with a Parthian
shot.

The first twenty-six stanzas are made portentous by constant scenes
of death: death in bed (ll. 27 – 8, 37 – 40); death by judicial execution
(ll. 53 – 6, 66 – 8, 97 – 100); death by self-starvation (ll. 69 – 70); death
by cannibalism (ll. 71 – 2); a glutton's death (ll. 78 – 80); necrophilia
(ll. 73 – 6). There are also the staple metaphors of courtship, such as
'siege warfare' with the lady turned into the 'Foe'.

There are unmistakable links between this poem and the first thirty
lines of 'To his Coy Mistress'. The necrophilia links up with 'Worms
shall try / That long-preserv'd Virginity'. The verb 'refuse' links up
with 'you should, if you please, refuse'. The 'State' in line 14 and 'so
high a rate' in line 68 link up with the couplet:

> For, Lady, you deserve this State;
> Nor would I love at lower rate.

But, most telling link of all, the second stanza here makes a
preliminary study of 'coyness' (niceness):

> Nature, her own Sexes foe,                                   5
> Long had taught her to be coy:
> But she neither knew t'enjoy,
> Nor yet let her Lover go.

It is a possible conclusion that 'Daphnis and Chloe', a poem on which he had lavished much care, was still in Marvell's mind when he first began 'To his Coy Mistress', but, as we shall see, there are good grounds for thinking that many years elapsed before he finished that masterpiece.

# 4 'Young Love'

This neat lyric found favour early on. Following its first appearance in the 1681 Folio, it was one of nine Marvell pieces printed in *Miscellany Poems* by Jacob Tonson senior in 1716 and one of four noticed by Giles Jacob in his *Historical Account of the Lives and Writings of Our Most Considerable English Poets* (1720). George Ellis printed it with 'Daphnis and Chloe' in the second edition of his *Specimens of the Early English Poets* (1801), having ignored Marvell in the first edition (1790). Thomas Campbell printed it in *Specimens of the British Poets* (1819).

Like the longer 'Daphnis and Chloe', it is composed in trochaic heptasyllabic quatrains. But its rhyme scheme goes *abab*, whereas that in 'Daphnis and Chloe' went *abba*.

We will take half of it at a time.

I

Come little Infant, Love me now,
    While thine unsuspected years
Clear thine aged Fathers brow
    From cold Jealousie and Fears.

II

Pretty surely 'twere to see          5
    By young Love old Time beguil'd:
While our Sportings are as free
    As the Nurses with the Child.

### III

Common Beauties stay fifteen;
   Such as yours should swifter move;      10
Whose fair Blossoms are too green
   Yet for Lust, but not for Love.

### IV

Love as much the snowy Lamb
   Or the wanton Kid does prize,
As the lusty Bull or Ram,       15
   For his morning Sacrifice.

In line 1 there is no stress on 'little' and somehow the word has to be reduced to one syllable, either by eliding it with 'Infant' or by slurring it into a colloquial 'lil'. The title crops up in line 6.

The poem is studded with internal rhymes. The method changes in stanzas V to VIII, but in I to IV the first word of the third line echoes part of the last word of the second. In I 'clear' echoes 'years'. In II 'While' echoes 'beguil'd'. In III 'Whose' echoes the vowel sound of 'move', and in IV 'as' repeats the last consonant of 'prize'. This pattern cannot be accidental.

The ninth line contains a pitfall. Everyone expects 'stay' to mean 'remain'. Thus H. E. Toliver in *Marvell's Ironic Vision* (Yale University Press, 1965), p.163, pictures the poet 'undoubtedly with tongue in cheek, as though to say "they don't remain young, of course, but they try to"'. The fact is that seventeenth-century adults regarded sexual intercourse by boys or girls of fourteen or younger as inexcusably precocious, but as something to be expected in a boy or girl who had turned fifteen. In those days 'stay' meant 'wait' (intransitive) or 'wait for' (transitive). As J. B. Leishman delicately put it in *The Art of Marvell's Poetry* (Hutchinson, 1966), p.173n., 'stay fifteen' means 'wait until they are fifteen before loving and being loved'. The Oxford *Andrew Marvell*, third edition (1971) wrongly translates it 'do not emerge (out of the awkward age) before they are fifteen years old'. The Victorian Goldwin Smith had no such illusions when he complained in his notes in the Andrew Marvell selection in T. H. Ward's *English Poets*, Vol. II (1880) that the poem was 'marred by the intrusion in the third and fourth stanzas of the fiercer and coarser passions'.

'Common Beauties' was a pet phrase of Thomas Carew's. In 'To A. L.', lines 14–16, he wrote:

> Thus common beauties and meane faces
> Shall have more pastime, and enjoy
> The sport you loose by being coy.

And in 'Ingrateful Beauty Threatned', lines 3–5, he told Celia:

> Thou hadst, in the forgotten crowd
> Of common Beauties, liv'd unknowne,
> Had not my verse exhal'd thy name.

It was typical of Marvell, however, to personify beauty and still in the same breath treat it as an abstract noun. 'Common Beauties stay fifteen;/Such as yours should swifter move;' is comparable to the 'Fond Lovers' in 'The Garden' who cut their mistress's name in these trees and do not stay to consider 'How far these Beauties Hers exceed!'

Stanza V gives the poem a fresh start, or at least a second wind, by picking up the 'Love me now' of line 1 and reversing it.

### V

> Now then love me: time may take
>    Thee before thy time away:
> Of this Need wee'l Virtue make,
>    And learn Love before we may.          20

### VI

> So we win of doubtful Fate;
>    And, if good she to us meant,
> We that Good shall antedate,
>    Or, if ill, that Ill prevent.

### VII

> Thus as Kingdomes, frustrating          25
>    Other Titles to their Crown,
> In the craddle crown their King,
>    So all Forraign Claims to drown,

### VIII

So, to make all Rivals vain,
   Now I crown thee with my Love:       30
Crown me with thy Love again,
   And we both shall Monarchs prove.

The subtle internal rhyming in stanzas I to IV is replaced in V to VIII by the repetition of whole words: 'Love' in V; 'Good' and 'Ill' in VI; 'crown' in VII; 'Love' and 'crown' in VIII. And all these are stressed words, as were the echoes in I to IV.

The classical symmetry in VI is helped by the synonyms 'antedate', 'prevent'; both meaning 'anticipate'. The stanza is tightly compressed. Amplified, it says: 'In that way we shall be stealing a march on Fate, while her intentions are still undisclosed. If she had good intentions towards us, we'll have enjoyed the good earlier. If she intended ill, we'll have had some good first.' Fate must, of course, prevail in the end or she would not be Fate. The argument cleverly reconciles the opposite forces of Free Will and Fate.

The terse dialectic of these stanzas, like those in the far greater poem 'The Definition of Love', is markedly reminiscent of Donne. But Donne was more dramatic than Marvell and Marvell is more musical than Donne.

Legouis, in *Andrew Marvell* (Oxford University Press, 1965), p.31, offered the suggestion that 'Young Love' 'might have been written for T. C. a little later (if she lived long enough), but before she became "ripe for man" '. So for him the little girl here was older than 'little T. C.'. He did not say how old he thought either was. But the reader needs to form a hypothesis.

It was the foible of parents and teachers in the mid-seventeenth century to rush little children ahead. Precocity was the order of the day. John Toy taught four-year-old boys to compose Latin verse. John Evelyn's five-year-old son knew swathes of Greek. 'Little Infant' in the first line of this poem might mean no more than four or five years old, 'While our Sportings are as free / As the Nurses with the Child' at two or three. What do the last eight lines tell us? 'As little boys are sometimes crowned in their cradles to frustrate foreign claimants during a regency and avert war, so the poet crowns the little girl to frustrate other claimants to her love.' Surely this is a very young girl, a six-year-old at most. The younger she is, the less opprobrious the proposition.

How then are we to picture the scene in stanza VIII?

> Now I crown thee with my Love:                    30
>   Crown me with thy Love again,
>     And we both shall Monarchs prove.

Bradbrook and Lloyd Thomas in *Andrew Marvell* (Cambridge University Press, 1940), p.50, saw in these lines 'the suggestion of a romping game like Ring a ring o'Roses'. But that relic of the plague, with its sneezes and 'we all fall down', was never a romping game for two; the 'pockets full of posies' were for disinfection, not for childish crowns. It is far more likely that here the young man ceremoniously places on the child's head a coronal of flowers, a daisy-chain crown, and then invites her to lift it off, and, in turn, crown him. They will be two crowned heads, if she does. Or they might have made two coronals and both could end up wearing crowns and laughing.

There is no apparent intention that the poem should be heard by the child, let alone understood. The poet is writing above the child's head, writing for other grown-ups.

# 5   'The Match'

With ten highly rational stanzas all spoken by the same man, this poem was clearly not designed as a pastoral or meant to be sung. As in 'On a Drop of Dew' later, two elaborately parallel developments are bridged in four final lines.

To make a spontaneous love match, 'The Match' of the title, one man and one woman must meet. In lines 1—16 here the perfect woman arrives, ripe for marriage.

### I

> Nature had long a Treasure made
>   Of all her choisest store;
> Fearing, when She should be decay'd,
>   To beg in vain for more.

### II

Her *Orientest* Colours there,                                        5
     And Essences most pure,
With sweetest Perfumes hoarded were,
     All as she thought secure.

### III

She seldom them unlock'd, or us'd,
     But with the nicest care;                                       10
For, with one grain of them diffus'd,
     She could the World repair.

### IV

But likeness soon together drew
     What she did separate lay;
Of which one perfect Beauty grew,                                    15
     And that was *Celia*.

In line 1 the 'Treasure' is a lock-up, an indoor Treasury. Dame Nature
is depicted as human and ageing and, like any prudent housewife of
diminishing charm, catering for the bad years to come. In line 5
'Orientest' means 'brightest', through association with the east and
the dawn. Colours gladden the eye, essences the palate, and perfumes
the smell. Thus composed, Celia must gladden the senses of Man.
Conversely, the fact that she does so must be due to some such rare
origin.

     But readers can look back at lines 1–16 with most pleasure when
they have read lines 17–36 and realised the parallelism with the man
of the match.

### V

Love wisely had of long fore-seen
     That he must once grow old;
And therefore stor'd a Magazine,
     To save him from the cold.                                      20

## VI

He kept the several Cells repleat
    With Nitre thrice refin'd;
The Naphta's and the Sulphurs heat,
    And all that burns the Mind.

## VII

He fortifi'd the double Gate,                    25
    And rarely thither came,
For, with one Spark of these, he streight
    All Nature could inflame.

## VIII

Till, by vicinity so long,
    A nearer Way they sought;                    30
And, grown magnetically strong,
    Into each other wrought.

## IX

Thus all his fewel did unite
    To make one fire high:
None ever burn'd so hot, so bright;              35
    And *Celia* that am I.

That is, 'No fire ever burn'd so hot, so bright; and, Celia, that fire am
I.' When the man confesses his ardour, he needs eight lines, not four.
Otherwise the parallelism is complete. The very word 'Magazine'
derives from the Arabic for treasury or storehouse.

It is a powder-magazine here, with separate compartments or cells
for the three ingredients of gunpowder: 'Nitre', which is saltpetre;
'Sulphur', which is brimstone; 'Naphta' or naphtha, which is more or
less petroleum. But there is no thought of making gunpowder here or
causing explosions; only of making the hottest possible love-flame.
Stanza IX pants with dramatic ardour.

The weakness in the poem comes now. There should be an interval
of time during which 'the match' can have taken effect. In this metre
the impetus is too great, and the last stanza arrives before the reader
can pause.

X

So we alone the happy rest,
 Whilst all the World is poor,
And have within our Selves possest
 All Love's and Nature's store.   40

# 6 'The Fair Singer'

For the first and only time, Marvell has copied here Shakespeare's stanza form in *Venus and Adonis*. Its six lines of decasyllabic iambics rhyme *ababcc* and would therefore do tolerably well for the sestet of a Petrarchan sonnet.

 In the first stanza the second pair of rhymes should be pronounced as the poet intended, and as his Age allowed, 'Enem-eye', 'Harmon-eye', or they will trespass on the neighbouring 'me' and 'agree' and that must affect the next stanza.

I

To make a final conquest of all me,
Love did compose so sweet an Enemy,
In whom both Beauties to my death agree,
Joyning themselves in fatal Harmony;
That while she with her Eyes my Heart does bind, 5
She with her Voice might captivate my Mind.

II

I could have fled from One but singly fair:
My dis-intangled Soul it self might save,
Breaking the curled trammels of her hair.
But how should I avoid to be her Slave,  10
Whose subtile Art invisibly can wreath
My Fetters of the very Air I breath?

### III

It had been easie fighting in some plain,
Where Victory might hang in equal choice,
But all resistance against her is vain,                    15
Who has th'advantage both of Eyes and Voice,
And all my Forces needs must be undone,
She having gained both the Wind and Sun.

This Cavalier lyric is a well-calculated mixture of gallantry and wit, but a musical mixture. Each stanza is a self-contained sentence. The motion is onward and forward in each; there are no inversions of word order in III, and elsewhere there are only the small changes needed to put the verbs 'agree', 'bind', 'save' in a position to rhyme. The markedly Latin syntax will later recur in 'The Mower to the Glo-Worms', another short poem.

The gallantry has its limits. While the poet singles the Lady out from her sex, he does not name her as Milton did his Leonora, or Lovelace and Carew their Gratiana and Celia, or Waller his Mrs Arden. Nor does Marvell concentrate on the Fair Singer to the total exclusion of the rest of the sex. His first two lines imply that his heart has been touched by women's beauty before. It was in order to make a final conquest of 'all me', he says, that the god Love devised so sweet a lady as this. And in lines 7—9 he can imagine another lady trying to hold him by physical beauty alone:

I could have fled from One but singly fair:
My dis-intangled Soul it self might save,
Breaking the curled trammels of her hair.

The 'Soul' here is distinct from the 'Heart' and the 'Mind' which are victims of the Fair Singer's two Beauties, and the 'her' in line 9 is distinct from the 'her' in line 10. 'Trammels' were nets of close mesh. Michael Drayton first coined 'curl'd tramels of hair' in *The Muses Elysium*, Nymphal II, lines 235—6, where Cleon fancied birds. . .

. . . caught ere they be ware
In the curl'd tramels of thy hair.

Marvell's poem is a masterpiece of decorous wit, though a miniature masterpiece. The wit takes several forms. It works through the imagery, for one thing. There is the early musical metaphor in 'compose' and 'Harmony'. There is the sustained metaphor of the sex war: the lady is an 'Enemy' in I, where she aims at his 'death'; she takes him prisoner in the second half of II; she out-manoeuvres him and defeats him and his 'Forces' in a pitched battle in III.

In addition, the wit works through puns. In line 5 'does bind' means at once 'trusses up' and 'charms with a spell'. In line 6 'captivate' similarly means 'take captive' and 'enchant'.

But the best wit plays with the twin beauties of eyes and of voice which compose the Fair Singer. This is surely the germ of the poem. Here he is on the same ground as Waller in 'Of Mrs Arden':

> Behold, and listen, while the fair
> Breaks in sweet sounds the willing air,
> And with her own breath fans the fire
> Which her bright eyes do first inspire.
> What reason can that love control,
> Which more than one way courts the soul?
> 　So when a flash of lightning falls
> On our abodes, the danger calls
> For human aid, which hopes the flame
> To conquer, though from heaven it came;
> But if the winds with that conspire,
> Men strive not, but deplore the fire.

Waller's lines cry out for a musical setting in a way in which Marvell's do not. But Marvell is Waller's master in the artistic compression of wit.

This gift shows here at the end of each stanza, where the couplet encourages epigrammatic effect. In lines 11–12 the lady's 'subtile Art' as a singer 'can wreath' (a circular image) invisible 'Fetters' (another circular image) about the feet of the poet with the circling notes of her song; it comes through the air that he breathes and its magic roots him to the ground. Milton described such imagined circles as 'mazes' in 'L'Allegro', lines 135–42:

> And ever against eating Cares,
> Lap me in soft Lydian Airs,
> Married to immortal verse
> Such as the meeting soul may pierce
> In notes, with many a winding bout

Of linked sweetness long drawn out, 140
With wanton heed, and giddy cunning,
The melting voice through mazes running.

He was using a larger scale than Marvell, but both had the same sort of music in mind and both were reacting as listeners.

In stanza III all these forms of wit are summed up together. 'It would have been easy to fight the lady on level ground and equal terms,' Marvell tells us. The metaphor 'hangs' is the classical image of scales suspended by gods in the air, in equipoise while the struggle was equal and the issue uncertain. So Zeus held the scales containing the Fates of Achilles and Hector in Homer's *Iliad*, XXII 209 ff., which Virgil copied in *Aeneid*, XII 725–7. Marvell may also have in mind Donne's 'The Ecstasy', lines 13–16:

> As, 'twixt two equal armies, Fate
>   Suspends uncertain victory,
> Our souls (which to advance their state
>   Were gone out) hung 'twixt her and me.

In the last four lines Marvell explains, with brilliant economy, why he has no chance in the battle with the Fair Singer:

> But all resistance against her is vain, 15
> Who has th'advantage both of Eyes and Voice,
> And all my Forces needs must be undone,
> She having gained both the Wind and Sun.

The point is that every General always wanted to fight with the wind behind him. Equally he liked to have the sun at his back. He was glad to have either of these advantages. But the Fair Singer has both, and the poet in her audience is lost. In her full-throated song she sweeps him with 'the wind' of her beautiful voice. At the same time, gazing only at him while she sings, she dazzles him with her beautiful eyes, which shine like the Sun. All his 'Forces' must needs be undone. The pun there sets the seal on the couplet, for the word 'Forces' means (1) 'troops' and (2) 'muscular powers' or 'powers of resistance'.

# 7 'An Elegy upon the Death of my Lord Francis Villiers'

This poem was first printed as Marvell's by Margoliouth in 1928. It came to him by way of C. H. Wilkinson from an unlicensed anonymous quarto in the collection which had been left to Worcester College, Oxford by the bibliophile–politician George Clarke (1660–1736), a collection begun by his father, Sir William (1623–66). On the first of the quarto's eight pages, the title page, the words 'by Andrew Marvell' are added in the hand of George Clarke. A second copy came to light in 1974 at the College of Wooster, Ohio, USA. There is as yet no third.

Lord Francis Villiers was killed by Parliamentarian troopers at Kingston-upon-Thames on 7 July 1648 in his twentieth year. It was the third day of the Earl of Holland's ill-fated rising, the immediate aim of which was to relieve the Royalists besieged in Colchester by General Thomas Lord Fairfax. Lord Francis's elder brother, George Duke of Buckingham, was the Earl of Holland's general of the horse.

The Elegy has thirteen paragraphs, but can be studied best in four parts: A, ll. 1–24; B, ll. 25–58; C, ll. 59–104; D, ll. 105–28. Many points in favour of Marvell's authorship will emerge.

## A

'Tis true that he is dead: but yet to chuse,
Methinkes thou Fame should not have brought the news.
Thou canst discourse at will and speak at large:
But wast not in the fight nor durst thou charge.
While he, transported all with valiant rage,    5
His name eternizd but cut short his age;
On the safe battlements of Richmonds bowers
Thou wast espyd, and from the guilded Towers
Thy silver Trumpets sounded a Retreat,
Farre from the dust and battails sulphry heat.    10
Yet what couldst thou have done? 'tis alwayes late
To struggle with inevitable fate.
Much rather thou I know expectst to tell
How heavy *Cromwell* gnasht the earth and fell.

Or how slow Death farre from the sight of day      15
The long-deceived *Fairfax* bore away.
But untill then, let us young *Francis* praise:
And plant upon his hearse the bloody bayes,
Which we will water with our welling eyes.
Teares spring not still from spungy Cowardize.      20
The purer fountaines from the Rocks more steep
Destill and stony valour best doth weep.
Besides Revenge, if often quencht in teares,
Hardens like Steele and daily keener weares.

The poet takes up his pen after the rumour of his friend's death has been verified and before the interment in Westminster Abbey. His rounding on 'Fame' is a typically angry reaction to the bringer of bad news. Unlike Virgil in *Aeneid*, Book IV, he makes Fame a man, but in placing his figure of Fame on Richmond's 'safe battlements and guilded Towers' he probably recalls Virgil's Fame '*aut summi culmine tecti turribus aut altis*' (either on the roof top or on the high towers) in lines 186–7.

In line 10 'sulphry heat' has its counterpart in Marvell's 'The Match', line 23, 'The Naphta's and the Sulphur's heat', while Marvell also has 'Where Sulphrey Phlegeton does ever burn' in 'Tom May's Death', line 90.

In line 11 the question 'Yet what couldst thou have done?' echoes Milton's elegy 'Lycidas', lines 56–7:

Ay me, I fondly dream!
'Had ye bin there' . . . for what could that have done?

There was no poem that Marvell echoed more often than 'Lycidas'. He echoed line 28, 'That last infirmity of Noble mind', twice: in 1646 at Rome in 'Fleckno', line 28, 'The last distemper of the sober brain', and in 1658 in 'A Poem Upon the Death of O.C.', line 22, 'Those nobler weaknesses of humane Mind'. He echoed line 112, where the angry St Peter 'shook his Miter'd locks and stern bespake', in 'Tom May's Death', line 32, where Ben Jonson's ghost in Elysium 'shook his gray locks' and broke into a fierce tirade. He echoed line 177, 'In the blest Kingdoms meek of joy and love', in 'The First Anniversary of the Government under O.C.', line 218, 'Unto the Kingdom blest of Peace and Love'; and in the same poem 'beaked Promontories' in

line 358 echoed 'beaked Promontory' in 'Lycidas', line 94. And these
are not the only examples.

It was the detestation of Lieutenant-General Cromwell and the
distaste for General Fairfax in lines 13–16 that caused Margoliouth
in 1927 to write: 'If the poem is Marvell's, it is his one unequivocally
royalist utterance; it throws into strong relief the transitional
character of "An Horatian Ode" where royalist principles and
admiration for Cromwell the Great Man exist side by side: it explains
"Tom May's Death": and it throws a backward light on the history of
Marvell's mind during the still obscure years since 1641.' (*The Poems
and Letters of Andrew Marvell*, 1st ed., Oxford University Press,
1927, I, 334.) That rather ignored the unequivocally royalist utterances in 'To his Noble Friend Mr Richard Lovelace', written six or
seven months before.

In line 18 'the bloody bayes' were the customary sprigs of blood-
soaked rosemary put on the coffin of a battle casualty. In line 20 'still'
means 'always': 'it is not always cowardly to weep'. In line 21 'the
fountaines' are the sources of rivers. In lines 23–4 the steel that goes to
the forging of swords is tempered or brought to a proper hardness and
elasticity by heating after quenching; the warrior's tears by the same
process can harden his revenge.

In line 22 the Latin derivative 'destill' (pour down in droplets) is a
true Marvellian word. He used it intransitively in 'On a Drop of
Dew', line 37, 'Such did the Manna's sacred dew destil', and he used it
transitively in 'Damon the Mower', line 43, 'On me the Morn her
dew distills'.

Lord Francis was born to Katharine Duchess of Buckingham on 2
April 1629, eight months after his famous father was assassinated on
23 August 1628. The poet now travels twenty years back to the
*conception* of the posthumous child.


B


Great *Buckingham*, whose death doth freshly strike        25
Our memoryes, because to this so like;
Ere that in the Eternall Court he shone,
And here a Favorite there found a throne;
The fatall night before he hence did bleed,
Left to his *Princess* this immortall seed.        30
As the wise *Chinese* in the fertile wombe

Of Earth doth a more precious clay entombe,
Which dying by his will he leaves consignd:
Til by mature delay of time refind
The christall metall fit to be releast     35
Is taken forth to crowne each royall feast:
Such was the fate by which this Postume breathd,
Who scarcely seems begotten but bequeathd.
    Never was any humane plant that grew
More faire then this and ácceptábly new.     40
'Tis truth that beauty doth most men dispraise:
Prudence and valour their esteeme do raise.
But he that hath already these in store,
Can not be poorer sure for having more.
And his unimitable handsomenesse     45
Made him indeed be more then man, not lesse.
We do but faintly Gods resemblance beare
And like rough coyns of careless mints appeare:
But he of purpose made, did represent
In a rich Medall every lineament.     50
    Lovely and admirable as he was,
Yet was his Sword or Armour all his Glasse.
Nor in his Mistris eyes that joy he tooke,
As in an Enemies himselfe to looke.
I know how well he did, with what delight     55
Those serious imitations of fight.
Still in the trialls of strong exercise
His was the first, and his the second prize.

The adroit simile of the 'Chinese' (Chinaman) in lines 31−6 tallies with the simile in Marvell's 'The First Anniversary of the Government under O.C.', lines 19−22, where Cromwell's executive speed is contrasted with the slow operation of Kings:

> Their earthy Projects under ground they lay,
> More slow and brittle then the *China* clay:
> Well may they strive to leave them to their Son,
> For one Thing never was by one King don.

It was still commonly believed that porcelain or china dishes were made of earth and lay underground maturing for generations; in which time they passed with other property from father to son.

The 'unimitable handsomeness' of Lord Francis is well attested by friend and foe alike. The Royalist Earl of Clarendon, recounting his death, wrote: 'And in this confusion the Lord Francis Villiers, a youth of rare beauty and comeliness of person, not being upon his horse so soon as the rest, or endeavouring to make some resistance, was unfortunately killed, with one or two more but of little note.' (*History of the Great Rebellion*, Oxford University Press, 1843, XI, 104). The Parliamentarian General Edmund Ludlow wrote in his account:

> The Lord Francis presuming perhaps that his beauty would have charmed the souldiers, as it had done Mrs Kirk, for whom he made a splendid entertainment the night before he left the town, and made her a present of plate to the value of a thousand pounds, stayed behind his company, where unseasonably daring the troopers, and refusing to take quarter, he was killed, and after his death there was found upon him some of the hair of Mrs Kirk sew'd in a piece of ribbon that hung next his skin. (*Memoirs*, ed. C. H. Firth, Oxford University Press, 1894, I, 198.)

It is in lines 55–8 that the voice of Andrew Marvell is most unmistakably heard. A reticent man, he did not often wax autobiographical; so it made all the greater impact when he did. There are three particularly good examples in his Cromwell poems in this metre. There is the passage in 'The First Anniversary of the Government under O.C.', lines 265–78, about a storm at seas, beginning:

> So have I seen at Sea, when whirling Winds,
> Hurry the Bark, but more the Seamens minds . . .

There is the passage in 'A Poem upon the Death of O.C.', lines 89–100, with the same beginning:

> So have I seen a Vine, whose lasting Age
> Of many a Winter hath surviv'd the rage.

And in the same poem there is the passage in lines 247–54:

> I saw him dead, a leaden slumber lyes,
> And mortal sleep over those wakefull eyes:

Here in the Villiers Elegy the poet says 'I know', not 'I saw', but the
artistic intention is the same, to bring authentic experience to bear and
so impress and convince the readers. And we can well believe that
what Marvell 'knew' about Francis Villiers in various martial
competitions on horseback he came to know in 1646–47 in Rome.

The poet next turns to the separate theme of Lord Francis among
the ladies. Marvell had done the same thing in the third section of
verses 'To his Noble Friend Mr Richard Lovelace' a few months
before.

## C

Bright Lady, thou that rulest from above
The last and greatest Monarchy of Love:      60
Faire *Richmond* hold thy Brother or he goes.
Try if the Jasmin of thy hand or Rose
Of thy red Lip can keep him alwayes here.
For he loves danger and doth never feare.
Or may thy tears prevaile with him to stay?      65
    But he resolv'd breaks carelessly away.
Onely one argument could now prolong
His stay and that most faire and so most strong:
The matchless *Chlora* whose pure fires did warm
His soule and only could his passions charme.      70
    You might with much more reason go reprove
The amorous Magnet which the North doth love.
Or preach divorce and say it is amisse
That with tall Elms the twining Vines should kisse
Then chide two such so fit, so equall faire      75
That in the world they have no other paire.
Whom it might seeme that Heaven did create
To restore man unto his first estate.
Yet she for honours tyrannous respect
Her own desires did and his neglect.      80
And like the Modest Plant at every touch
Shrunk in her leaves and feard it was too much.
    But who can paint the torments and that pain
Which he profest and now she could not faigne?
He like the Sun but overcast and pale:      85
Shee like a Rainbow, that ere long must faile,

Whose rosiall cheek where Heaven it selfe did view
Begins to separate and dissolve to dew.
    At last he leave obtaines though sad and slow,
First of her ánd then of himselfe to goe.                    90
How comely and how terrible he sits
At once and Warre and well as Love befits!
Ride where thou wilt and bold adventures find:
But all the Ladies are got up behind.
Guard them, though not thy selfe: for in thy death     95
Th'Eleven thousand Virgins lose their breath.
    So *Hector* issuing from the Trojan wall
The sad *Iliades* to the Gods did call
With hands display'd and with dishevell'd haire
That they the Empire in his life would spare.          100
While he secure through all the field doth spy
*Achilles* for *Achilles* only cry.
Ah ignorant that yet e'er night he must
Be drawn by him inglorious through the dust.

The 'bright Lady' in line 59 and 'faire Richmond' in line 61 was
Mary Villiers, sister of Francis and wife of James Stuart, Duke of
Richmond and Lennox, whose seat at Richmond was two miles
from Kingston-upon-Thames. She had the family's good looks.
    The age-old romantic combination of Lily and Rose for white skin
and red lips is refreshingly changed here to Jasmine and Rose. In line
62 'or he goes' means 'ere he goes'; the verb would be subjunctive,
'go', but for the need to rhyme.
    In the poetically idealised lines 67—88, 'the matchless Chlora' was
the Mrs Kirk of Ludlow's *Memoirs* above. She had been born Mary
Townshend, daughter of the Court poet Aurelian Townshend
(1583—1651) whose last years were sadly decayed. Mary, however,
thrived on her beauty at Court and in 1646 was given in marriage by
the King himself to George Kirke, Groom of the King's Chamber, at
Oxford. Either the poet here did not know of her reputation for
'gallantry' (Marvell was abroad in 1643—47) or he chose to ignore it;
lines 79—80 assert that out of respect for the tyrant Honour 'she
neglected her own desires and his' and modestly shrank from
adultery; in lines 69—70 'her pure fires did warm /His soule'; in lines
77—8 she and he were fit partners for a 'Paradise Restored'.
    On that basis the poetry ascends at line 83 to the higher level of
epic, and for forty lines there it remains. The question 'Who can

paint?' challenges the inward eye of the reader. The details are graphic. The language is memorably balanced and musical.

On horseback in lines 91–2 Lord Francis is 'at once' (simultaneously) 'comely' and 'terrible'. The comeliness fits him for love and the terror for war. He is an Arthurian knight errant, ready to strike down the next foe or rescue a damsel. Only here there is a limit.

> Ride where thou wilt and bold adventures find:
> But all the Ladies are got up behind.

The key word is 'bold'. 'Challenge any number of foemen, but expect no amorous adventures ahead, because all the ladies are already behind you.' Lines 95–6 go on: 'Guard your life for their sake, if not for your own; your death would leave "the eleven thousand virgins" with nothing to live for'.

The reference here is to the legend of St Ursula. She was the daughter of the fifth-century King of Brittany and a Christian. When wooed by the heir to the kingdom of Britain, she bade him first bring ten British noblewomen, each with one thousand virgins in attendance, and an eleventh thousand more for herself. He did this, and she converted them all. She then took them over the Alps to Rome, where they were blessed by the Pope. But on the way back she and her eleven thousand were slain by the Huns at Cologne.

The Homeric simile in lines 97–104 maintains the new epic dimension. 'Hector issuing' is absolute in construction and means 'when Hector issued'. In Homer's *Iliad*, XXII, Hector went out of Ilion (Troy) to seek mortal combat on foot with Achilles the Greek, careless of his own safety and of the fate of the daughters of Troy (*Iliades* or *Troades*). 'He looks for Achilles and he shouts for Achilles.' The Iliades (a trisyllable here, with the stress on 'li') mounted the walls and prayed frantically to their gods for the hero's deliverance, as the virgins do now for Villiers. But Hector, like Villiers, was killed. There the parallel ended, for Hector was dishonourably dragged through the dust at the tail of the chariot of Achilles, which Villiers was not.

Before we go on to D, there are several signposts to Marvell in C. He used the same name Chlora for the mourner in 'Mourning' and he used Clora (with no 'h') for the heroine in 'The Gallery'. In line 74 'the twining Vines' have an echo in 'Upon Appleton House', lines 609–10:

> Bind me ye *Woodbines* in your twines,
> Curle me about ye gadding *Vines*.

In lines 81–2 the simile of the *mimosa pudica* or modest plant is
repeated in 'Upon Appleton House', lines 357–8, where it is likened
to 'that Heaven-nursed Plant', conscience:

> A prickling leaf it bears, and such
> As that which shrinks at ev'ry touch.

Finally, let us look again at the two couplets, lines 83–6:

> But who can paint the torments and that pain
> Which he profest and now she could not faigne?
> He like the Sun but overcast and pale:                      85
> Shee like a Rainbow, that ere long must faile.

The balance and grace in the second couplet are matched by Marvell's
lines 37–8 in 'To his Noble Friend Mr Richard Lovelace':

> Whose hand so rudely grasps the steely brand,
> Whose hand so gently melts the Lady's hand.

And it is more than the common factor of 'feign', meaning 'dissemble
and cloak', that is reminiscent of Marvell's lines 61–2 in 'A Poem
upon the Death of O.C.', though that was to come ten years later. He
is linking the mortal illnesses of Oliver and his favourite daughter in
September 1658:

> She lest He grieve hides what She can her pains,
> And He to lessen hers his Sorrow feigns.

### D

> Such fell young *Villiers* in the chearfull heat          105
> Of youth: his locks intangled all with sweat
> And those eyes which the Sentinell did keep
> Of love clos'd up in an eternal sleep.
> While *Venus* of *Adonis* thinks no more
> Slaine by the harsh tuske of the Savage Boare,           110

Hither she runns and hath him hurried farre
Out of the noise and blood, and killing warre:
Where in her Gardens of Sweet myrtle laid
Shee kisses him in the immortall shade.
    Yet dyed he not revengelesse: Much he did      115
Ere he could suffer. A whole Pyramid
Of Vulgar bodies he erected high:
Scorning without a Sepulcher to dye.
And with his steele which did whole troopes divide
He cut his Epitaph on either Side.      120
Till finding nothing to his courage fit
He rid up last to death and conquer'd it.
    Such are the Obsequies to *Francis* own:
He best the pompe of his owne death hath showne.
And we hereafter to his honour will      125
Not write so many, but so many kill.
Till the whole Army by just vengeance come
To be at once his Trophee and his Tombe.

In line 105 'heat' is pronounced 'het' to rhyme with 'sweat', as in Marvell's 'Damon the Mower', lines 45—6:

> And, if at Noon my toil me heat,
> The Sun himself licks off my Sweat.

'Intangled' and 'closed' are participles in an absolute construction. The 'Sentinel of love' keeps the eyes open and Lord Francis had little use for sleep. The present tenses in lines 108—14 break into the past tenses of lines 98—122. The poet has Shakespeare's 'Venus and Adonis' in mind. In line 110 the iambic rhythm is deliberately distorted in order that the reader may hear the crunch of the tusk of the boar:

> Sláine by | the hársh | túske of | the Sáv | age Boáre.

Lord Francis was an Adonis, and Venus must take care of all lovers, of course. She spirits him away, but in his last minutes he had already managed his own funeral rites. Even the engraving of his epitaph on both sides of his sepulchre or altar tomb had already been done by his sabre to right and left of the troops on horseback that he fought his way through.

> And with his steele which did whole troopes divide
> He cut his Epitaph on either Side.

The same rhymes appear in Marvell's Horatian Ode', lines 15–16, where Cromwell, in his rise to the Irish command,

> Did thorough his own Side
> His fiery way divide.

The poet ends with a noble resolution for himself and the other Royalists who have survived the dead man. They will avenge him with deeds and not words. Their victorious army will be both the trophy that Greek victors raised and the sepulchral monument that he personally has earned. King Charles I was, of course, still alive.

Marvell ended two other poems in a similar way. 'The unfortunate Lover', another posthumous son and young lover, ends:

> And he in Story only rules,
> In a Field *Sable* a Lover *Gules*.

And the last stanza of 'The Mower's Song', before the refrain, reads:

> And thus, ye Meadows, which have been          25
> Companions of my thoughts more green,
> Shall now the Heraldry become
> With which I shall adorn my Tomb.

It was much more natural for him to end thus if he had already written 'Upon the Death of my Lord Francis Villiers'.

The fact that this elegy was privately printed on its own suggests that it was unsolicited. I believe that Marvell was Francis's friend and admirer from their months together in Rome; that Marvell keenly regretted his death; that the poet wrote these lines in a concentrated burst of energy and sent them to the Duke and Duchess of Richmond. The printing of them is evidence that the recipients were pleased.

The time has surely come to admit them with pleasure into the received Marvell canon.

# 8  'Mourning'

## I

You, that decipher out the Fate
Of humane Off-springs from the Skies,
What mean these Infants which of late
Spring from the Starrs of *Chlora's* Eyes?

The question so artistically framed is addressed to astrologers, but in the mid-seventeenth century their ranks still included most doctors. They were as adept at casting a horoscope and working out a new baby's fate from the stars as any clever decoder of ciphered despatches. Who, then, could better interpret the tears that Chlora had been shedding 'of late'?

Lovers and poets commonly liken the eyes of a lady to stars. Here, by a natural extension, Chlora's tears are the 'Infants' or 'Off-springs' of her starry eyes. In the next stanzas Marvell describes these.

## II

Her Eyes confus'd, and doubled ore,                    5
With Tears suspended ere they flow;
Seem bending upwards, to restore
To Heaven, whence it came, their Woe.

## III

When, molding of the watry Sphears,
Slow drops unty themselves away;                      10
As if she, with those precious Tears,
Would strow the ground where *Strephon* lay.

The two stanzas are one sentence really. The alliterative introduction of 'w' in line 8, 'whence' and 'Woe', continued with 'When' and 'watry' in line 9, serves as a kind of cement. Nor does the 'w' end there.

In II the gathered tears in each eye have the prismatic effect of making them seem double. The word 'bend' means 'incline' and involves the suggestion of movement, which in this case is 'upwards'. In much the same way lines 35–6 of 'On a Drop of Dew' describe the human soul as a sphere at the moment of imminent lift-off.

> Moving but on a point below,
> It all about does upwards bend.

Stanza III opens with a small problem. How does 'molding of the watry Sphears' slot into 'When . . . slow drops unty themselves away' and what does it mean? Since 'molding' is not plural, it can hardly be a noun in apposition to 'drops'; there is no collective noun 'molding' and, though there is a collective noun 'offspring', Marvell has just used 'Off-springs' above. It must be the present participle, then, of an intransitive 'mold'. Clearly 'the watry Sphears' are Chlora's eyes, but the phrase is as clearly derived from *sphaera aquae* (the sphere of water) which in pre-Copernican astronomy circulated outside *sphaera terrae* (the sphere of earth). Between 'molding' and 'the watry Sphears' the preposition 'of' means 'from' (not 'off'); so it did in the Nicene Creed's 'God of God, Light of Light, very God of very God', and so it does in Marvell's 'Young Love', line 21, 'So we win of doubtful Fate'. Thus lines 9—10 mean: 'When slow tear-drops, taking their shape from the watery spheres of Chlora's wet eyes, set themselves free and fall . . .'.

Marvell knew nothing of gravity's pull and his verb 'unty' makes the captive tears release themselves as by a human act of will. The indirect speech in lines 11—12 similarly implies that Chlora said to herself: 'I will strow these precious tears on Strephon's grave.' That would make a classical libation.

Can 'Strephon' have been Lord Francis Villiers and 'Chlora' Mrs Mary Kirke? She was the Chlora in the Villiers Elegy and Marvell was far too kind to her there. The Elector Palatine had been her lover in 1635, ten years before she married George Kirke, and she could still captivate young Lord Francis two years after that. Now he was dead.

Whether this is the same 'Chlora' or not, society tongues start gossiping in stanzas IV and V:

IV

> Yet some affirm, pretending Art,
> Her Eyes have so her Bosome drown'd,
> Only to soften near her Heart                15
> A place to fix another Wound.

### V

And, while vain Pomp does her restrain
Within her solitary Bowr,
She courts her self in am'rous Rain;
Her self both *Danae* and the Showr.                    20

Danae (a disyllable here) was the Greek maiden confined in a windowless tower whom the amorous Zeus nevertheless contrived to reach through the roof in a golden shower; she bore him Perseus. Chlora's isolation is the same, self-confined to her upstairs bedroom. Her iconoclastic critics despise convention, which they call 'vain Pomp'. Since her mind must run on courtship, her tears can only be mental substitutes for Zeus's amorous shower.

In IV the difficult phrase is 'pretending Art'. James Winny in *Andrew Marvell* (Hutchinson, 1962), p.99, explains it as 'pretending to be well versed in feminine guile'. That works if the 'Art' is not Chlora's. But are not the gossips *alleging* that Chlora's tears are less tears of 'mourning' than the sly product of art? They doubt her constancy. They doubt her sincerity. They think she is looking forward, not back. Either she already has another lover in mind or she is indulging in erotic fantasy. Other tongues are more bold:

### VI

Nay others, bolder, hence esteem
Joy now so much her Master grown,
That whatsoever does but seem
Like Grief, is from her Windows thrown.

### VII

Nor that she payes, while she survives,                    25
To her dead Love this Tribute due;
But casts abroad these Donatives,
At the installing of a new.

Their extra boldness is marked by the extra stress on the first syllable in lines 21 and 22. The tone becomes masculine and assertive. 'Her tears are tears of Joy.' 'She celebrates the opening of a new epoch.'

In Marvell's London the women tipped bedroom slops out of the projecting upper windows into the 'channel' that went down the middle of the road. In a vulgar image the gossips imply that Chlora's tears are not 'precious', but mere bedroom slops.

In ancient Rome the *donativum* was a mass distribution of small coins by great men on festive occasions. In the Middle Ages it was called 'largesse'. In a more patrician image, the same gossips describe these tears as 'Donatives' at the Installation of Strephon's Successor.

The two final stanzas are markedly different, both from each other and from all that has gone before:

### VIII

How wide they dream! The *Indian* Slaves
That sink for Pearl through Seas profound,          30
Would find her Tears yet deeper Waves
And not of one the bottom sound.

### IX

I yet my silent Judgment keep,
Disputing not what they believe:
But sure as oft as Women weep,                      35
It is to be suppos'd they grieve.

Stanza VIII is a candid aside to the reader. The poet's ejaculation 'How wide they dream!' covers both sets of gossips and means 'How far from the truth their surmises are!' And why so? Because Chlora's tears are all deep. This contrast of dimensions is deliberate; the dreams *wide* and the tears *deep*. Every detail is carefully controlled. In each line the caesura comes exactly half-way. Each half-line descends a stage nearer the ocean-bed. The musical progression is downward, but by degrees, not a falling cadence. The consonants are skilfully marshalled, the vowels most gracefully varied.

Stanza IX harks back to the title and indirectly answers the opening question. We see how the poet who has just confided in us behaves when he rejoins his circle; a listener, inscrutable and sphinx-like. This was the same man who in 1675 would write in a letter: 'I am naturally and now more by my Age inclined to keep my thoughts private.' That is what in his youth he does now, as he privately resolves to err on the side of the angels and trust women's displays of emotion. But he will not display any emotion himself. Hence the ironic tone here.

# 9 'The Nymph complaining for the death of her Faun'

This tender lyric is much more than another Catullan lament for the death of a pet. It is a dramatic monologue brimming with sweetness and charm. It is a study in Stuart girl portraiture. The Nymph speaks all 122 lines. In the process her young heart is laid bare.

How old should we take her to be? Far older than the 'little infant' in 'Young Love' or the small girl in 'The Picture of little T.C. in a Prospect of Flowers'. Older than the Mary Fairfax aged twelve, who is Caelia in Marvell's lines 'To his worthy Friend Doctor Wittie', or the same Mary Fairfax who, at thirteen or fourteen, is 'the young Maria' and 'Blest Nymph' in 'Upon Appleton House'. Fifteen years old at least. More likely, seventeen.

The poet is not concerned to compress or economise here. Since spontaneous grief is diffuse, he lets his nymph pour out all that she feels. He will hold her to octosyllabic couplets throughout, but not to a set stanza form. The eleven paragraphs vary in length from twenty-four lines to four. As it happens, the first is the longest.

> The wanton Troopers riding by
> Have shot my Faun and it will dye.
> Ungentle men! They cannot thrive
> To kill thee. Thou neer didst alive
> Them any harm: alas nor cou'd          5
> Thy death yet do them any good.
> I'me sure I never wisht them ill;
> Nor do I for all this; nor will:
> But, if my simple Pray'rs may yet
> Prevail with Heaven to forget          10
> Thy murder, I will Joyn my Tears
> Rather then fail. But, O my fears!
> It cannot dye so. Heavens King
> Keeps register of every thing:
> And nothing may we use in vain.        15
> Ev'n Beasts must be with justice slain;
> Else Men are made their *Deodands*.
> Though they should wash their guilty hands
> In this warm life-blood, which doth part

69

From thine, and wound me to the Heart,          20
Yet could they not be clean: their Stain
Is dy'd in such a Purple Grain.
There is not such another in
The World, to offer for their Sin.

The opening couplet provides a crisp start. It gives us the situation
and the metre. In its jog-trot we may hear the horses' hoofs going
past.

The word 'Troopers' helps to date the poem. The *New English
Dictionary* gives 1640 as the year of its first known appearance in print
and the 'trooper' then was a Scottish Covenanter. But the word
quickly spread to the south. In the English Civil Wars both sides had
their Troops of Horse, all consisting of sixty mounted men and two
officers, armed with sabres and pistols. Oliver Cromwell was Captain
of the famous 67th Troop at Edgehill in 1642. At Marston Moor in
1644, as Lieutenant-General to the Earl of Manchester, he led the left
wing and had 4200 Troopers under him, half of them English, half
Scots; for the Parliament had recently 'taken the Covenant' to secure
Scottish support.

Marvell was out of the country for the four years up to 1647, but
his sympathies were Royalist when he came back. As we have seen,
he wrote a Royalist elegy on his friend Lord Francis Villiers, killed in
action on 7 July 1648 at Kingston-upon-Thames in the Second Civil
War. The word 'troopers' appears in the Parliamentarian General
Edmund Ludlow's brief account of that action: 'The Lord
Francis . . . stayed behind his company, where unseasonably daring
the troopers, and refusing to take quarter, he was killed.' ( *Memoirs*,
Oxford University Press, 1894, I, 198.)

'The Nymph complaining for the death of her Faun' has every
appearance of being likewise based on fact. It is Cavalier in tone. The
nymph is patrician. 'The wanton Troopers' are Parliamentarian. The
scene is the south. Even a detail like her calling God 'Heaven's King' is
suggestive of Royalist sympathies. After the execution of King
Charles on 30 January 1649 the war moved to Ireland. All this points
to Marvell's having started this autumnal poem in the autumn of
1648, however much he may have polished it later.

In line 3 'ungentle' means 'ill-bred'. One mark of the nymph's
good breeding is her saturation in Bible learning and Christian
thought. Young though she is, she knows that to bear malice is
wrong; that she should pray for her enemies; that tears can add force

to prayers. But she also remembers that men are accountable ultimately to God, who 'keeps register of every thing'. To her a 'register' meant a blank book for handwritten memoranda. Her notion is Bible-based. For instance, in Malachi, III 16, 'a book of remembrance was written before the Lord for them that feared him and that thought upon his name'. And at the Last Judgment in Revelation, XX 12, 'the books were opened, and the dead were judged out of those things which were written in the books according to their works'. Clearly also she is referring in the last couplet to the sacrifice of Jesus Christ on the Cross, the Lamb of God that taketh away the sins of the World, the Redeemer of Mankind.

But the troopers have put themselves beyond redemption. They have killed the best fawn in the world. No fawn now remains that is good enough for an expiatory sacrifice. In lines 18–22 there seems to be a mixture of the Macbeths' blood-stained hands, which a little water would or would not wash clean, and the robes of the saints in Revelation, which were washed white in the Blood of the Lamb. No conscious effort of the troopers would wash the filthy witness from their hands, not even if they dipped them in the blood of the fawn while still warm.

The girl's candour and youth are conveyed by simplicity of diction and rawness of syntax. What are we to make of 'They cannot thrive to kill thee', in strict grammatical terms? In line 13 'it cannot dye so' is a cryptic way of saying that 'it cannot die with the murder generously forgotten by God in response to my prayers'. And it takes time to see that 'life-blood, which doth part /From thine, and wound me to the Heart' is her raw way of saying 'life-blood which issues from thy heart, and wounds me to mine'. As for simplicity of diction, six of these twenty-four lines are totally monosyllabic, including the successive lines 19, 20, 21; while nine others contain six monosyllables, including lines 4, 5, 6, 7.

The one arcane word is 'Deodands'. Beasts causing the death of humans were forfeit by law to the Crown; they were *Deo dandi* (meet to be given to God) and the money from their sale was put to pious uses. In a witty paradox here, the girl states it as a juridical fact that humans who cause the death of a beast are forfeit in the same way. There cannot be one law for humans and another for beasts, in her view.

The poem goes on to give the brief history of this fawn.

Unconstant *Sylvio*, when yet                                    25
I had not found him counterfeit,
One morning (I remember well)
Ty'd in this silver Chain and Bell,
Gave it to me: nay and I know
What he said then; I'me sure I do.                               30
Said He, look how your Huntsman here
Hath taught a Faun to hunt his *Dear*.
But *Sylvio* soon had me beguil'd.
This waxed tame; while he grew wild,
And quite regardless of my Smart,                               35
Left me his Faun, but took his Heart,
    Thenceforth I set my self to play
My solitary time away,
With this: and very well content
Could so mine idle Life have spent.                             40
For it was full of sport; and light
Of foot, and heart; and did invite,
Me to its game; it seem'd to bless
Its self in me. How could I less
Than love it? O I cannot be                                     45
Unkind, t'a Beast that loveth me.
    Had it liv'd long, I do not know
Whether it too might have done so
As *Sylvio* did: his Gifts might be
Perhaps as false or more than he.                               50
But I am sure, for ought that I
Could in so short a time espie,
Thy Love was far more better then
The love of false and cruel men.

In Latin there would have been no disguising the gender of the
fawn. In English 'it' and 'this' are neuter. But after line 32 the reader
can safely presume that, as Sylvio's proxy huntsman, the fawn is a
buck. 'Sylvio', with its 'sylvan' associations, is a good name for a
woodland hunter. The girl's account of him illuminates our view of
her. Well she remembers the morning he came and gave her the fawn.
Very clever his speech seemed at the time. With or without 'this silver
Chain and Bell', no gift could have been more pleasing. But Sylvio
soon proved 'unconstant', 'counterfeit', 'false', 'cruel' because 'heedless of her smart'. With his departure went her good opinion of men.

All were 'false and cruel' in her eyes after that. The wantonness of the troopers was typical of the male sex. She did not stay to consider that only one trooper fired the lethal pistol shot.

Her virgin modesty is such that she has to excuse herself for petting a *male* fawn at all. 'How could I less /Than love it? O I cannot be / Unkind t' a Beast that loveth me.' This modesty re-appears later on.

Her wit shines through her simplicity. No creation of Marvell's lacks wit. She enjoyed Sylvio's pun on 'dear' and 'deer' and his calling himself 'her Huntsman'. She matches that with her own equally trite pun on 'heart' and 'hart'. She does not know that it is trite.

Marvell is subtle in his manipulation of sound. For instance, in lines 35–6 there is a flurry of stressed monosyllables ending in 't'; they are italicised below:

> And *quite* regardless of my *Smart*,
> *Left* me his Faun, but took his *Heart*.

This device he renews and redoubles in lines 41–2, after rhyming *content* with *spent*:

> For *it* was full of *sport*; and *light*
> Of *foot*, and *heart*; and did *invite*

Not only do the dentals ('did' included) display her white teeth, but each italicised word raises the musical pitch after a fall, so suggesting the upward springs of the skipping fawn. The rhythm is frisky.

The new feature in the next lines is the whiteness of the fawn. M. C. Bradbrook and M. G. Lloyd Thomas in their *Andrew Marvell* (Cambridge University Press, 1940), p. 49, state that 'The whiteness of the fawn is insisted on throughout the poem', but this is not so. We hear of it now for the very first time.

> With sweetest milk, and sugar, first                55
> I it at mine own fingers nurst.
> And as it grew, so every day
> It wax'd more white and sweet than they.
> It had so sweet a Breath! And oft
> I blusht to see its foot more soft,                60
> And white, (shall I say then my hand?)
> NAY any Ladies of the Land.
>         It is a wond'rous thing, how fleet

'Twas on those little silver feet.
With what a pretty skipping grace,                    65
It oft would challenge me the Race:
And when 'thad left me far away,
'Twould stay, and run again, and stay.
For it was nimbler much than Hindes;
And trod, as on the four Winds.                       70

In the first eight lines above, no fewer than fifty-two of the fifty-eight words are monosyllabic. The diction could hardly be simpler or the expression more juvenile. Again her virginal modesty is brought out. 'Many times she found herself blushing at the sight of the whiteness of the male foot exposed, whiter not merely than *her* hand but *any Lady's of the Land*'. She had used 'nay' in line 29, but here it is the one word in all Marvell's verse to be printed in block capitals. The main object is to surpass the neighbouring stresses in 'my hand' and 'any', but its sheer energy is beautifully girlish. She is being her normal self and has for the moment forgotten to grieve.

In lines 63—70 the emphasis shifts on to the buck's agile speed. A series of disyllabic words, all trochees, convey this: 'wond'rous', 'little silver' ('argent' being the heraldic term for white), 'pretty skipping', 'challenge'. And in their races the fawn's speed and playful stops are marked by the broken rhythm of:

'Twould stay, and run again, and stay.

'Stay' means 'stop and wait'. The buck seems to tread, not on four feet, but four winds. 'Four' is a disyllable here.

In the next paragraph the poem reaches new heights.

I have a Garden of my own,
But so with Roses over grown,
And Lillies, that you would it guess
To be a little Wilderness.
And all the Spring time of the year                   75
It onely loved to be there.
Among the beds of Lillyes, I
Have sought it oft, where it should lye;
Yet could not, till it self would rise,
Find it, although before mine Eyes.                   80
For, in the flaxen Lillies shade,

> It like a bank of Lillies laid.
> Upon the Roses it would feed,
> Until its Lips ev'n seem'd to bleed:
> And then to me 'twould boldly trip, 85
> And print those Roses on my Lip.
> But all its chief delight was still
> On Roses thus its self to fill:
> And its pure virgin Limbs to fold
> In whitest sheets of Lillies cold. 90
> Had it liv'd long, it would have been
> Lillies without, Roses within.

In likening her overgrown garden to 'a little Wilderness' the nymph was using a well-understood gardening term. Under I (c) the *New English Dictionary* defines 'wilderness' as 'A piece of ground in a large garden or park, planted with trees and laid out in an ornamental or fantastic style, often in the form of a maze or labyrinth'. Francis Quarles wrote in 1644:

> I cut me Aqueducts, whose current flees
> And waters all my Wilderness of Trees.

At the time of the fawn's death in the autumn, the nymph's garden was neglected and out of control. This picture of the white lilies and red roses is a picture of the garden as it had been in its prime, in 'the Spring time of the year', the season that lasted from late March to mid-June. The tenses are uniformly historic from line 74 on.

The two flower names dominate both the sense and the sound. In line 72 all four stressed syllables are heavy with the long O of 'Rose':

> But só | with Ró | ses ó | ver grówn.

The word 'Roses' comes four more times after that, including 'thóse Róses' in line 86. As for 'Lillies', they are more prominent still. The word comes six times. Ten other times we have words that begin with the same initial 'l': 'little', 'loved', 'lye', 'like', 'laid', 'Lips', 'Lip', 'Limbs', 'liv'd', 'long'. Every one of them is stressed. So is the 'light' in 'delight'. The short 'i' in 'Lillies' keeps cropping up elsewhere too. We hear it ten times in the last couplet alone (for 'been' is to be pronounced, as Milton spelt it, 'bin'):

> Had it liv'd long, it would have been
> Lillies without, Roses within.

The perfect balance between the two halves of this last line epitomises the larger, more elaborate balance between lines 77–82 (lilies) and 83–8 (roses). The white fawn at rest was invisible among the white lilies. On its feet it stood up and ate red rose petals until its white muzzle was blood-red.

In this choice seventh paragraph a change has come over the scene. The fawn was previously pure animal, a four-footed beast. When the nymph accepted its challenge to 'the race', she ran like a hind and of course was outrun by the buck. Now in this seventh paragraph she is pure nymph again and the fawn waxes human. It 'rises' intelligently in the garden to let her know where it is. It 'boldly trips' to her and with a long kiss 'prints' the red rose stain on her lip. The outdoor 'beds of Lillies' in line 77 become domestic indoor beds almost in lines 89–90, when the white fawn delights 'to fold its pure virgin Limbs in whitest sheets of Lilies cold'. The gain from this indoor suggestion and this anthropomorphising of the fawn is exploited in the twelve lines which follow:

> O help! O help! I see it faint:
> And dye as calmely as a Saint.
> See how it weeps. The Tears do come                95
> Sad, slowly dropping like a Gumme.
> So weeps the wounded Balsome: so
> The holy Frankincense doth flow.
> The brotherless *Heliades*
> Melt in such Amber Tears as these.                100
>     I in a golden Vial will
> Keep these two crystal Tears; and fill
> It till it do o'reflow with mine;
> Then place it in *Diana's* Shrine.

Was ever pathos more delicately handled than in these first eight lines? All the secrets of the art are observed. A minimum of words, each scoring because the pace is kept slow. A hushed voice, and the lingering sibilants of 'Saint', 'See', 'Sad', 'slowly', 'So', 'so' – syllables which are all stressed. And behind the clear voice, at the heart of the speaker, genuine love and genuine grief.

Saints die calmly in their beds. One thinks of the medieval

sculpture at Chartres of the Death of the Virgin, above the Cathedral's north porch; of Our Lady's arms folded at rest and the horizontal white drapery folds.

The 'Gumme' simile in line 96 links eyes with trees. They both exude gum. So Hamlet, with a sideglance at Polonius, spoke of 'old men's eyes purging thick amber and plumtree gum' (III, ii). Marvell thinks of three trees that 'weep'. Balm or balsam, medicinal resin, is wept by the balsam tree, if 'wounded' like the dead fawn. The 'holy' incense used at altars is a gum resin from the frankincense tree. The yellow fossil resin amber in mythology came from the poplar trees into which, on the death of their only brother Phaethon, the three daughters of the Sun and Clymene were turned. In Greek the Sun was *Helios* and the Daughters of the Sun *Helíadés*, rhymed here with 'these'. In Ovid's *Metamorphoses* the bark closed over the girls' last sad words 'and from that bark there flowed tears which, dropping from the new-made branches, were hardened into amber by the sun' (II 364–5). They fell into the river Eridanus, which bore them off to be an ornament later for Roman brides. In X 91 a grove of poplars is *'nemus Heliadum'*, 'the grove of the daughters of the Sun', and in X 263 a list of small presents that girls particularly welcome includes amber, which Ovid calls *'Heliadum lacrimas'*, 'tears of the daughters of the Sun', dropping from poplars. Ovid went on to tell the story of the myrrh tree that wept, but Marvell did not need a fourth tree. He had achieved his perfect terminal couplet in:

> The brotherless *Heliades*
> Melt in such Amber Tears as these.

'Diana's Shrine' was doubly appropriate. Diana was the virgin goddess of chastity; the fawn and nymph were virgins too. 'Golden vial' comes straight from Revelation, V 8, where 'the four and twenty elders fell down before the Lamb, having every one of them harps and golden vials full of odours, which are the prayers of saints'. 'Golden vial' incidentally confirms the patrician rank of the nymph. From here on she is lavish and heedless of expense. Yet Bradbrook and Lloyd Thomas (op. cit., p.50) dubbed her 'a Puritan country girl'.

The same authors also broke completely new ground by identifying the fawn with Christ and the nymph with the Church, basing this allegorical interpretation on a parallelism between lines 71–92 and the Old Testament *Song of Solomon*, which to Christians prefigures the mutual love of Christ and the Church.

Margoliouth gave qualified assent to their thesis in the *Review of English Studies*, vol. 17, p.221. 'I am not convinced that they are wrong. If they are right, the poem takes on altogether new colour and significance'. But E. S. Le Comte attacked them in *Modern Philology*, vol. 50 (1952). Unfortunately he misrepresented them as alleging that the poem was 'an allegory on the Crucifixion'; they had alleged nothing of the kind. In the same periodical, vol. 51 (1954) Karina Williamson pointed this out. Her article was scrupulously fair and she concluded that Marvell's poem had strong 'religious overtones' drawn mainly from the Song of Solomon, but that no allegory was involved.

Now it is reasonably certain that no English lyrical poet in Marvell's day would write of a garden with lilies in it and a buck fawn and not think of that most popular of love lyrics, the Song of Solomon. In the Authorised Version its 3000 words include 'lily' or 'lilies' eight times; the male Lover (Christ) is seven times likened to a roe or a young hart, and the female (the Church) says in VI 2−3: 'My beloved is gone down into his garden, to the beds of spices, to feed in the garden and to gather lilies. I am my beloved's and my beloved is mine: he feedeth among the lilies.' There is surely a connection between the Song of Solomon and lines 71−92 of 'The Nymph complaining for the death of her Faun'.

But is it not reasonable, taking the poem as a whole, to start further back and suppose that, when Marvell contemplated making a lyric out of the known death of a girl's white pet fawn, he came to think of white lilies and so of the Song of Solomon and then had the idea of giving this English girl an English garden of her own, at a suitable stage of the poem, to share with the fawn? He needed incident and variety and colour, but he needed no allegory at all.

It was surely a comment on his own procedures when he wrote in praise of Milton's *Paradise Lost*:

> Thou hast not miss'd one thought that could be fit,
> And all that was improper dost omit.

His own assembly and selection and arrangement of materials were always most carefully done.

The frankincense tree in line 98 may be an offshoot of the verse in the Song of Solomon (IV 14) which includes in a list 'all trees of frankincense', though it is mentioned also in *Metamorphoses*, X, 309, some forty lines after the Heliades. A more certain gain from the Song of Solomon is apparent in lines 77—80:

> Among the beds of Lillyes, I
> Have sought it oft, where it should lye;
> Yet could not, till it self would rise,
> Find it, although before mine Eyes.    80

For we read in the Song of Solomon, III 1—2: 'By night on my bed I sought him whom my soul loveth: I sought him, but I found him not. I will rise now, and go about the city in the streets, and in the broad ways I will seek him whom my soul loveth: I sought him but I found him not.' And again we read in V 6: 'I opened to my beloved; but my beloved had withdrawn himself, and was gone: I sought him, but I could not find him.'

With the arrival of 'Diana's shrine' in line 104, the way is open for a classical pastoral ending. These are the concluding lines:

> Now my Sweet Faun is vanish'd to    105
> Whether the Swans and Turtles go:
> In fair *Elizium* to endure,
> With milk-white Lambs, and Ermins pure.
> O do not run too fast: for I
> Will but bespeak thy Grave, and dye.    110
>     First my unhappy Statue shall
> Be cut in Marble; and withal,
> Let it be weeping too: but there
> Th'Engraver sure his Art may spare;
> For I so truly thee bemoane,    115
> That I shall weep though I be Stone:
> Until my Tears, still dropping, wear
> My breast, themselves engraving there.
> There at my feet shalt thou be laid,
> Of purest Alabaster made:    120
>     For I would have thine Image be
> White as I can, though not as Thee.

In Greek mythology Elysium or the Islands of the Blest lay on the western edge of the world, washed by Oceanus. The Latin Elysium or Elysian fields were by Virgil's time part of Hades, the underworld whose entrance was near Lake Nemi. In post-Renaissance pastoral poetry Elysium was a heaven for sheep or shepherds in the sky. Marvell, as we shall see in chapter 29, made Thyrsis describe it thus to Dorinda:

> There, sheep are full
> Of sweetest grass and softest wooll;
> There, birds sing Consorts, garlands grow,
> Cool winds do whisper, springs do flow.

The nymph's white fawn goes to an Elysium where the denizens are all equally white — swans, turtledoves, lambs and ermines. It is so desirable a goal that they hurry to reach it. Her plea, 'O do not run too fast', links up with the one-sided races in lines 63–70. She wants to travel there with him. Her skin too is white.

Her own imminent death in line 110 comes as a painful surprise to the reader. Yet, if we look back, it was foreshadowed in lines 19–20 when she was wounded 'to the Heart'. Romance required that great loves and great friendships should finish in near-simultaneous death.

The last twelve lines form a sort of Last Will and Testament; 'First' in line 111 is the *Imprimis* of a Will. Patrician Wills in the seventeenth century often provided for the erection of a monument at the testator's 'cost and charges'. The nymph's monument is to be of costly marble.

In line 117 'still' means 'always', as it did in line 87. The idea that perpetual action will in the end mark even the hardest stone was part of the folk wisdom of the Middle Ages. Chaucer made use of it in *The Franklin's Tale*, lines 829–31:

> By proces, as ye knowen everichoon,
> Men may so longe graven in a stoon,
> Til som figure there-inne emprinted be.

Marvell is influenced in the matter of the nymph's statue by the sad story of Niobe. By boasting of her children and her ancestry she so infuriated the goddess Leto, mother of Apollo and Diana, that Leto sent those two expert archers down to earth and they shot Niobe's seven sons and seven daughters dead. Niobe's husband Amphion then killed himself and she was turned by grief into a marble statue which wept and wept.

Alabaster is chosen for the image of the fawn because of its whiteness, but it was the stock monumental stone. The poem thus ends with the nymph's tribute to the whiteness of the fawn.

There are some resemblances between the two poems of Catullus on Lesbia's sparrow, brief though these were, and Marvell's poem on the Nymph and fawn. Both men were writing in their twenties: both girls' pets were male. In the first poem, on the living cocksparrow, Catullus makes Lesbia give it her forefinger and goad it into sharp little pecks; both girls thus play with their pets. In the second poem, on the dead sparrow, there are at least four points of contact. Catullus states flatly in line 3 'my girl-friend's sparrow is dead': Marvell announces the death in his title and in line 2 states flatly that the shot fawn 'will die'. When Marvell says in line 41 'For it was full of sport: and light /Of foot, and heart', one thinks of Catullus's '*Nam mellitus erat*' ('For it was honey-sweet') and the hopping about of the sparrow — 'It never moved far from her lap; hopping now this way, now that, it kept coming back chirping to its one and only mistress'. Lesbia's sparrow 'goes the shadowy way to the place whence there is no returning', namely the underworld: the nymph's fawn runs to Elysium. Both girls end up in tears.

Though much more than that, Marvell's lyric *is* a Catullan lament.

# 10 'The Definition of Love'

After the title, which in effect says, 'Here Love is defined!', this poem does not make a single *literal* statement. All is imagery and personification, and the imagery is for the most part audaciously far-fetched. Conceit follows conceit. Every subject of the academic trivium and quadrivium is exploited in turn. The reader must either rise to the intellectual challenge or be content to enjoy the poem in terms of sensation and sound.

The stanza form used is the same as in 'Mourning' and 'The Mower to the Glo-Worms', an octosyllabic iambic quatrain with alternate lines rhyming. It is not a glib measure and all three poems are noticeably short. This has eight stanzas, compared to their nine and four.

What distinguishes 'The Definition of Love' from the other two technically is its confident, resonant tone and exceptional speed.

### I

My Love is of a birth as rare
As 'tis for object strange and high:
It was begotten by despair
Upon Impossibility.

### II

Magnanimous Despair alone                                    5
Could show me so divine a thing,
Where feeble Hope could ne'r have flown
But vainly flapt its Tinsel Wing.

### III

And yet I quickly might arrive
Where my extended Soul is fixt,                              10
But Fate does Iron wedges drive,
And alwaies crouds it self betwixt.

### IV

For Fate with jealous Eye does see
Two perfect Loves; nor lets them close:
Their union would her ruine be,                              15
And her Tyrannick pow'r depose.

### V

And therefore her Decrees of Steel
Us as the distant Poles have plac'd,
(Though Loves whole World on us doth wheel)
Not by themselves to be embrac'd.                            20

### VI

Unless the giddy Heaven fall,
And Earth some new Convulsion tear;
And, us to joyn, the World should all
Be cramp'd into a *Planisphere*.

## VII

As Lines so Loves *oblique* may well          25
Themselves in every Angle greet:
But ours so truly *Paralel*,
Though infinite can never meet.

## VIII

Therefore the Love which us doth bind,
But Fate so enviously debarrs,          30
Is the Conjunction of the Mind,
And Opposition of the Stars.

The poet achieves his speed by suppressing caesuras and running together the two lines of each half-stanza, particularly the first half since it achieves no rhyme. Only in four of the thirty-two lines can one hear a caesura and then it comes as a concession to the sense. Lines 7 and 8 are the only pair to slow down to the usual Marvellian pace and exhibit the usual antiphonal balance:

Where féeble Hópe | could né'r have flówn
But váinly fiápt | its Tínsel Wíng.

So often in his early attempts at courtship the young male finds Hope a bird whose performance in flight falls far short of its gaudy plumage. His hope then turns into despair. But he did hope at first; 'flapt' is a finite verb here.

The psychology of despair in lines 3−6 corresponds closely to human experience. The male *can* win the female by blindly pressing an impossible suit. The most perfect understanding *can* be reached on the Wings of Despair, just as the heroism which achieves the impossible in battle can be the courage of despair.

The villain of the poem is the ungovernable third party, Fate, introduced as neuter in gender at lines 11−12:

But Fate does Iron wedges drive,
And alwaies crouds it self betwixt.

The verb 'crowds' means 'pushes, thrusts'. Marvell used it again of an individual action in 'Tom May's Death', line 36: 'As he (May) crowds in, he (Jonson) whips him ore the pate.' The 'iron wedges' are those made by blacksmiths and used by carpenters to split a newly felled tree. Spenser used them allegorically in *The Faerie Queene*, II, v, 25:

> His name was Care; a blacksmith by his trade,
> That neither day nor night from working spared,
> But to small purpose yron wedges made;
> These be unquiet thoughts, that carefull minds invade.

Shakespeare used the same wedge in *Troilus and Cressida*, I, i, 34−5, where Troilus said: 'When my heart, as wedged with a sigh, would rive in twain.' Thus Fate here is a force which 'drives iron wedges', that is, hammers them in, so splitting true lovers apart. Fate perpetually 'thrusts itself' in between them.

At this point Fate becomes feminine and from now on 'she' is a sovereign Queen 'with jealous Eye'. The union of any 'perfect Love' would be 'her ruine' and would dethrone 'her Tyrannick power'. Accordingly she issued 'Decrees of Steel' against what she 'so enviously debarrs'.

Marvell spoke briefly of Fate's 'malice' in 'Daphnis and Chloe', lines 93−4:

> Fate I come, as dark, as sad,
> As thy Malice could desire.

But in 'The Definition of Love' Fate is a full character drawn in the round. Her interfering malevolence is based on envy and Machiavellian statecraft; her tyranny can only thrive in a kingdom of thwarted and stunted subjects. To some extent the poet has gone back to Homeric times when the Olympian gods were themselves subject to 'Moira', a singular Fate. Classical Greece then made the Fates plural sisters, 'Moirai', and these are still active in Greek folklore today.

But to some extent also the poet has in mind the religious wrangling in his own day over 'Free Will versus Fate'. In *Paradise Lost*, II, 559−61, Milton's fallen Angels in Hell sat apart and 'reasoned high':

> Of Providence, Foreknowledge, Will, and Fate,
> Fixt Fate, Free Will, Foreknowledge absolute,
> And found no end, in wand'ring mazes lost.

In just the same way Marvell's Fate is aware that, if lovers are allowed

complete free will to 'close' with the perfect partner of their own
choice, then her 'Tyranny' will be superseded and she will perish.

But ordinary loves are imperfect, illicit or clandestine, and they are
the 'Loves oblique' in VII. As two 'oblique Lines' meet in all
geometrical angles, so two 'oblique Loves' may well greet each other
in angles of town walls, or of courtyards, or doorways, or rooms. In
*The Winter's Tale*, I, ii, 289, Shakespeare listed 'skulking in corners'
among the adulterous signs. Compared to such moral obliquities,
clean parallel lines had an air of wholesome perfection. 'Our lines, so
truly parallel, though infinite, can never meet.'

That statement leads logically to the final definition of love in VIII:

> Therefore the Love which us doth bind,
> But Fate so enviously debarrs,
> Is the Conjunction of the Mind,
> And Opposition of the Stars.

And such a 'Definition', proclaimed in the title, is the goal and
terminal point of the poem.

But the word needs to be looked at through seventeenth-century
eyes. The Logic that Marvell learnt at Cambridge included the recent
thinking of the Frenchman, Petrus Ramus, and 'definition' was one
of its pet technical terms. Marvell reproduced it in the last year of his
life in *Remarks upon a Late Disingenuous Discourse* (1678): 'A definition
always consists, as being a dialectical animal, of a body, which is the
genus, and a difference, which is the soul of the thing defined.' But he
had put this same Ramist doctrine to poetic use twenty to thirty years
earlier at the end of his 'Eyes and Tears':

> Thus let your Streams o'reflow your Springs,
> Till Eyes and Tears be the same things:
> And each the other's difference bears;          55
> These weeping Eyes, those seeing Tears.

Logically here the genus 'Eyes' has the difference 'seeing' and the
genus 'Tears' has the difference 'weeping'. But let eyes and tears 'be
the same Things' and then the differences can be exchanged; the result
is 'These weeping Eyes' and, more paradoxically, 'those seeing Tears'.

The definition of love in stanza VIII is equally Ramist, but double-
headed. The love 'which us doth bind' has the genus 'Conjunction'
and the difference 'of the Mind' ('of the Soul' would not rhyme). The

love which 'Fate so enviously debarrs' has the genus 'Opposition' and difference 'of the Stars'. They enter as the allies of Fate. As Carew put it in 'To his mistris': 'Fate and the Planets sometymes bodies part'. Opposition and conjunction are antonyms, but not merely astronomical metaphors here, despite the attendant 'Stars' and despite the sustained astronomical imagery in stanzas V and VI above.

They form one intricate sentence, but complete a train of reasoning which began in IV: 'Fate feels threatened whenever she sees two perfect loves, and she always frustrates their consummation.' That is the major premise. The minor has to be supplied: 'We are two such loves'. The conclusion follows in V: 'Therefore her Decrees of Steel/Us as the distant Poles have plac'd.' The distant Poles are the celestial, not terrestrial, Poles. Already the word order has wedged 'Us' apart from 'have plac'd'. Now 'the Poles' are wedged apart from 'embraced' by the slow parenthetical line: '(Though Loves whole World on us doth wheel)'. The eight monosyllables, six of them stressed, seem to make one long axis. Round it love's sphere revolves. This is a sphere created by poets and reserved for the rare romances which make impression upon time. Richard Lovelace described it in stanza III of 'To Lucasta, Going beyond the Seas':

> Though Seas and Land betwixt us both,
>     Our Faith and Troth,
>   Like separated soules,
>     All time and space controules:
> Above the highest sphere wee meet
> Unseene, unknowne, and greet as Angels greet.

These last two lines of Lovelace endorse, if they do not repeat, what Thomas Carew had just written in 'To my Mistresse in absence', lines 9–10:

> Yet let our boundless spirits meet
> And in love's spheare each other greet.

It is in this imagined sphere that Marvell fancies his 'extended Soul' to be fixed. Here dwells the 'object strange and high', the love which is in his eyes 'so divine a thing'; not wholly out of reach, but fated to remain that distance away.

On 9 August 1671 Marvell replied at some length to a letter from a male friend in Persia and in the fourth sentence wrote:

God's good Providence, which hath thro so dangerous a Disease and so many Difficultys preserved and restored you, will, I doubt not, conduct you to a prosperous Issue, and the Perfection of your so laudable · Undertakings. And, under that, your own good Genius, in Conjunction with your Brother here, will, I hope, tho at the distance of *England* and *Persia*, in good Time operate extraordinary Effects; for the Magnetism of two Souls, rightly touched, works beyond all natural Limits.

The voice of the lyrical poet spoke there. Here in this poem the two distant celestial Poles are 'Not by themselves to be embrac'd' (Not able to be clasped and possessed by each other) unless three marvels happen, the three stated with such economy in stanza VI. First, the spinning spheres of the Ptolemaic system must lose their balance and fall flat, each hemisphere on its own side of the equatorial plane. Second, Earth's unturning pendent globe must be torn by a new convulsion and forced out of shape; presumably an old convulsion gave it that shape. Third, the whole created world (the collapsed heaven and convulsed earth), in order to bring the lovers together, must be constricted and cramped into the flat thickness of a cartographer's planisphere. In the centre of that surface, with the obstructing earth-globe removed, the celestial Poles could then coincide. Impossible though each of these three stipulations must seem, the reader must remember that the poet's love was the child of 'Impossibility'.

The lines of the meridians on such a planisphere may be the unacknowledged stepping-stone to the 'Lines oblique' that begin stanza VII.

In *Andrew Marvell* (Cambridge University Press, 1940), p. 44, Bradbrook and Lloyd Thomas remark that 'there is no temporal process' in 'The Definition of Love'. Certainly it has no 'now', 'before' or 'after'; there is no conjunction of time and the only temporal adverbs are 'always' and 'never' (twice). But time is a matter of tenses, and we meet the historic tenses 'was' (l.3), 'could' (ll.6—7), 'flapt' (l.8) before we reach the primary tenses in lines 10—32. And of these primary tenses the conjunctives 'fall' (l.21), 'tear' (l.22) and 'should be' (ll.23—4) refer to the future; 'can never meet' (l.28) refers to the future too. So there *is* a temporal sequence, on which a sonnet sequence could well have been built. There were the false dawns of Hope. There was the tedium and inertia; the resultant Despair; then this new friendship and its progress to an exchange of faith and troth.

At that point it attracted the hostility of 'Fate', who parted the 'perfect Loves' for ever, or until such time as a miraculous re-arrangement of the universe should reunite them. In the meantime their Platonic relationship will continue and their lives will run parallel, as they do now.

And all this the poet conveys to our intelligences and our sensitive souls in 32 lines or 190 words, 145 of which are words of one syllable. It is an astonishing achievement. The poem is a rare work of art.

## 11    'Eyes and Tears'

Metrically this poem is in the main stream of Marvell's development as a lyrical writer. A pair of octosyllabic couplets gives him his iambic quatrain. Soon a pair of these quatrains will give him his favourite stanza, the iambic octet.

As it is, the first two of this poem's fourteen quatrains could almost be reckoned one stanza. They launch a very personal poem in deceptively impersonal terms (for 'These Tears' turn out to be from the poet's own eyes).

### I

How wisely Nature did decree,
With the same Eyes to weep and see!
That, having view'd the object vain,
They might be ready to complain.

### II

And, since the Self-deluding Sight,                    5
In a false Angle takes each hight;
These Tears which better measure all,
Like wat'ry Lines and Plummets fall.

In line 4 'They' are the eyes. For man's spiritual health the Creator made His decree. At the back of the purpose clause in lines 3–4 is

*Ecclesiastes*, the book of the preacher who laments ('complains') that the eye sees nothing but vanity. 'I have seen all the works that are done under the sun: and, behold, all is vanity and vexation of Spirit.' (I 14)

In the second stanza the images combine to suggest life at sea. The eyes do not look vertically upwards. They have to judge the height of a star by triangulation and they often judge wrong. But tears do fall vertically downwards and make truer assessments, like plumblines taking the depth of salt water correctly.

The superiority of tears to eyes in one way or another is the point of each succeeding stanza. But the poet is largely concerned now with himself. He writes from experience.

### III

Two Tears, which Sorrow long did weigh
Within the Scales of either Eye,       10
And then paid out in equal Poise,
Are the true price of all my Joyes.

### IV

What in the World most fair appears,
Yea even Laughter, turns to Tears:
And all the Jewels which we prize,       15
Melt in these Pendants of the Eyes.

### V

I have through every Garden been,
Amongst the Red, the White, the Green;
And yet, from all the flow'rs I saw,
No Hony, but these Tears could draw.       20

### VI

So the all-seeing Sun each day
Distills the World with Chymick Ray;
But finds the Essence only Showers,
Which straight in pity back he poures.

## VII

Yet happy they whom Grief doth bless,                    25
That weep the more, and see the less:
And, to preserve their Sight more true,
Bath still their Eyes in their own Dew.

## VIII

So *Magdalen*, in Tears more wise,
Dissolv'd those captivating Eyes,                         30
Whose liquid Chaines could flowing meet
To fetter her Redeemers feet.

## IX

Not full sailes hasting loaden home,
Nor the chast Ladies pregnant Womb,
Nor *Cynthia* Teeming show's so fair,                     35
As two Eyes swoln with weeping are.

## X

The sparkling Glance that shoots Desire,
Drench'd in these Waves, does lose it fire.
Yea oft the Thund'rer pitty takes
And here the hissing Lightning slakes.

## XI

The Incense was to Heaven dear,
Not as a Perfume, but a Tear.
And Stars shew lovely in the Night,
But as they seem the Tears of Light.

These nine stanzas amount to a logical proof that the eyes of man do better to weep than to see. What we have here is more than a paradox. It is a poetical theorem. The steps can be paraphrased thus:

Two matching tears from eyes of deep sorrow are worth all my joys (ll.9−12).

All that the world reckons most beautiful ends in tears. Even laughter does (ll.13−14).

The emotion with which we view precious jewels brings tears, the best jewels of all, to our eyes (ll. 15–16).

Like a bee I have seen Western Europe's best gardens, but drawn no nectar from the flowers except tears (ll. 17–20). So too the sun sees everything by day and its hot beams extract moisture – as the alchemist's heat extracts the fifth essence or 'quintessence' – which moisture it later returns to the earth in tears of pity; that is, rain (ll. 21–4).

Happy are they who, blest with grief, weep more than see; constant tears do them good and keep their sight true (ll. 25–8). It was so with the sinful Mary Magdalene, when her seductive eyes dissolved in penitential tears and her Saviour stood still while her tears bathed his feet (ll. 29–32).

No other full curve has the beauty of two eyes swollen with weeping: not the bellying sails of a ship on the homeward run; not the housewife with child by her husband; not Cynthia the Moon at the full (ll. 33–6).

The roving eye that shoots arrows of desire loses its heat, if drowned in a tear. Yes, even the lightnings of thundering Jupiter go out with a hiss in his tears when, as he often does, he feels pity (ll. 37–40).

The original attraction of incense for Heaven was not its smell, but its appearance on the frankincense tree as a resinous tear (ll. 41–2).

In the night sky the stars are beautiful only because they seem tears of light (ll. 43–4).

The Magdalene stanza VIII was so central to his argument that Marvell translated it into two Latin elegiac couplets, though he translated no other. He had been reading or he was recalling Crashaw's poems on Mary Magdalene, 'The Weeper' and 'The Teare', the first two poems in *Steps to the Temple* (1646). Though not actually echoing Crashaw, 'Eyes and Tears' does use some of his material.

In 'The Weeper', for instance line 126, Mary's tears wait to be born 'from her eyes' swolne wombes of sorrow'. Marvell's stanza IX would seem to derive from this phrase.

Again Marvell's lines 15–16, 'And all the Jewels which we prize / Melt in these Pendants of the Eyes', may be reminiscent of Crashaw. For not only has he in 'The Weeper', lines 47–8, the couplet:

> Sorrowes best Jewels lye in these
> Caskets, of which Heaven keeps the Keyes.

but also in 'The Teare', lines 10–12, he makes the sun stoop and take up a tear and give it to Artemis, his sister, and Crashaw then comments:

> Proud will his sister be to weare
> This thine eye's Jewell in her Eare.

So the Magdalene's tear becomes 'a pendant' in the goddess's ear. In Marvell conversely the tears are 'pendants' of the eyes while still wet, but the connection with Crashaw is there. And there are other hints of 'The Teare' later in Marvell's 'The Garden' and 'On a Drop of Dew', as we shall see.

Having proved to his own satisfaction that eyes do better to weep than to see, Marvell orders his own eyes to follow St Mary Magdalene's example and the example of all good weepers, and so ends his poem with power.

### XII

> Ope then mine Eyes your double Sluice,                45
> And practise so your noblest Use.
> For others too can see, or sleep;
> But only humane Eyes can weep.

### XIII

> Now like two Clouds dissolving, drop,
> And at each Tear in distance stop:                50
> Now like two Fountains trickle down:
> Now like two floods o'return and drown.

### XIV

> Thus let your Streams o'reflow your Springs,
> Till Eyes and Tears be the same things:
> And each the other's difference bears;                55
> These weeping Eyes, those seeing Tears.

The phrase 'double Sluice' means his 'two eyelids' and its inclusion here proves that Marvell took the 'Eyes and Tears' of the title and line

54 from the passage in Shakespeare's *Venus and Adonis*, lines 955–63, where Venus dissolved into tears at the thought of the boar:

> Here overcome, as one full of despair,
> She vail'd her eyelids, who like sluices stopp'd
> The crystal tide, that from her two cheeks fair
> In the sweet channel of her bosom dropp'd.
>   But through the flood gates breaks the silver rain,
>   And with his strong course opens them again.
>
> O how her eyes and tears did lend and borrow,
> Her eye seen in the tears, tears in her eye,
> Both crystals, where they view'd each other's sorrow.

Those last lines of Shakespeare have also prompted Marvell's finishing stanza, but he adds the spice of Ramist logic already detailed in our analysis of the ending to 'The Definition of Love' on p. 85 above.

In line 45 'others' are animals; they, Marvell says, do not weep. Nevertheless, in 'The Nymph complaining for the death of her Faun' he makes great play with the tears of the fawn; and rightly, because animals certainly do weep.

The key to the meaning of line 50, 'And at each Tear in distance stop', is perhaps found in Crashaw's 'The Weeper', stanza 18, where Mary Magdalene is praying with the metaphorical aid of a rosary:

> Still at each sigh, that is, each stop,
> A bead, that is, a teare doth drop.

Her prayers, in other words, are punctuated by sighs and tears. The poet's tears punctuate his devotions as milestones provide traveller's stops.

After that, he weeps continuously: the tears trickle down thinly like rivers not far from their source, but then grow uncontrollably copious, like broad rivers overflowing their banks. In religious terms these changes mark mounting degrees of contrition and self-abasement. We have a Marvell here not seen before.

The poem was first printed in the 1681 Folio, and almost at once was reprinted in 1688 in an anthology, *Poetical Recreations*, for one Benjamin Crayle. This version left out stanzas II and III, V, IX, and XI. The omission of V was most damaging to the structure.

A manuscript copy in Bodleian MS. Tanner 306, f388, omits stanza IX and is headed 'by Mr. Marvil'. He might well have thought that stanza too nearly grotesque. But none of the dozen variants in Tanner is an improvement and its last line is disastrous: 'These seeing eyes these weeping teares'.

# 12   'Upon the Death of Lord Hastings'

This set of heroic couplets was written for *Lachrymae Musarum; The Tears of the Muses, Exprest in Elegies*, which appeared late in 1649. Hastings had died on 24 June.

Marvell's eight paragraphs contain 8, 10, 8, 6, 8, 6, 8, 6 lines. We see him drawing nearer the regular eight-line stanzas which he used for 'The unfortunate Lover' and 'The Gallery' and went on using at Appleton House; their lines were a foot shorter.

His opening paragraph on the nineteen-year-old Hastings sets the elegiac pace and dictates the dignified tone.

> Go, intercept some Fountain in the Vein,
> Whose Virgin-Source yet never steept the Plain.
> *Hastings* is dead, and we must finde a Store
> Of Tears untoucht, and never wept before.
> Go, stand betwixt the *Morning* and the *Flowers*;        5
> And, ere they fall, arrest the early *Showers*.
> *Hastings* is dead; and we, disconsolate,
> With early *Tears* must mourn his early *Fate*.

'We' in lines 3 and 7 are Marvell himself and the thirty-three other poets from whom Richard Brome was coaxing contributions. Marvell may even have known that the volume was to be called *The Tears of the Muses*. They needed to be 'original Tears' (l.4) and they needed to be 'early Tears' (l.8), in the sense of arriving in good time.

The repeated 'Go', 'early' and 'Hastings is dead' do perhaps indicate the learning of the value of repetition from Milton's 'Lycidas', particularly its eighth and ninth lines:

For Lycidas is dead, dead ere his prime
Young Lycidas, and hath not left his peer.

The second and third paragraphs are much more difficult:

Alas, his *Vertues* did his *Death* presage:
Needs must he die, that doth out-run his *Age*.      10
The Phlegmatick and Slowe prolongs his day,
And on Times Wheel sticks like a *Remora*.
What man is he, that hath not *Heaven* beguil'd,
And is not thence mistaken for a *Childe*?
While those of growth more sudden, and more bold,    15
Are hurried hence, as if already old.
For, there above, They number not as here,
But weigh to Man the *Geometrick* yeer.
    Had he but at this Measure still increast,
And on *the Tree of Life* once made a Feast,      20
As that of *Knowledge*; what Loves had he given
To Earth, and then what Jealousies to Heaven!
But 'tis a *Maxime* of that State, That none,
Lest He become like Them, taste more then one.
Therefore the *Democratick* Stars did rise,      25
And all that Worth from hence did *Ostracize*.

The reader has to distinguish clearly between those pronouns and possessives that refer to Hastings and those which speak of Man. The argument in lines 9–18 runs:

The very virtues of Hastings foreshadowed his early death; anyone who develops too quickly must die. It is the man of slow, phlegmatic humour who lives on, clinging to time. Every man of slow growth gives Heaven a false impression of his age and is consequently mistaken for a child and left to mature, while those of rapid and obvious growth are taken to be old men and hurried hence. For in Heaven the gods do not use our arithmetic, but weigh man's portion of life by their geometric year.

The 'Remora' (pronounced 'reemoray') in line 12 is the sucking-fish *Echeneis remora* (Latin *mora* means 'delay'), which attached itself to a ship's side and was thought to delay its progress. The phlegmatic man clings to 'Times Wheel', avoiding eternity, and by so doing he slows down the wheel's revolution.

'The Geometrick Yeer' in line 18, as Mrs E. E. Duncan—Jones has pointed out, exploits an idea of Dr John Wilkins in *Mathematical Magic* (1648): 'It is possible geometrically to contrive such an artificial motion as shall be of greater swiftness than the revolutions of the heavens.' In 1649 Marvell is therefore putting to witty use the latest mathematical idea. For it is the revolutions of the sun and moon that give man his days, months, years. They open the third paragraph, which means:

If Hastings had ceaselessly grown in terms of arithmetical years and had once eaten from the Tree of Life as well as from the Tree of Knowledge, just imagine the series of loves that he would have given to the earth (and of 'Jealousies to Heaven')! But the 'State' of Heaven has a strict law prohibiting any man from eating of the Tree of Life, lest he thereby become immortal like the gods. And so the citizen stars cast their democratic votes (one star, one vote) in favour of banishing the virtuous Hastings from here to Heaven.

This last quip grafts Greek history on to Genesis, III 22—4: 'And the Lord God said, Behold, the man is become as one of us, to know good and evil: and now, lest he put forth his hand, and take also of the tree of life, and eat, and live for ever: therefore the Lord God sent him forth from the garden of Eden, to till the ground from whence he was taken. So he drove out the man.' All that held good too for Hastings, except the tilling of the land. Marvell substitutes for the Expulsion from Eden the ostracism from Athens which was part of the new Democratic Constitution of Cleisthenes in 510 B. C. The male citizens in his Ecclesia had one vote each and with it the power of 'ostracising' or exiling one Athenian a year. Marvell makes the stars his citizen voters in this world, with Heaven the land of exile beyond the grave.

His next step must be to exonerate Hastings from any suggestion of Adam's sin or the disgrace of expulsion.

> Yet as some *Prince*, that, for State-Jealousie,
> Secures his neerest and most lov'd *Ally*;
> His Thought with richest Triumphs entertains,
> And in the choicest Pleasures charms his Pains:          30
> So he, not banisht hence, but there confin'd,
> There better recreates his active Minde.

Before the *Chrystal Palace* where he dwells,
The armed *Angels* hold their *Carouzels*;
And underneath, he views the *Turnaments*                    35
Of all those Sublunary *Elements*.
But most he doth th'*Eternal Book* behold,
On which the *happie Names* do stand enroll'd;
And gladly there can all his Kinred claim,
But most rejoyces at his *Mothers* name.                     40

In line 28 'secures' means 'imprisons, confines'. It takes a
Machiavellian Prince to imprison his guest and 'neerest Ally' and then
soften the blow by entertaining him with martial spectacles and
cultural delights. But it makes a fine simile for the treatment of
Hastings in Heaven. He is 'confined' there, not 'banished' from here.
He is entertained there with angelic tournaments, but can also look
down on tournaments on earth *sub luna* (under the moon). He views
the Roll of the Elect and rejoices to find his kinsmen's names there,
both living and dead – his mother's especially. Her place in Heaven is
booked, he can see.

She was the Countess of Huntingdon and very much alive. She had
been born Lucy Davies, daughter of the Sir John Davies (1569–
1626) who was an Oxford poet and the attorney-general for Ireland.
A poet herself, she authorised this memorial volume on her son. A
copy of the second issue (1650) in the Henry E. Huntington Library,
U.S.A., has an elegy in her autograph on the flyleaf.

Her husband Ferdinando, the fourth Earl of Huntingdon, appeared
in the Parliament cavalry at Edgehill in 1642, but, according to the
Royalist Clarendon, he fled the field when fighting began. No
mention of him is made here by the Royalist Marvell. He stays
submerged among the 'Kinred'. (This was the Middle English form
of the word which, for no good reason, changed to 'kindred'.)

Three more paragraphs complete the tale of the poem:

The gods themselves cannot their Joy conceal,
But draw their Veils, and their pure Beams reveal:
Onely they drooping *Hymeneus* note,
Who for sad *Purple*, tears his *Saffron*-coat;
And trails his Torches th'row the Starry Hall            45
Reversed, at his *Darlings* Funeral.
     And *Aesculapius*, who, asham'd and stern,
Himself at once condemneth, and *Mayern*;

Like some sad *Chymist*, who, prepar'd to reap
The *Golden Harvest*, sees his Glasses leap.                    50
For, how Immortal must their race have stood,
Had *Mayern* once been mixt with *Hastings* blood!
How Sweet and Verdant would these *Lawrels* be,
Had they been planted on that *Balsam*-tree!
  But what could he, good man, although he bruis'd    55
All Herbs, and them a thousand ways infus'd?
All he had try'd, but all in vain, he saw,
And wept, as we, without Redress or Law.
For *Man*(alas) is but the *Heavens* sport;
And *Art* indeed is Long, but *Life* is Short.                  60

The full stop and paragraph break at line 46 are artificial. Syntactically lines 43−50 constitute one sentence, in which 'note' has the direct objects 'Hymeneus' and 'Aesculapius' (each scanned with four syllables), while 'condemneth' has the direct objects 'himself' and 'Mayern'. As the Latin god of marriage, Hymen(a)eus is sad because he was due to marry Hastings to Mayern's daughter next day and had to go to the funeral instead. As the Latin god of medicine, Aesculapius damns himself for bad doctoring and at the same time damns Sir Theodore de Mayerne, court physician and doyen of French doctors in England. No good doctor loses a patient. Mayerne, for his part, in losing his own daughter's intended groom on the eve of the wedding, suffers a disappointment like that of the alchemist who has just turned base metal to gold when the glass beakers shatter and all is lost. The alchemist's ripe harvest would have been imperishable gold: the union of Lord Hastings and Miss Mayerne would have been the birth of an unending dynasty.

But the great physician could not save his own daughter's bridegroom from a premature death, because the forces of Heaven are inevitably too great for Man. Here Marvell invokes the Shakespearian image in *King Lear* (IV, i, 39−40):

> As flies to wanton boys, are we to the gods:
> They kill us for their sport.

And, to rhyme with 'sport', Marvell uses the start of the five-fold *Aphorism* of Hippocrates, Greek father of medicine: 'Life is short; Art is long, Opportunity fleeting, Experiment perilous, Judgment hard.'
  He thus brings the wheel full circle (to use another image from

*King Lear*), for the 'early Fate' of Lord Hastings began the poem and 'Alas' began its second paragraph.

It is because 'Art is long' that the sadness and the irony of this young man's death have been handed down to posterity in these verses and the verses of Denham and Herrick and Cotton and, yes, of Dryden, then an eighteen-year-old Westminster School boy. Dryden's 108 lines in 'The Tears of the Muses' included a tasteless dwelling on the dread smallpox (unmentioned by Marvell) which killed the young man:

> Was there no milder way but the small-pox,
> The very filthiness of Pandora's box!
> So many spots like naeves on Venus' soil,
> One jewel set off with so many a foil;
> Blisters with pride swell'd, which through's flesh did sprout
> Like rose-buds, stuck i' th' lily-skin about.
> Each little pimple had a tear in it,
> To wail the fault its rising did commit.

# 13 'A Dialogue between the Resolved Soul and Created Pleasure'

Thus headed, this courtly and Christian poem is the first in the 1681 Folio. But it can also be found in the seventeenth-century Bodleian MS. Rawlinson A. 176 with the title 'A Combat Between the Soule And Sense', with 'Sense' as the second speaker, not 'Pleasure'. The Folio title fits the final Chorus in lines 75–8, while the Bodleian MS. title echoes 'Combat' in line 8 and suits the first Chorus in lines 45–50. This it calls 'Charge': signifying the Body's 'exhortation' to the Soul.

> Courage my Soul, now learn to wield
> The weight of thine immortal Shield.
> Close on thy Head thy Helmet bright.
> Ballance thy Sword against the Fight.
> See where an Army, strong as fair,                    5

With silken Banners spreads the air.
Now, if thou bee'st that thing Divine,
In this day's Combat let it shine:
And shew that Nature wants an Art
To conquer one resolved Heart.                    10

Behind this speech lies St Paul's Epistle to the Ephesians, VI 10—17:

Finally, my brethren, be strong in the Lord, and in the power of his might. Put on the whole armour of God, that ye may be able to stand against the wiles of the devil . . . Wherefore take unto you the whole armour of God . . . Above all, taking the shield of faith, wherewith ye shall be able to quench all the fiery darts of the wicked. And take the helmet of salvation, and the sword of the Spirit, which is the word of God.

Marvell takes shield, helmet, sword in the Pauline order and in Pleasure's person tries all 'the wiles of the devil' against the Resolved or Resolute Soul. The supporting devil army in mid-air is his amplification of Ephesians, II 2, where Satan is called 'the prince of the power of the air'.

In line 8 'it' stands for 'thy being that thing Divine'. In line 9 'wants' means 'lacks'.

'Pleasure' now enters the scene, a suave gentleman who seizes the initiative by confidently playing the host. He speaks trochaic heptasyllabics.

### Pleasure

Welcome the Creations Guest,
Lord of Earth, and Heavens Heir.
Lay aside that Warlike Crest,
And of Nature's banquet share:
Where the Souls of fruits and flow'rs                    15
Stand prepared to heighten yours.

### Soul

I sup above, and cannot stay
To bait so long upon the way.

### Pleasure

On these downy Pillows lye,
Whose soft Plumes will thither fly:               20
On these Roses strow'd so plain
Lest one Leaf thy Side should strain.

### Soul

My gentler Rest is on a Thought,
Conscious of doing what I ought.

### Pleasure

If thou bee'st with Perfumes pleas'd,             25
Such as oft the Gods appeas'd,
Thou in fragrant Clouds shalt show
Like another God below.

### Soul

A Soul that knowes not to presume
Is Heaven's and its own perfume.                  30

### Pleasure

Every thing does seem to vie
Which should first attract thine Eye:
But since none deserves that grace,
In this Crystal view *thy* face.

### Soul

When the Creator's skill is priz'd,               35
The rest is all but Earth disguis'd.

### Pleasure

Heark how Musick then prepares
For thy Stay these charming Aires;
Which the posting Winds recall,
And suspend the Rivers Fall.                      40

### Soul

Had I but any time to lose,
On this I would it all dispose.
Cease Tempter. None chain a mind
Whom this sweet Chordage cannot bind.

### CHORUS

*Earth cannot shew so brave a Sight*                    45
*As when a single Soul does fence*
*The Batteries of alluring Sense,*
*And Heaven views it with delight.*
    *Then persevere: for still new Charges sound:*
    *And if thou overcom'st thou shalt be crown'd.*      50

The Chorus is an independent group of performers who have a mind of their own, like the later Chorus in Marvell's 'Two Songs at the Marriage of the Lord Fauconberg and the Lady Mary Cromwell' in 1657. Their honest iambics proclaim them to be on the side of the angels and their last line echoes the Book of Revelation, in which the clause 'he that overcometh' or 'him that overcometh' occurs eight times, four of them in chapter II, where in verse 10 we read: 'Be thou faithful unto death, and I will give thee a crown of life.'

In lines 46—7 'fence /The Batteries' means 'withstand the on-slaughts' but may more particularly suggest the Soul's 'fencing with sword and buckler. If 'Sense' were the name of the attacker, as in the Bodleian MS., 'the Batteries of alluring Sense' would have extra force. In the Folio text, it means that 'Pleasure' tempts with thrusts of each sense in turn: taste, touch, smell, sight and sound. And indeed the words 'Sight' and 'sound' end lines 45 and 49, and are rhymed. The couplet in 'Upon Appleton House', lines 287—8, also uses the same fence — sense rhyme:

> And with five Bastions it did fence,
> As aiming one for ev'ry Sense.

That reads like a reminiscence of this poem, rather than the other way round.

To 'bait' in line 18 was to 'stop for food on a journey'. But the Soul cannot stop now and still be in Heaven for supper. He says so. 'Pleasure' therefore suggests that the 'Plumes' in the pillows on the luxurious bed of rose petals will fly the Soul to Heaven without more ado. The Soul speaks of duty. To the third temptation, to stay on earth in perfumed godhead, the Soul gives a tarter reply: 'it would be presumptuous'.

There might seem to be little harm in the Soul's seeing his face in the proffered mirror, but 'Pleasure' knows better and the Soul knows better. To accept would be selfish vanity. The Soul's cryptic response means: 'When one has given God the Father due credit for moulding one's head and body, all that remains is clay in disguise.' There is nothing to be vain about. Man did not make his own face.

As poetry, lines 37–40 are the most pleasant so far. The ravishing power of stringed music is able to bring back winds that have passed by at express speed; they come back to listen. Nay more, it can arrest the flowing river and can silence the noise of water falling; again, this is because the water wants only to hear the sweet music. In turn, the Soul's answer accepts the attraction of music. Had he only the time, he would spend it like this (for stringed music is actually playing). But, not having the time, he stops the mouth of the tempter. Yet he softens his veto with a jest. For the spelling 'chordage' demonstrates a pun on the 'cordage' that physically binds and the 'chordage' that consists of spell-binding musical 'chords'. The same play on 'bind' and the same 'mind–bind' rhyme occurred in lines 5–6 of 'The Fair Singer'. Well may the Chorus applaud!

The four remaining temptations are beauty, riches, glory, and knowledge or science. 'Pleasure' sublimates his tone now by mixing trochaics with hexasyllabic iambics. The appeal is to manly ambition.

*Pleasure*

> All this fair, and soft, and sweet,
>     Which scatteringly doth shine,
> Shall within one Beauty meet,
>     And she be only thine.

*Soul*

> If things of Sight such Heavens be,                    55
> What Heavens are those we cannot see?

### Pleasure

Where so e're thy Foot shall go
   The minted Gold shall lie;
Till thou purchase all below
   And want new Worlds to buy.                    60

### Soul

Were't not a price who'ld value Gold?
And that's worth nought that can be sold.

### Pleasure

Wilt thou all the Glory have
   That War or Peace commend?
Half the World shall be thy Slave                         65
   The other half thy Friend.

### Soul

What Friends, if to my self untrue?
What Slaves, unless I captive you?

### Pleasure

Thou shalt know each hidden Cause;
   And see the future Time:                       70
Try what depth the Centre draws;
   And then to Heaven climb.

### Soul

None thither mounts by the degree
Of Knowledge, but Humility.

### CHORUS

*Triúmph, triúmph, victorious Soul;*                      75
*The World has not one Pleasure more:*
*The rest does lie beyond the Pole,*
*And is thine everlasting Store.*

The making of 'Beauty' in lines 51 – 4 is strongly reminiscent of the making of Celia in 'The Match'. Pleasure's fourth line offers sensual gratification and lascivious delight; he plays the Pandar. The innocent Soul thinks only of beauty as sight and rejects here on earth what he is sure will be bettered in Heaven. Marvell's 'All this fair, and soft, and sweet' was a re-modelling of Cowley's line 18 in 'The Soul', 'Either soft, or sweet, or fair'. Both poets were summing up the pleasures of the five senses. Cowley's poem had been printed in *The Mistress* (1647).

The offer of gold is spurned on the ground that the metal has no intrinsic value. It represents power to purchase, but nothing is valuable that can be bought and sold. In the same way the Soul denies that glory can bring friends or slaves; it is Pleasure that a true Soul must enslave.

The greatest temptation is held back to the end. A seventeenth-century university wit most of all valued knowledge. His Plato had taught him that the rational part of the soul should be sovereign. His Virgil had called 'knowledge of causes' true happiness. He wanted to know the future. He wanted to find out such physical facts as the distance to the centre of the terrestrial globe. Knowing all that, he could climb up to Heaven.

But in knowledge the Resolute Soul sees the prospect of pride. By the 'degree' of humility, not of knowledge, he says, one 'mounts' to Heaven. He puns on 'degree'. It is a university degree, marking a step in the academic hierarchy. It is equally a step or mounting-block, so placed as to give the horseman a leg up. Thus the Soul cues each Chorus in with a pun and with consequent clapping and laughter.

Each 'triumph' in line 75 is accented on the second syllable and is an iambus. After the Roman victory came the Roman triumph. All nine temptations have failed and the world has no more 'created' and therefore fallen 'pleasures'. What pleasure remains is eternal and unrationed and boundless for pure souls in heaven.

It is an exhilarating conclusion. Good triumphs. One soul is saved.

Internal evidence in this poem and 'The Gallery' suggests that the date of their composition was close to that of 'An Horatian Ode'. If so, they were Marvell's first essays in the stanza form that he went on to use in 'Upon Appleton House', 'The Hill and Grove at Bill-borow', 'Damon the Mower' and 'The Garden', all of which we think he wrote in 1651–2, his Nun Appleton years.

Pierre Legouis professed a poor opinion of the form. 'Marvell makes stanzas of a sort with groups of four octosyllabic couplets separated by Roman figures. These units have little to do with the art of versification; at best they answer to the desire of dividing the movement of thought into equal time-lengths.' (*Andrew Marvell*, Oxford University Press, 1965, p.83) But, two sentences later, he had to admit of 'The Garden': 'This last poem comes so near perfection that one hesitates to disparage the metrical pattern on which it is built and the poet who probably preferred this pattern to all others.'

The fact is that Marvell wrote no fewer than 1136 lines in this stanza form, which he handled increasingly well. He seems to have imported it from France. Saint-Amant used groups of five octosyllabic couplets, which Legouis would presumably allow to be 'stanzas of a sort', and in the 1640s Saint-Amant's reputation stood high.

'The unfortunate Lover' opens on a paradoxical note. The word 'Alas', coming after such a title, does not surprise the reader; but 'Alas, how pleasant' most decidedly does.

I

> Alas, how pleasant are their dayes
> With whom the Infant Love yet playes!
> Sorted by pairs, they still are seen
> By Fountains cool, and Shadows green.
> But soon these Flames do lose their light,          5
> Like Meteors of a Summers Night:
> Nor can they to that Region climb,
> To make impression upon Time.

In line 3 'still' means 'always', its regular seventeenth-century adverbial sense. In line 4 the 'Fountains' are not artificial jets of water, but *fontes aquarum*, the 'water-brooks' that 'the hart desireth' in Psalm 42. This is no patrician garden scene, but a pastoral setting for the courtship of ordinary folk. In line 7 'that Region' means 'the region of timelessness and incorruptibility beyond the moon'. Meteors were regarded as exhalations from the earth's centre, which burnt out when they reached the sphere of fire, far short of the moon. What hope, then, had lovers' flames? The 'climb-Time' rhyme figures also in 'An Horatian Ode', lines 33−4.

The next six stanzas are, like the loving couples, 'sorted by pairs'. Numbers II and III register the Lover's unfortunate birth, IV and V his unfortunate upbringing, VI and VII his unfortunate end. The past tenses of II and III take the reader back at least eighteen years and give the poem a new, narrative start.

### II

   'Twas in a Shipwrack, when the Seas
   Rul'd, and the Winds did what they please,    10
   That my poor Lover floting lay,
   And, e're brought forth, was cast away:
   Till at the last the master−Wave
   Upon the Rock his Mother drave;
   And there she split against the Stone,    15
   In a *Cesarian Section*.

### III

   The Sea him lent these bitter Tears
   Which at his Eyes he alwaies wears.
   And from the Winds the Sighs he bore,
   Which through his surging Breast do roar.    20
   No Day he saw but that which breaks,
   Through frighted Clouds in forked streaks.
   While round the ratling Thunder hurl'd,
   As at the Fun'ral of the World.

In line 11 'my poor Lover' means 'the unfortunate Male Lover who is the subject of my poem'; the word 'unfortunate' is not used until line 30. The medical term 'Cesarian Section' is moulded into the iambic rhythm by trisyllabising both words; the old-fashioned 'shi-own' sound in the last foot rhymes with 'stone'. No father is mentioned at all. We are left to work out the literal fact that a boy baby was delivered by surgery from a mother who did not survive. Allegorically, Nature is made to achieve this after a shipwreck in a storm. The poet goes on to exploit the superstition that a Caesarian baby will have as strange a career as Julius Caesar, the original Caesarian babe.

In line 22 the clouds and the forked lightning streaks are another reminder of the Horatian Ode with its 'three-fork'd Lightning first / Breaking the Clouds where it was nurst'. Detonations of thunder reverberate all around in line 23, where 'hurl'd' is intransitive and means 'roared or blustered as the wind'.

The present tenses in 'wears' and 'do roar' give us our first intimation that the baby does grow up. But how, we must wonder, could that have come about? Stanzas IV and V supply an answer of sorts.

### IV

While Nature to his Birth presents                    25
This masque of quarrelling Elements;
A num'rous fleet of Corm'rants black,
That sail'd insulting o're the Wrack,
Receiv'd into their cruel Care,
Th'unfortunate and abject Heir:                       30
Guardians most fit to entertain
The Orphan of the *Hurricane*.

### V

They fed him up with Hopes and Air,
Which soon digested to Despair.
And as one Corm'rant fed him, still                   35
Another on his Heart did bill.
Thus while they famish him, and feast,
He both consumed, and increast:
And languished with doubtful Breath,
Th' *Amphibium* of Life and Death.                    40

In line 25 'presents' means 'presented', but Marvell likes to imitate the Latin use of the present tense after *dum*; it is the same with line 37. In line 30 'Heir' does double duty. It shows that paternal estates are involved. It provides the basis for the punning 'Air' in line 33. Shakespeare used the same pun in similar circumstances when he made Hamlet, the disappointed heir, tell Claudius: 'I eat the Air, promise-crammed' (III, ii).

The greed of the cormorant is proverbial. It makes sense if the 'numerous fleet of cormorants black' are taken to signify black-suited functionaries from the Court of Wards, who in an intestacy acted as guardians of an orphan and administered the estate till his coming of age. At their worst they were cormorants indeed. At their best they still had to be paid.

There are not just two cormorants at work on the rock in lines 35–6, as the Oxford third edition of the *Poems* (1971) alleges on p.255. 'One' and 'another' do not equal 'the one' and 'the other'. One *relay* 'fed him' and feasted him so that he increased, and another *relay* was always ('still') pecking at his heart, the vital organ of the lover; as a result of their pecking, their famishing him, he 'consumèd', he wasted away. An 'Amphibium' is equally at home in water and on dry land: the orphan adapted in the same way to life and death. The antitheses are cleverly presented in a succession of strong verbs.

In stanzas VI and VII the whining schoolboy has grown up into Shakespeare's third age of man, 'the lover sighing like furnace', the condition foreshadowed in stanza III. The tenses can now become present again.

### VI

And now, when angry Heaven wou'd
Behold a spectacle of Blood,
Fortune and He are call'd to play
At sharp before it all the day:
And Tyrant Love his brest does ply                45
With all his wing'd Artillery.
Whilst he, betwixt the Flames and Waves,
Like *Ajax*, the mad Tempest braves.

### VII

See how he nak'd and fierce does stand,
Cuffing the Thunder with one hand;                50
While with the other he does lock,
And grapple, with the stubborn Rock:
From which he with each Wave rebounds,
Torn into Flames, and ragg'd with Wounds.
And all he saies, a Lover drest                  55
In his own Blood does relish best.

With these two stanzas the long marine metaphor ends. The poor young man dies. Without ever having left his rock, he, the orphan of the hurricane, the ward of the cormorants, succumbs to Fortune and Love.

'Angry Heaven' (another phrase in the Horatian Ode) thunders at him through 'the mad Tempest'. For its own sport it also ordains a mortal combat between Fortune and him. 'To play at sharp' was to duel with unblunted foils. Gladiators did it professionally for a limited number of rounds, but this pair have to do it 'all the day'. In mid-ocean, Fortune's weapon has to be the waves; their ebb and flow bear some resemblance to the swordsman's retreat and attack.

Independently of Heaven 'Tyrant Love', no longer the tame 'Infant Love' of stanza I, assumes the offensive and shoots volleys of 'wing'd' arrows at the naked man. Every hit draws blood and lights a flame of desire, like the flames in stanza I, except that they did not last.

Thus in lines 47–8 the unfortunate lover tries to surmount his crisis in the face of three forms of attack:

> Whilst he, betwixt the Flames and Waves,
> Like *Ajax*, the mad Tempest braves.

He braves the Tempest as Ajax the son of Oileus did, but with no more success. Shipwrecked on the way back from Troy, Ajax swam safely ashore with the aid of Poseidon but arrogantly took all the credit himself, whereupon angry Poseidon stormed at him and he was drowned. Virgil's account in *Aeneid*, I 41–5, is full of lightning and fire, but here the flames are of Cupid's making and heaven merely thunders.

In VII the heroic last stand wins our admiration. The young man turns athlete. As a boxer, he 'cuffs' the thunder, counter-punching with his free hand. As a wrestler, he uses his other hand to 'lock' and 'grapple' with his native rock, trying desperately to secure a hold. But 'the stubborn Rock' sides with Fortune and each time fends him off till the next wave once more plucks him away. With his body 'Torn into Flames, and ragged with Wounds' from Cupid's arrows, the fierce Lover cannot survive 'all the day'.

The final couplet of VII is distinctly perplexing:

> And all he saies, a Lover drest
> In his own Blood does relish best.

However, 'relish' is clearly a transitive verb and, as clearly, its only possible object is 'all (that) he saies'. So the sentence means: 'Better than anybody else, a lover dressed in his own blood relishes all that the unfortunate lover *saies*.' If 'saies' or 'says' meant 'speaks', it would not be easy to imagine what the unfortunate lover says or who could hear it or how. He has not spoken so far. Clutching at straws, one might argue that the stanza with its opening 'See how' is an emblem, an engraving, and painted words could issue in conventional banners from his mouth. On the other hand, Marvell began 'On a Drop of Dew' and 'Upon the Hill and Grove at Bill-borow' and two separate stanzas of 'Upon Appleton House' with 'See how' and they are no more emblematic than 'Three blind mice, see how they run'.

There is another solution, and that is to take 'says' as the aphetic form of 'assays', meaning 'endeavours', 'attempts'. It was so used in the seventeenth century both as verb and as noun. The vexed sentence would then mean: 'A Lover covered in his own blood can best appreciate all that the unfortunate Lover endeavours (against overwhelming odds).' This novel interpretation links perfectly well with the final stanza and with the probable source of its opening idea:

## VIII

This is the only *Banneret*
That ever Love created yet:
Who though, by the Malignant Starrs,
Forced to live in Storms and Warrs;       60
Yet dying leaves a Perfume here,
And Musick within every Ear:
And he in Story only rules,
In a Field *Sable* a Lover *Gules*.

Marvell's London circle would recognise in that 'Banneret' couplet a backward glance at the Richard Lovelace quatrain in 'Dialogue: Lucasta, Alexis' (1649):

Souldiers suspected of their courage goe,
That Ensignes and their Breasts untorne show:
Love neere his Standard when his Hoste he sets,
Creates alone fresh-bleeding *Bannerets*.

A monarch created a Banneret when he knighted a brave soldier on the battlefield. The poet is saying that love only does this on the visible evidence of a wounded breast. He promotes the newly-smitten when he gives pride of place near his standard. Marvell goes further and makes his unfortunate lover the only Banneret ever created by love so far ('yet').

From line 61 the hero is treated as dead, and the paradox of the poem is unfurled. Though he was fated to *live* in storms and wars, yet his *death* has brought him fame and repute. The twin metaphors 'Perfume' and 'Musick' derive from Ecclesiasticus, XLIX 1: 'The remembrance of Josias is like the composition of the perfume that is made by the art of the apothecary: it is sweet as honey in all mouths, and as musick at a banquet of wine.' Thus this last stanza inverts stanza I. For the happy lovers were quickly forgotten and made no impression upon time, regrettable though that was (hence the 'Alas, how pleasant' start), but the unfortunate lover's name goes down to posterity, to be mentioned with honour and approval, to be 'Musick within every ear'.

The word 'Story' poses a problem in line 63. Legouis in the Oxford third edition of the *Poems* (1971) thinks the line 'may mean either "he is supreme in the world of fiction [the romances of chivalry]" or "it is only in the world of fiction that he rules".' But, adds Legouis more hopefully, '"Story" might mean "a painting . . . representing a historical subject. Hence any work of pictorial . . . art containing figures"(O.E.D. . . .) This would agree better with the next line, and confirm the emblematic character of the poem.'

But in the seventeenth and eighteenth centuries 'story' could mean 'epitaph' too. Gray used it in that sense in his 'Elegy' when he asked:

> Can storied urn or animated bust
> Back to its mansion call the fleeting breath?

Ben Jonson used it in that sense when he began his Epitaph on Salomon Pavy, the bright boy-actor:

> Weep with me, all you that read
> This little story;
> And know, for whom a tear you shed
> Death's self is sorry.

The twenty lines of Jonson's elegy that follow contain no narrative *fiction* at all. They tell us that the boy was thirteen and had been for three years 'the stage's jewel' and that he was particularly good at acting old men's parts. But Jonson's elegy ensured the boy's fame.

The heraldry of 'a Field Sable' (a funeral-black background to the shield) and 'a Lover Gules' (a blood-red full-length male, corresponding to the 'Lover drest in his own blood' of lines 55–6) most naturally suggests a patrician Tomb. Where we put perishable flowers, they hung durable scutcheons. The last stanza of 'The Mower's Song' has these four lines before the refrain:

> And thus, ye Meadows, which have been          25
> Companions of my thoughts more green,
> Shall now the Heraldry become
> With which I shall adorn my Tomb.

Likewise Marvell's 'Elegy upon the Death of my Lord Francis Villiers' ended with the words 'his Trophee and his Tombe'; and, as we have seen, Lord Francis was a posthumous son slain in a Civil War action in July 1648 at the age of nineteen and leaving 'the matchless Chlora' forlorn. Some such tragedy may have inspired 'The unfortunate Lover'.

Marvell always contrived a strong finish to his poems and, if this interpretation of lines 63–4 is correct, he contrives a strong finish here; for the whole poem then becomes an elegy to adorn 'the unfortunate's' tomb. And the Lover rules 'only in Story' because he did not live to 'rule' his paternal estate.

## 15   'The Gallery'

From the unnerving obscurities of 'The unfortunate Lover' one turns with relief to 'The Gallery', which is superficially as clear as glass. It opens with an invitation to a shepherdess.

I

> *Clora* come view my Soul, and tell
> Whether I have contriv'd it well.
> Now all its several lodgings lye
> Compos'd into one Gallery;

And the great *Arras*-hangings, made        5
Of various Faces, by are laid;
That, for all furniture, you'l find
Only your Picture in my Mind.

'Soul' and 'mind' are synonyms here. All his thoughts, he tells Clora, are of her. The old sets of separate apartments or 'lodgings' are merged into one long gallery now. He has taken down the large tapestry hangings, embroidered with the faces of his former loves, and they are stowed away ('by are laid'). She will find her portrait ('picture') the only furnishing there. She is invited to inspect the gallery and pronounce ('tell') whether the result is good.

He addresses her at first with some formality, using the respectful 'you' and 'your'; but from line 9 onwards he slips into 'thou' and 'thy'.

## II

Here Thou art painted in the Dress
Of an Inhumane Murtheress;        10
Examining upon our Hearts
Thy fertile Shop of cruel Arts:
Engines more keen than ever yet
Adorned Tyrants Cabinet;
Of which the most tormenting are        15
Black Eyes, red Lips, and curled Hair.

She has accepted his invitation and he is showing her round. His first picture teases her, but it is not unflattering.

In line 9 'Dress' means 'guise' more than 'robe', but carries the suggestion of a full-length portrait. 'Cabinet' in line 14 is a crucial word. It contains two meanings at once, 'study' and 'gallery'. It is the malevolent tyrant's study or closet where he keeps his instruments of torture for 'examining' victims. (See D. I. B. Smith (ed.), *The Rehearsal Transpros'd*, Oxford University Press, 1971, p.60 and n.) It is the benevolent tyrant's picture-gallery, 'adorned' with valuable paintings. Thus her good looks are her instruments of torture ('Engines'), her assorted stock-in-trade ('Shop'), which she enjoys trying out ('Examining') on the susceptibilities of men ('our Hearts'), regardless of the pain she inflicts.

The last line is dramatic. It has two caesuras and six of its eight syllables are stressed. The effect is to stamp her head, seen full-face, on each subsequent portrait.

An otherwise opposite picture hangs on the opposite wall; no standing 'Murtheress' this time, but a reclining nude.

### III

> But, on the other side, th' art drawn
> Like to *Aurora* in the Dawn;
> When in the East she slumb'ring lyes,
> And stretches out her milky Thighs;                    20
> While all the morning Quire does sing,
> And *Manna* falls, and Roses spring;
> And, at thy Feet, the wooing Doves
> Sit perfecting their harmless Loves.

This outdoor scene, graphically detailed, is a crowded canvas. Clora lies full-length asleep, naked as the Latin dawn-goddess Aurora. Raillery gives way to romance. The dim sky at first light, the dawn chorus of birds, the manna descending, the roses erect, can easily be imagined in colour; doves courting or mating in the foreground complete the erotic effect.

The same alternation of indoor with outdoor, of what torments men with what pleases them, governs the pictures in the two stanzas that follow.

### IV

> Like an Enchantress here thou show'st,                 25
> Vexing thy restless Lover's Ghost;
> And, by a Light obscure, dost rave
> Over his Entrails, in the Cave;
> Divining thence, with horrid Care,
> How long thou shalt continue fair;                     30
> And (when inform'd) them throw'st away,
> To be the greedy Vultur's prey.

### V

> But, against that, thou sit'st a float
> Like *Venus* in her pearly Boat.
> The *Halcyons*, calming all that's nigh,               35

> Betwixt the Air and Water fly.
> Or, if some rowling Wave appears,
> A Mass of Ambergris it bears.
> Nor blows more Wind than what may well
> Convoy the Perfume to the Smell.                    40

The tone of raillery returns in IV, but this time the picture borders on the blood-curdling. In the dim light of the cave Clora bends over her dead lover (whom she has killed) like an ancient Roman *haruspex* bending over a sacrificial victim, meticulously inspecting the entrails for abnormalities that will disclose the future. Nine words of Latin origin make an unusually large concentration in eight lines. The effect is classical, though the setting is straight out of Shakespeare's *Macbeth*. But this is a very young and egotistical witch, anxious only to know how long her good looks will last. There is a note of satire here.

The next picture is a daylight seascape. Clora sits in a boat naked (or she would be no Venus). Sibilants are the dominant sound: 'sit'st', 'Venus', 'Halcyons', 'betwixt', 'Mass', 'Ambergris', 'Smell'. Marvell is at his most sensuous. There are whisperings to hear, an unruffled ocean to see, the richest of all perfumes to smell. All is idle and static. Venus poses, and does not row. Only the halcyons, travelling low on the water in the foreground, appear to be in mid-flight.

Bird-life fascinated Marvell. Most of his lyrics have birds in them and his birds are always well-observed. Kingfishers (halcyons) come in four other poems; it seems that they gave him a special thrill. Compare this picture with the twilight river scene in 'Upon Appleton House', lines 669–72.

> The modest *Halcyon* comes in sight,
> Flying betwixt the Day and Night;                    670
> And such an horror calm and dumb,
> *Admiring Nature* does benum.

The final stanzas VI and VII discard the idea that Clora is viewing the gallery. To pursue that would be tedious. Instead, she is back on her own ground and he is telling her what he sees in his mind.

### VI

> These Pictures and a thousand more,
> Of Thee, my Gallery do store;
> In all the Forms thou can'st invent

Either to please me, or torment:
For thou alone to people me,                    45
Art grown a num'rous Colony;
And a Collection choicer far
Then or *Whitehall's*, or *Mantua's* were.

### VII

But, of these Pictures and the rest,
That at the Entrance likes me best:            50
Where the same Posture, and the Look
Remains, with which I first was took.
A tender Shepherdess, whose Hair
Hangs loosely playing in the Air,
Transplanting Flow'rs from the green Hill,      55
To crown her Head, and Bosome fill.

Stanza VI is a good example of Marvell's irrepressible wit. Its last couplet has an editorial interest too, as being a guide to the poem's date:

> . . . a Collection choicer far
> Then or *Whitehall's*, or *Mantua's* were.

Margoliouth noted in his 1927 and 1952 Oxford editions of Marvell's poems that the Duke of Mantua's Collection was bought by King Charles I, who added it to his pictures at Whitehall. These in turn, he noted, were being sold and dispersed from February 1649 to July 1650. On the verb 'were' he wrote: '*Were*, if read as past tense not as subjunctive, may date the poem or its revision later than their dispersal'.

Reprinting this in the Third Edition of 1971, Legouis, the new editor, went on: 'Grierson's ingenious conjecture that Marvell first wrote "are" before, and altered it to "were" after, the dispersal, was based on the badness of the rhyme. Unfortunately Marvell was not fastidious in this respect; in lines 15−16 of this same piece he rhymes "are" with "hair".'

Now, as regards the rhyming, it should be noted that in 'Upon Appleton House', lines 695−6, Marvell again rhymed 'Fair' with 'are', and in the Second Song 'at the Marriage of the Lord Fauconberg and the Lady Mary Cromwell' he rhymed 'are' with 'Hair'. He was relying on the Stuart Scottish pronunciation of 'are' as 'air'. He reckoned to use every option in rhyming. And since 'er' was then commonly pronounced 'ar', one pronunciation of 'were' was 'war', the same sound as his noun 'war' made when he rhymed it with 'star' and 'car', with 'Dunbar' and 'far' and 'Oliver'. 'Were' is therefore a whole rhyme here to 'far'. There would be no gain in Grierson's 'are'.

As regards the parsing of *were*, Margoliouth's point was that, if subjunctive, it would be present subjunctive; and if present subjunctive, the line could have been written when King Charles was alive. Such a supposition ignores the history of English grammar. Charles Butler in *The English Grammar* (1633) had no conjunctive or subjunctive mood. He made *were* invariably indicative while recording its use instead of the singular *was* after 'if', 'though', etc., and after words of wishing such as 'I would', 'would to God'. John Wallis in *Grammatica linguae Anglicanae* (1653) included a conjunctive mood in association with a long line of possible conjunctions, but he made *be* the present conjunctive and *were* the preterite conjunctive. This was still the doctrine when Samuel Johnson wrote the English Grammar which he prefixed to his Dictionary in 1755. So Marvell was undoubtedly referring to the past when he wrote *were*.

Furthermore, King Charles's agents did not buy all the pictures in the Duke of Mantua's Collection at its sale in 1626 nor did the King hang all that he bought at Whitehall. The largest and costliest item, the nine canvases of Mantegna's 'Triumph of Julius Caesar' (each nine feet square) went to Hampton Court. Cromwell later had them hung in his state apartments there. Caesar appealed to him.

In short, Marvell is referring to two quite distinct historic collections. He is saying that the imaginary Clora collection of over a thousand portraits of her was a far more choice one than either Whitehall's pictures 'were' before 1650 or Mantua's 'were' before 1626. Mantua's were reputed the finest in Europe before Charles I collected Whitehall's. And Whitehall's, when Marvell wrote this poem, were a 'Collection' no more.

In stanza VII the tone changes completely. The teasings and exaggerations stop. He ceases to embroider or invent. He means all he says. And what he says accords with the traditional romantic idealisation of love at first sight. The picture that pleases ('likes') him best is his first sight of her. He remembers her posture and her look. He was captivated ('took') then and there. And he uses the present tense now, for that picture is still in the front of his mind.

> A tender Shepherdess, whose Hair
> Hangs loosely playing in the Air,
> Transplanting Flow'rs from the green Hill, 55
> To crown her Head, and Bosome fill.

On this note of vivid candour the poem comes to a beautiful close. It was engineered to carry this conclusion and the end justifies the means.

Did the shepherdess come from real life? Marvell never married in all his 57 years. But many a bachelor was in love once and men have a way of remembering their first sight of the girl in their lives. In Marvell's case there is that other reference in 'The Coronet' to 'the fragrant Towers', the sweet-smelling tall flower-crowns, 'That once adorn'd my Shepherdesses head'. If 'The Gallery' is entirely fictional, however, one can almost admire it the more for coming so close to real life.

The 'transplanting' metaphor had earlier been employed by Thomas Carew at the start of his heroic couplets 'On a Damaske rose sticking upon a Ladies breast' (1640):

> Let pride grow big my rose, and let the cleare
> And damaske colour of thy leaves appeare.
> Let scent and lookes be sweete and blesse that hand,
> That did transplant thee to that sacred land.

Carew's 'leaves' were rose petals, of course. So are they on various occasions in Marvell.


# 16 'An Horatian Ode upon Cromwel's Return from Ireland'

General Oliver Cromwell returned from Ireland in May 1650 at the Parliament's behest and had a triumphant reception in London on the last day of the month. He was appointed second-in-command to General Fairfax on 12 June for the Scottish campaign, and on the withdrawal of Fairfax was promoted to the General's place on 26

June. He entered Scotland with his army on 22 July. By that time Marvell had evidently finished the Horatian Ode begun in June; it makes no mention of Fairfax and ends before the start of the Scottish campaign. The poet was then in his thirtieth year. His new hero was fifty-one. The infant Commonwealth was eighteen months old.

The Ode has the unity that comes of careful construction. Its 120 lines divide up into five principal parts, which it will be convenient to letter. Between two stanzas of prologue (A, ll.1—8) and two of epilogue (E, ll.113—20) are three sections of unequal length. The longest (B, ll.9—72) deals with time past; C (ll.73—96) deals with time Present and D (ll.97—112) with future time. The metre is iambic throughout. In every stanza an octosyllabic couplet is followed by a shorter hexasyllabic one. Quiller-Couch in *The Oxford Book of English Verse* printed the stanzas with spaces between, but in that arrangement the loss outweighs the gain; the shorter couplet more than once starts a new phase and three couplets may go to one sentence. The poem is too closely knit for such treatment, Horatian though it may look.

Nevertheless the stanza is the musical unit and Marvell exploits all the scope that it offers for symmetry and balance. In places he also imparts an antiphonal character. Indeed this registers in the opening stanzas at once. Two voices could read alternate lines here.

A

> The forward Youth that would appear
> Must now forsake his *Muses* dear,
>      Nor in the Shadows sing
>      His Numbers languishing.
> 'Tis time to leave the Books in dust,                5
> And oyl th'unusèd Armours rust;
>      Removing from the Wall
>      The Corslet of the Hall.

In 1650, eleven years after taking his Bachelor's degree, Marvell was a man and not a youth. He was calling adventurous under-graduates from the shadows of Oxford and Cambridge colleges or country manor houses to the sturdier arena of war. 'The Muses' stand for university studies; 'the Books' are chiefly Greek and Latin texts; 'numbers languishing' are Greek and Latin undergraduate verses —

and English love-poems, no doubt. June and July were not the busiest months in the academic year.

Already in these eight lines the English is laced with Latin word order and idiom. 'Nor' in line 3 is a Latinism for 'And not'; it will come again in lines 61, 81, 111 and will start a new couplet each time. In lines 7–8 'The Corslet of the Hall' is a corslet hung on the Wall of the Hall, the baronial hall in a castle or moated house.

Marvell's stanza form was not his own invention. Sir Richard Fanshawe (1608–66) used it more than once in *Selected Parts of Horace, Prince of Lyricks*, a collection of English verse translations of his which he printed in 1652; and though that year used to seem too late to serve Marvell, we now know that the British Museum has a manuscript ode of Fanshawe's (Add. MS. 15228, folios 29 and 29b), written in this same stanza form in 1626. William Simeone pointed it out in *Notes and Queries* (1952), pp.316–8, and N. W. Bawcutt printed the Ode in *Shorter Poems and Translations by Sir Richard Fanshawe* (Liverpool University Press, 1964). The two poets could have met in London or Spain. In the first half of 1647 they were both in Spain, and they were both in London in the autumn of the same year.

Marvell improved Fanshawe's stanza quite remarkably. Subtitled in Latin '*Splendidis longum valedico nugis*' ('I pay a long farewell to glittering trifles'), this 1626 'Oade' of Fanshawe's marks the boundary between his leaving Jesus College, Cambridge and its classical studies and his arrival at the Inner Temple to study law. It begins:

> Yee Vanity's of humane Race,
> That lead fond youth the Wildgoose-chace,
>     Mindless of after good;
>     Bee-gone y'are understood.
> Butt thou, my darling Vanity,
> Foe to my thriveing, Poetry,
>     Whose Love, begunne at first,
>     My unwise Tutour nurst;
> What witch, with her inchanting rodd;
> Can loose me from thy Charms, what God?
>     Not Pegasus cann mee
>     From thy Chymera's free.

Marvell's treatment of the stanza form gives the rest of his poem an added interest after that. Lines 9–72 (time past) can best be handled in three numbered stages.

B 1

So restless *Cromwel* could not cease
In the inglorious Arts of Peace,                                    10
   But through adventrous War
   Urged his active Star.
And, like the three-fork'd Lightning, first
Breaking the Clouds where it was nurst,
   Did thorough his own Side                                15
   His fiery way divide.
(For 'tis all one to Courage high
The Emulous or Enemy;
   And with such to inclose
   Is more then to oppose.)                                 20
Then burning through the Air he went,
And Pallaces and Temples rent:
   And *Caesars* head at last
   Did through his Laurels blast.
'Tis Madness to resist or blame                                    25
The force of angry Heavens flame:

In line 20 the adverb 'more' is another Latinism, meaning 'worse'.
Lucan's *Pharsalia* has in its very first line the phrase '*Bella . . . plus
quam civilia*' ('Wars more than civil'), which J. D. Duff in the Loeb
edition translates 'war worse than civil'. The highly compressed
parenthetical lines 17–20 amount to this, when expanded: 'The
soldier of exceptional spirit has the dynamism to outdo fellow-soldier
and foe alike; such a man finds it worse to be confined by rivals than to
be confronted by the other side.' Cromwell's 'own side' in line 15 was
the Parliament side and nothing more, though some critics have seen
in it also a strange sort of Caesarian birth. In line 18 'Emulous' and
'Enemy' are singular nouns; hence their capital letters. English
normally uses 'emulous' as adjective only, though the Latin *aemulus*
could be adjective or noun. The *New English Dictionary*, overlooking
this passage, gives no instance of 'emulous' as a noun.

   The 'lightning' simile in lines 13–16 is developed into a metaphysical conceit in lines 21–6. Superhuman forces were at work.
His 'active Star' fought for Cromwell and 'angry Heaven' fought
against King Charles ('Caesar') in spite of his crown ('laurels'). But it
still needed 'restless Cromwell' to *urge* 'his active Star'. Much credit,
then, must be given at the human level to 'the Man'.

B 2

> And, if we would speak true,
> Much to the Man is due.
> Who, from his private Gardens, where
> He liv'd reserved and austere,                            30
>   As if his highest plot
>   To plant the Bergamot,
> Could by industrious Valour climbe
> To ruine the great Work of Time,
>   And cast the Kingdome old                               35
>   Into another Mold.
> Though Justice against Fate complain,·
> And plead the antient Rights in vain:
>   But those do hold or break
>   As Men are strong or weak.                              40
> Nature that hateth emptiness,
> Allows of penetration less:
>   And therefore must make room
>   Where greater Spirits come. ⁻

In line 27 who are meant by 'we'? The word is unstressed, but important. It might mean 'we English' and, if printed in 1650, would have been interpreted thus. In fact, though, the poem only circulated in manuscript among Marvell's friends and he intended no more at that time; 'we' consequently meant, when he wrote it, 'we former loyal subjects of the late King Charles', men who with Marvell must now re-assess General Cromwell, their *de facto* ruler, the hero of the hour.

'The Bergamot' was a southern Italian pear tree, *pero bergamotto*, lately introduced into England and felicitously introduced here; it brightens the poem after some rather drab lines. In lines 33–40, however, the poetry takes wing and metaphors begin to abound. A craftsman melts old metal down and runs it into a new mould. A civil lawsuit, 'Justice versus Fate', is pleaded in court; Fate prevails. Rope cables can hold or break aboard ship; so can 'Rights' operated by men.

The last four lines invoke a seventeenth-century physical law, 'the penetration of dimensions', to which Marvell had already playfully alluded in 'Fleckno, an English Priest at Rome' in March 1646:

> ... I, that was
> Delightful, said there can no Body pass
> Except by penetration hither, where
> Two make a crowd ... (ll.97– 100)

According to this law, no two bodies in Nature can occupy the same space. (Better known was the other law: 'Nature abhors a vacuum'.) The poet now goes on to show that Cromwell was 'a greater Spirit' than the King and so by this natural law Charles had had to make room.

### B 3

> What Field of all the Civil Wars,    45
> Where his were not the deepest Scars?
>     And *Hampton* shows what part
>     He had of wiser Art:
> Where, twining subtile fears with hope,
> He wove a Net of such a scope,    50
>     That *Charles* himself might chase
>     To *Cares-brooks* narrow case:
> That thence the *Royal Actor* born
> The *Tragick Scaffold* might adorn:
>     While round the armed Bands    55
>     Did clap their bloody hands.
> *He* nothing common did, or mean,
> Upon that memorable Scene;
>     But with his keener Eye
>     The Axes edge did try:    60
> Nor call'd the *Gods* with vulgar spight
> To vindicate his helpless Right,
>     But bow'd his comely Head
>     Down, as upon a Bed.
> This was that memorable Hour    65
> Which first assur'd the forced Pow'r.
>     So when they did design
>     The *Capitols* first Line,
> A bleeding Head where they begun,
> Did fright the Architects to run;    70
>     And yet in that the *State*
>     Foresaw it's happy Fate.

Cromwell's better battle record takes up two rhetorical lines and no more. His 'Scars' in line 46 are the cuts he inflicted on the enemy with his cavalry sabre. His own body went miraculously unscathed. So in 'A Poem upon the Death of O. C.', lines 195—6, Marvell would later write:

> . . . though in battle none so brave or fierce,
> Yet him the adverse steel could never pierce.

His statecraft or 'wiser Art' takes up ten lines, of which 49—51 have been most frequently misunderstood. The meaning is not, as Margoliouth proposed, 'wove a net of such a scope as might chase Charles himself'. No net or scope ever chased anyone. There is no correlative here. 'That *Charles* himself might chase' is as straightforward an adverbial clause of purpose as the next is: 'That thence the *Royal Actor* born (escorted) the *Tragick Scaffold* might adorn'. Both have the same grammatical order: subject, object, verb. There is no difficulty in the idea of King Charles chasing himself. (Cf. 'The Fair Singer', line 8, 'My dis-intangled Soul it self might save.' and 'The Coronet', line 10, 'So I myself deceive.') Charles was the stag that fetched up in the 'narrow case' (cramped cage) of Carisbrooke Castle. But no one hunted him there. He hunted himself, having quietly escaped from Hampton on horseback on the dark night of 17 November 1647 with his two chosen friends. He was not pursued or challenged. He was not recognised until he introduced himself to a shocked Colonel Hammond, Parliamentary Governor of the Isle of Wight, who had to be sent for.

What the 'wiser Art' and the 'Net' amount to in lines 47—50 is a poetical re-statement of the popular belief that the King's flight from Hampton to Carisbrooke was a master-stroke of Cromwell's. Cromwell had multiplied the King's fears for his safety as a prisoner, people said. Cromwell had fostered the King's hope of a secure future elsewhere. 'A Net of such a scope' meant simply 'so far-sighted and intricate a scheme'. Everything that happened to Charles on the way to his doom was said by Cromwell's admirers to have been intended in that original scheme. Cromwell let Charles escape; Cromwell let him be at once both hunter and stag on the trail to the inevitable cage, in order that he might be 'borne thence' under close guard to the scaffold.

The theatrical metaphor begun by 'Actor' in line 53 lasts for twelve lines, the longest image in the poem. It capitalises on the fact that 'scaffolds' were run up for plays even more than for executions, or had been till the Puritans outlawed public plays. In a classical ode tragedies had a natural place. Great actors were 'ornaments' of the stage.

With the word 'adorn' in line 54 the tone changes to explicit approval of the king and implicit disapproval of the military power. No literal hand-clapping, of course, was intended in line 56. It was just that the standing-room for groundlings on three sides of the normal theatrical stage or scaffold or scene was on this memorable occasion taken up by serried ranks of battle-proved infantry. In his own tragedy, then, King Charles played the King to perfection. He did nothing to demean himself. With eyes sharper than the executioner's axe he tested its cutting edge; he did not quail. He made the usual condemned speech without ranting to high heaven or basely repining at his lot. He had right on his side, but did not uselessly invoke it. His head was 'comely' indeed. He bowed it down on the low block as a man might on a pillow in bed. (Perhaps there is also a suggestion here of an actor making his last bow to the audience.) The final effect is inexpressibly tender. So in Horace's Actium Ode (I, 37) the Roman poet was tender towards Cleopatra and Octavian, on opposite sides in another Civil War.

From the moment that Charles's head was struck off, the Republic took the place of the Monarchy and the power gained by force of arms was confirmed, subject only to the proviso which would conclude the poem:

> The same *Arts* that did gain
> A *Pow'r* must it *maintain*.

The far-away Roman precedent invoked in lines 67–72 swiftly neutralises the pathos and at the same time reinforces the Horatian element in the Ode, for this was a piece of history known to Horace himself. It was Varro (116–27 B.C.) who first derived CAPITOLIUM from the *caput humanum* (human head), which they found when they dug the site for the Temple of Jupiter. Livy referred to this in his Book I. The elder Pliny, repeating the story a century later, added that the prophet Olenus Calenus of Etruria saw in it at the time 'a clear and lucky omen'. No Latin author said anything about the head 'bleeding' or about frightened builders running away. Marvell embroidered the story for his own topical ends. It provided at once a scholarly parallel and a useful diversion.

There is further embroidery in the Irish section that follows, but it had an English propagandist basis as well. One cannot know how much of it Marvell believed. He is happy to write as a prejudiced Englishman gloating over foreign conquest and unexpectedly complete success.

### C

And now the *Irish* are asham'd
To see themselves in one Year tam'd:
    So much one Man can do,               75
    That does both act and know.
They can affirm his Praises best,
And have, though overcome, confest
    How good he is, how just,
    And fit for highest Trust:            80
Nor yet grown stiffer with Command,
But still in the *Republick's* hand:
    How fit he is to sway
    That can so well obey.
He to the *Commons Feet* presents       85
A *Kingdome*, for his first year's rents:
    And, what he may, forbears
    His Fame to make it theirs:
And has his Sword and Spoyls ungirt,
To lay them at the *Publick's* skirt.      90
    So when the Falcon high
    Falls heavy from the Sky,
She, having kill'd, no more does search,
But on the next green Bow to pearch;
    Where, when he first does lure,     95
    The Falkner has her sure.

The six lines 79–84 represent direct speech, the testimony of the native Irish. In 81–2 'yet' and 'still' are temporal adverbs, but not synonyms; 'still' means 'always'. The metaphor is from wax; soft and malleable 'in the hand', but away from it stiffer and stiffer. In line 87 'what he may' is another Latinism, a literal translation of the *'qua licet'* that Marvell uses in 'Ros', line 8, for 'as best it can':

Exprimit aetherei qua licet Orbis aquas.

Cromwell was appointed to the Irish command on 15 March 1649. He landed his army in Dublin on 15 August. His men stormed Drogheda on 18 September after ten days of siege and slew 3500 without quarter, including those burnt alive in St Peter's Church. He dealt with Wexford as harshly and met little opposition after that. He certainly did keep his word, even if it was to his own disadvantage, as when outwitted at Clonmel in his last action on 27 April 1650.

The likening of Cromwell to a falcon and Parliament to the falconer could not be more apt — except that trained falcons were females. The intransitive verb 'lure' (l.95) meant 'call to a hawk when casting the lure'. This lure was a bunch of feathers with a long cord attached. The falcon under training had its food inserted in the lure. To recall one, the falconer swung the cord round his head as he 'lured' aloud. The obedient falcon heard him and promptly flew in.

All this was as familiar to Marvell's generation as a motoring simile would be to ours. Equally familiar was the deer-hunting in the next section.

D

What may not then our *Isle* presume
While Victory his Crest does plume!
　　What may not others fear
　　If thus he crown each Year!　　　　　　　　100
A *Caesar* he ere long to *Gaul*,
To *Italy* an *Hannibal*,
　　And to all States not free
　　Shall *Clymaterick* be.
The *Pict* no shelter now shall find　　　　　　105
Within his party-colour'd Mind;
　　But from this Valour sad
　　Shrink underneath the Plad:
Happy if in the tufted brake
The *English Hunter* him mistake;　　　　　　110
　　Nor lay his Hounds in near
　　The *Caledonian* Deer.

This is the most rhetorical section of the Ode and its unusually high proportion of italicised words invites the reader to impart special force and gusto to them. One of the most effective is '*Clymaterick*' in line 104. Editors commonly explain it as an adjective meaning 'critical', 'marking an epoch'. If so, it would be the only predicative adjective to open with a capital in Marvell; attributive adjectives sometimes do, but it is a treatment normally reserved for nouns and *Clymaterick* (the form derived from French and used in Thompson's second MS. book) or *Clymacterick* (the form derived from Greek and used in the 1681 Folio) is a perfectly good noun. It means 'critical or fatal period in life'. Some said that 'Clymactericks' came every seven years in the human life cycle, some every nine. Either way the Grand Clymacterick was the age of 63, seven times nine.

There is another reason for thinking that Marvell was using the noun. His political position or standpoint in this poem accords with that urged by Marchamont Needham (1620–78) in April 1650 in a pamphlet entitled *Case of the Commonwealth of England stated or the Equity Utility and Necessity of a submission to the present Government*. The author was himself a recent convert from the Royalist cause. His first two chapter headings were: (1) 'That Governments have their Revolutions and fatall periods.' A fatal period is a climacteric, of course. (2) 'That the Power of the Sword is and ever hath been the Foundation of all Titles of Government.' This is very much Marvell's argument here. Witness the last two stanzas.

E

> But thou the War's and Fortune's Son
> March indefatigably on;
>     And for the last effect                                    115
>     Still keep thy Sword erect:
> Besides the force it has to fright
> The Spirits of the shady Night,
>     The same *Arts* that did *gain*
>     A *Pow'r* must it *maintain*.                             120

The four italicised words in the final couplet help to give it an oracular force. The 'Arts' are a reminder of the Hampton episode. In line 113 'Fortune's Son' is a direct translation of Horace's '*Fortunae filius*' in *Sermones*, ii, 6, 49, and aptly sums up the influence of Fate on Cromwell's rise; 'the War's Son' is a tribute to 'the Man'. 'The Spirits of the shady Night' are evil spirits which can harm the unprotected, but will back away from naked steel.

Marvell never saw his Horatian Ode in print. For a century very few did. In the posthumous 1681 Folio it was included at first, and two extant copies contain it; but soon, on someone's instructions, the printers left it out. Cooke's editions did not include it in 1726 or 1772. Captain Edward Thompson added it just in time at the end of his final volume in 1776. He had probably found it in manuscript.

Marvell's brilliant performance here at the age of twenty-nine is the complete answer to those critics who want to delay the date of his best poems until 'he was sufficiently mature'. One remembers the Earl of Clarendon's expression of surprise at Edmund Waller's poetical flowering 'at the age when other men used to give up writing verses, (for he was near thirty years of age when he first engaged himself in that exercise, at least that he was known to do so)' (*The Life of Edward earl of Clarendon*, 1668).

# 17   'The Mower against Gardens'

This poem is Marvell's one Epode. Its pattern of iambic couplets had been used twice by Ben Jonson; the Londoner in him was praising life in the country each time. In *The Forrest* (1616) he used it for his Epode 'To Sir Robert Wroth', a title which went on in the manuscript 'in praise of a Country life'. In *The Under-Wood* (1640) he used it again for his translation of the Second Epode of Horace and this time they printed the title 'The praises of a Countrie life'. His translation began:

> Happie is he, that from all Businesse cleere,
>   As the old race of Mankind were,
> With his owne Oxen tills his Sire's left lands,
>   And is not in the Usurers bands.

Marvell's Mower hates gardens because he loves meadows. In his eyes gardens are artificial man-made enclosures and meadows are God-given natural growths.

The Mower's twenty Jonsonian couplets are uniformly end-stopped and slow. They exclude all suggestion of bustle. They move at a countryman's pace and express a countryman's passion.

Sixteen of the twenty couplets form hidden quatrains; the first eight do, and the last two do. This underlying organisation is a factor to be borne in mind when interpreting the sense. It helps more than once.

Luxurious Man, to bring his Vice in use,
   Did after him the World seduce:
And from the fields the Flow'rs and Plants allure,
   Where Nature was most plain and pure.
He first enclos'd within the Gardens square      5
   A dead and standing pool of Air:
And a more luscious Earth for them did knead,
   Which stupifi'd them while it fed.
The Pink grew then as double as his Mind;
   The nutriment did change the kind.      10
With strange perfumes he did the Roses taint.
   And Flow'rs themselves were taught to paint.
The Tulip, white, did for complexion seek;
   And learn'd to interline its cheek:
Its Onion root they then so high did hold,      15
   That one was for a Meadow sold.
Another World was search'd, through Oceans new,
   To find the *Marvel of Peru.*
And yet these Rarities might be allow'd,
   To Man, that sov'raign thing and proud;      20
Had he not dealt between the Bark and Tree,
   Forbidden mixtures there to see.
No Plant now knew the Stock from which it came;
   He grafts upon the Wild the Tame:
That the uncertain and adult'rate fruit      25
   Might put the Palate in dispute.
His green *Seraglio* has its Eunuchs too;
   Lest any Tyrant him out-doe.
And in the Cherry he does Nature vex,
   To procreate without a Sex.      30
'Tis all enforc'd; the Fountain and the Grot;
   While the sweet Fields do lye forgot:
Where willing Nature does to all dispence
   A wild and fragrant Innocence:
And *Fauns* and *Faryes* do the Meadows till,      35
   More by their presence then their skill.
Their Statues polish'd by some ancient hand,
   May to adorn the Gardens stand:
But howso'ere the Figures do excel,
   The *Gods* themselves with us do dwell.      40

The poem is not a pastoral. It is a postgraduate exercise in academic debate. The Mower moralises but does not mow, or even mention his scythe. No woman comes into the picture, nor does his own name. He remains an anonymous misanthrope. His friends are 'the sweet Fields' of line 32; they and he are the partners who in line 40 constitute 'us'. His enemy is arrogant 'Man'; in line 20 he calls Man 'that sov'raign thing and proud', and in line 28 he more or less calls him a tyrant.

The Mower throughout is championing Nature against Art. In places, particularly at the start, he is also championing the country against the town. Mrs E. E. Duncan-Jones has given us the clue. At least, she gave it to J. B. Leishman, who quoted her extensively in *The Art of Marvell's Poetry* (Hutchinson, 1966), pp.134–5. She believed that in this poem Marvell drew on the Elder Pliny, whose *Naturalis Historia* in thirty-seven books was translated by Philemon Holland and published in 1601 and 1634–5. In Holland's Book XIX, chapter 4, as she pointed out, the invention of city gardens was ascribed to Epicurus in the following terms:

> The invention to have gardens within a citie, came up first by Epicurus the doctor and master of all voluptuous idlenesse, who devised such gardens of pleasance in Athens: for before his time, the manner was not in any citie to dwell (as it were) in the countrey, and so to make citie and countrey al one, all their gardens were in the villages without.

To this one may add that in the lifetime of Epicurus (341–270 B.C.) his school in Athens was known as 'Gardens' (*Keroi*), after the gardens in which he taught. (Harvey, *The Oxford Companion to Classical Literature*, 1937, p.162).

So the likelihood is that the 'Man' in Marvell's first line was not Adam after the fall, but the much-maligned Epicurus. 'Luxury' to the Elizabethans and Stuarts meant 'lechery'. 'Luxurious Man' to them, was 'Lecherous Man'. The adjective fits the description of Epicurus in Holland's Pliny as 'The doctor and master of all voluptuous idlenesse' and it explains the first finite verbs, 'did seduce' and '(did) allure', and other sexual metaphors later. Epicurean Man invented city gardens in order 'to bring his Vice in use'; that is, 'to promote his voluptuousness'. And the world that he seduced after him was the vegetable world of wild flowers and plants, the Mower's primitive world.

His first step was to build walls round his square gardens and imprison the air, which became as slavishly inferior to a free current of air as a standing pool or standing pond in the country was to a free water-course. The pejorative image of 'a standing pond', with its ugly coating of green scum, had been used by Gratiano to jest at self-important, unsmiling men in *The Merchant of Venice* (I, i).

> There are a sort of men whose visages
> Do cream and mantle like a standing pond,
> And do a wilful stillness entertain,
> With purpose to be dressed in an opinion
> Of wisdom, gravity, profound conceit,
> As who should say, I am Sir Oracle,
> And when I ope my lips, let no dog bark.

Sir Henry Wotton, in *The Elements of Architecture* (1624, 1651), used the precise phrase 'standing Poole of Aire' to translate, as he said, the Latin of Alberti (*De Re Aedificatoria*, 1485). James Howell also used the precise phrase without acknowledgement in his *Instructions for Foreign Travel* (1642, 1650), a very popular book. It was thus a phrase in current use. Marvell somewhat dilutes it. For his caesura separates 'A dead and standing' from 'pool of Air'.

His metaphor 'knead' (pronounced 'ned') was taken from the making of bread, a culinary metaphor extended by 'luscious' and 'nutriment'. Each 'them' in lines 7–8 means 'Gardens' and a third 'them' is the understood object of 'fed'; in the same way, line 37 of 'The unfortunate Lover' understood 'him' – 'Thus while they famish him and feast'.

It is these accusatives that destroy Professor Frank Kermode's emendation of 'gardens square' to 'garden's square' (*The Selected Poetry of Marvell*, Signet Classics, 1967, p.97) i.e. 'the square of the garden'. One pool of air to one garden makes good democratic sense, no doubt. But if 'Garden' and 'square' were singular nouns, 'them' would have to refer back to 'Flow'rs and Plants' in line 3, which belonged to a separate quatrain; the time-sequence of the poem starts in line 5 with 'He first'. In any case, we have plural 'Gardens' in the title and in line 38, and this is a poem whose 1681 Folio text was left intact by Cooke and Thompson; even the correcting hand in Thompson's second MS. book left this poem alone, though adding some fifteen apostrophes elsewhere.

A new section begins in line 9 and ends after line 18. In these ten lines the Mower condemns one set of garden flowers as unnatural and another set as exotic and foreign. The double pink (clove-scented *dianthus* or carnation) is a product of man's double mind. By 'tainting' the roses with alien smells he not only marred them, but made them pestiferous and diseased. White flowers were taught to paint themselves, like women before their mirrors making-up. What sort of women did that? In Shakespeare's day, harlots did. That was how Hamlet classed Ophelia, when he raged at her kind in III, i: 'I have heard of your paintings too, well enough. God hath given you one face, and you make yourselves another.' Though things might have changed in the fifty years since, we find Marvell pillorying painted women in 'Upon Appleton House', lines 729–36:

> Go now fond Sex that on your Face
> Do all your useless Study place,                    730
> Nor once at Vice your Brows dare knit
> Lest the smooth Forehead wrinkled sit:
> Yet your own Face shall at you grin,
> Thorough the Black-bag of your Skin;
> When *knowledge* only could have fill'd          735
> And *Virtue* all those *Furrows till'd*.

Clearly, in the Fairfax household the ladies 'themselves did not paint'.

Mrs Duncan-Jones has pointed out that in Holland's Pliny the same perversions of flowers were being censured in the first century A.D. In Book II Holland's English condemned 'the artificial colouring and dying of Lilies' and the 'surmounting of the natural savor of flowers'. In Book XXI roses grew double and were given sophisticated smells. It does not follow, however, that either of these was in Marvell's mind. Though still using past tenses, with the tulip he was coming close to his own day. It was in about 1600 that it first became a prized flower and it was in the 1630s that speculators staked their last penny on breeder bulbs. The most humorous touch in the poem is the Mower's naive understatement:

> Its Onion root they then so high did hold,
> That one was for a Meadow sold.

He on his few pence a day would never buy a meadow, but a few pounds would have bought several acres. Yet they valued a new tulip so highly that they paid hundreds of pounds for just one. However, he goes to the opposite extreme when he says in lines 17–18:

> Another World was search'd, through Oceans new,
>   To find the *Marvel of Peru*.

This was the bushy, sweet-scented plant *Mirabilis jalapa*, whose flowers opened only in the late afternoon. It had already reached England by 1629 when the gardener John Parkinson published his *Paradisi in Sole Paradisus Terrestris* (The Earthly Paradise of *Park-in-Sun*) 'or a garden of all sorts of pleasant flowers which our English ayre will permitt to be nursed with us'. He called it '*Mirabilia Peruviana*, the Mervaile of Peru' and noted that it grew 'naturally in the West Indies'. So it does today. The Mower's hyperbole maintains that a special expedition set out to the New World to find it!

A second long section comprises lines 19–30, three sentences each four lines long (if we disregard the intrusive full stop at the end of line 28). This is the passionate part of the Mower's complaint. The germ of the poem may therefore lie here. It will pay to inspect one quatrain at a time.

> And yet these Rarities might be allow'd,
>   To Man, that sov'raign thing and proud;      20
> Had he not dealt between the Bark and Tree,
>   Forbidden mixtures there to see.

Mixtures were forbidden in the Bible by Mosaic Law. In Leviticus, XIX 19, God said: 'Thou shalt not let thy cattle gender with a diverse kind: thou shalt not sow thy field with mingled seed: neither shall a garment mingled of linen and woollen come upon thee.' In Deuteronomy, XXII 9, God said: 'Thou shalt not sow thy vineyard with divers seeds: lest the fruit of thy seed which thou hast sown and the fruit of thy vineyard, be defiled.' So there was a scriptural objection to 'mixtures' in gardens.

In line 21 Marvell is referring to the mixed operation of budding. A 'bud' sliced off the stem is bound to the cambium of the selected wild stock where a matching section of bark is removed; when the bud has 'taken', the stock above is cut off. But that operation is not the sole point here. The closeness of bark and tree proverbially symbolised true marriage and it only needed a third party, a paramour, with the probability of adulterate offspring, to set tongues wagging on the dark subject of 'coming', or 'going', or 'dealing', 'between the Bark and Tree'.

In line 23 the new 'mixture' attacked is grafting:

> No Plant now knew the Stock from which it came;
>   He grafts upon the Wild the Tame:
> That the uncertain and adult'rate fruit                    25
>   Might put the Palate in dispute.

The grafter saws branches off the trunk of a wild stock and inserts scions of one or more orchard trees into the surfaces exposed. The scions draw sap from the stock and burgeon and fruit from then on. Thomas Randolph (1605–35) had a picture of multiple grafting in his poem 'Upon Love fondly refused for Conscience sake', written in this same metre and printed four times between 1638 and 1652:

> If the fresh Trunke have sap enough to give
>   That each insertive branch may live;
> The Gardner grafts not only Apples there,
>   But addes the Warden and the Peare;
> The Peach, and Apricock together grow,
>   The Cherry and the Damson too.
> Till he hath made by skilfull husbandry
>   An intire Orchard of one Tree.

Randolph's audacious argument, more jesting than serious, was that in adult society monogamy was unnatural and promiscuity much to be preferred. J. B. Leishman (*The Art of Marvell's Poetry*, pp.132–3), recalling a broadcast talk of Frank Kermode's in 1953, argued that Marvell's poem was prompted by Randolph's; but there is no proof of this.

Mrs Duncan-Jones found a parallel condemnation of grafting or 'graffing' in Holland's Pliny, Book XV, chapter 9: 'As for all other fruits of trees, they are hardly to be numbred and reckoned by their forme and figure: much lesse by their sundry tasts and divers juices that they yeeld, so intermingled they are together by varietie of graffing one into another.' Marvell means the same thing by 'put the Palate in dispute'; namely, that the palate of the eater is puzzled to determine which fruit it is tasting. She was also able to point to Holland's use in Book XVII, chapter 15, of 'wild' and 'tame' in this connection: 'Generally all trees that are tame and gentle may well be graffed into stocks and roots of the wild.'

In the construction of Marvell's poem these same four lines play an interesting technical role. Every finite verb in the twenty-two lines before them was in the past tense: in the fourteen lines after them the tenses are all in the present. The words I have italicised here show how the poet achieves his transition:

> No Plant *now knew* the Stock from which it *came*;
>   He *grafts* upon the Wild the Tame:
> That the uncertain and adult'rate fruit          25
>   *Might put* the Palate in dispute.

The poet was still in past time all through that quatrain. His 'now' meant 'at that time' or 'by that time' and his 'grafts' was an imitation of the Latin historic present, with which Roman authors brought the past closer; he clearly meant 'grafted', for his subordinate verb in the next couplet was '*might* put' and not '*may*'. Effectively, however, without the reader quite realising it, the 'now' and the 'grafts' pave the way for the string of present tenses from line 27 to the end. Marvell was not being wanton or slovenly. He had a transition to manage and he managed it well. His historical excursion was over. What follows is contemporaneous with him.

From the age-old budding and grafting he proceeds in the next quatrain to make a new point about Man, but this time about contemporary Man.

> His green *Seraglio* has its Eunuchs too;
>   Lest any Tyrant him out-doe.
> And in the Cherry he does Nature vex,
>   To procreate without a Sex.          30

The original 'Seraglio' was the palace in Constantinople which housed government offices and the Sultan's harem. Subsequently other Middle Eastern tyrants built walled enclosures, which they called 'seraglios', solely for their harems; and they always put eunuchs in charge. These were, of course, castrated men; in the language of Marvell's day they were 'stoneless' and 'without a Sex'. That is the point here. Not to be outdone by any Eastern tyrant, man has eunuchs in his walled *garden* enclosure too; a significant stress falls on 'green' in the line 'His green Seraglio has its Eunuchs too'. These metaphorical eunuchs are trees that yield stoneless fruit. The example given here is the cherry tree, but the plum would have done equally well. Nature can grow new trees from cherry stones or plum stones, but man now sets her the vexing problem 'How to reproduce stoneless cherries without cherry stones'; for Nature can do nothing unnatural.

One has to bear in mind that sex in plant-life was then misunderstood. Not till the 1670s did the keen eye of Dr Nehemiah Grew discover the reproductive functions of the male stamen and female pistil in flowers. Not till 1682 did he print his discoveries in *The Anatomy of Leaves, Flowers, Fruits and Seeds*. By then Andrew Marvell was dead.

The Mower's next sentence becomes relaxed and tender after a passionate start:

> 'Tis all enforc'd; the Fountain and the Grot;
>     While the sweet Fields do lye forgot:
> Where willing Nature does to all dispence
>     A wild and fragrant Innocence:
> And *Fauns* and *Faryes* do the Meadows till,    35
>     More by their presence then their skill.

The wielder of the 'force' in 'enforc'd' is tyrant man, despicably sovereign and proud. In his gardens all is 'enforc'd'; the old intensive spadework and perversion of flowers and plants that we have heard of already, and the new provisions for patrician comfort that we hear of now — the artificial jet fountain and the artificial grotto or cave, two forced ways of ensuring some coolness. So the main sense of 'enforc'd' seems to be 'dictated and constrained'. In 'Upon Appleton House', line 756, the Spanish royal garden near Madrid, the Bel-Retiro, is dismissed as 'constrain'd'.

The delectable picture in the next five lines implicitly amplifies this. For what the fields have, the gardens have not. A fair paraphrase might be: 'The sour gardens receive all the attention, while the sweet fields are ignored. Yet, in these, bountiful Nature dispenses to all in common the joys of a primitive innocence. The meadows grow without any human hands being put to work. Fauns and fairies inspire growth by their mere presence or encourage it by their skill.' The verb 'till' (cultivate) is not really applicable to meadows, but it covers gardening and that is why it is there.

In the Mower's idealisation of meadow life there are parallels with the ideal republic that Gonzalo dreams of in *The Tempest* (II, i):

> No occupation, all men idle, all.
> No sovereignty . . .
> All things in common Nature should produce
> Without sweat or endeavour.

So the beauty of meadows is ideal and manifold. Gardens are no match for them.

It is tempting to see 'innocence' in line 34 as the opposite of the sexuality that began in the gardens with lecherous man and was still there in the 'green Seraglio' and stoneless cherry. But, as L. N. Wall has pointed out, in lines 33–4 Marvell was recalling a thought and a rhyme in 'To Zephirus' by William Habington (1605–54):

> Where nature doth dispence
> Her infant wealth, a beautious innocence.

There is a distinct grammatical break at the end of line 36. The four final lines form a unit on their own. Whereas each 'their' in line 36 looks back to the fauns and fairies of line 35, the 'their' in 37 looks forward.

> Their Statues polish'd by some ancient hand,
>  May to adorn the Gardens stand:
> But howso'ere the Figures do excel,
>  The *Gods* themselves with us do dwell.　　40

No ancient hand polished statues of fairies, and the Roman fauns were not gods; rather they were urchin spirits of the countryside and in pictures had horns and tails. The statues that stood on pedestals in seventeenth-century garden walks were larger-than-mortal figures of the chief Greek or Roman gods, or were said so to be. The Mower knew what he meant by figures, however vague he was about gods.

The quatrain is so arranged as to culminate in the last line. There 'Gods' is the big word in the first half and 'us' the big word in the second. They balance each other. The 'ell' of 'dwell' likewise balances the 'ell' of 'selves'. By 'us' he means 'me and my meadows'.

So different is this Mower poem from the other three that to generalise about 'the four Mower poems' is to court critical disaster. Probably this should be added to the pre-1651 compositions. I have put it as late as I dare. The Jonsonian influence was strong in November 1650 at the time of writing *Tom May's Death*. It was a London influence and after 1650 it would be some years before Marvell became a Londoner again.

# 18 'To his worthy Friend Doctor Wittie upon his Translation of the Popular Errours'

Early in 1651 Marvell ended three years of independence in London and Hull and entered the service of Lord and Lady Fairfax at Appleton House. He went there as tutor in French and Italian to Mary, their one surviving child. She had been born on 30 July 1638 and was twelve and a half. Her sister was dead.

We have to deduce the date of Marvell's arrival there from his own works. No such appointment can have been in prospect when he wrote his satirical elegy on the Parliament historian Thomas May, who died on 13 November 1650. He wrote that for royalist readers in full-blooded royalist vein attacking May as a turncoat.

> But thou base man first prostituted hast
> Our spotless knowledge and the studies chast.
> Apostatising from our Arts and us,
> To turn the Chronicler to *Spartacus.*
> Yet wast thou taken hence with equal fate,
> Before thou couldst great *Charles* his death relate.
>
> (ll.71−6)

May's *Breviary of the History of the Parliament of England* had appeared in 1650 and his last sentence read:

> But by what means, or what degrees, it came at last so far, as that the king was brought to trial, condemned, and beheaded: because the full search and narration of so great a business would make an History by itself, it cannot well be brought into this BREVIARY, which having passed over so long a time, shall here conclude.

Though Fairfax would have nothing to do with the trial and condemnation of the king and though Lady Fairfax heckled the proceedings more than once, he was General of the Parliament Army until his resignation in June 1650 and was one of May's heroes. He had been anathema to the royalist Marvell in July 1648, when the 'Elegy upon the Death of my Lord Francis Villiers' apostrophised Fame:

Much rather thou I know expectst to tell
How heavy *Cromwell* gnasht the earth and fell.
Or how slow Death farre from the sight of day
The long-deceivèd *Fairfax* bore away.

(ll.13–16)

And Marvell's new admiration for Cromwell, proclaimed in 'An Horatian Ode' in July 1650, did not yet extend to Fairfax.

Still, the logical time for Fairfax to bring a tutor into Appleton House was the end of the twelve days of Christmas, when all the boys' grammar schools up and down the country were re-assembling for the new half-year's work. And it was clearly from Appleton House that Marvell sent his English and Latin commendatory poems to Hull for his friend Robert Witty's prose translation of the *De Vulgi in Medicina Erroribus Libri quatuor* (1638) of Dr Primrose of Hull.

Now Witty's own dedication was dated 30 November 1650 and his address to the reader ended 'From my house at Hull, Decemb. 2. 1650', and the British Museum's copy of the book has 'May 3' handwritten by George Thomason against the imprint of 1651. Though the nine Latin elegiac couplets of Marvell give us no clue, in his English verses (printed below) the 'Caelia' of lines 17–27 is manifestly Mary Fairfax and they must have been written shortly after Marvell's tutorship began. The text here is that of 1651.

Sit further, and make roome for thine own fame,
Where just desert enroles thy honour'd name
*The good Interpreter.* Some in this task
Take off the Cypresse veile, but leave a mask,
Changing the Latine, but doe more obscure          5
That sense in English which was bright and pure.
So of *Translatours* they are *Authours* grown,
For ill *Translatours* make the booke their own.
Others do strive with words and forced phrase
To adde such lustre, and so many rayes,           10
That but to make the vessell shining, they
Much of the pretious Metall rub away.
He is *Translations* theefe that addeth more,
As much as he that taketh from the Store
Of the first *Authour.* Here he maketh blots       15
That mends; and added beauties are but spots.
    *Caelia* whose English doth more richly flow

Then *Tagus*, purer then dissolved snow,
And sweet as are her lips that speake it, she
Now learnes the tongues of *France* and *Italie*;                     20
But she is *Caelia* still: No other grace
But her own smiles commend that lovely face;
Her native beauty's not *Italianated*,
Nor her chaste minde into the *French* translated:
Her thoughts are *English*, though her sparkling wit     25
With other language doth them fitly fit.
*Translatours* learne of her. But stay I slide
Downe into *Errour* with the *vulgar* tide;
Women must not teach here: The *Doctor* doth
Stint them to Cawdles, Almond milk, and broth.          30
Now I reforme; and surely so will all
Whose happy eyes on thy *Translation* fall.
I see the people hasting to thy booke,
Liking themselves the worse the more they look,
And so disliking, that they nothing see                35
Now worth the liking but thy Booke and Thee.
And (if I judgement have) I censure right;
For something guides my hand that I must write.
You have Translations statutes best fulfil'd,
That, handling neither sully nor would guild.          40

*Andrew Marvell* A. F.

The initials A.F. stand for *Andreae Filius* (Son of Andrew). In a Hull
author's book this reference to their famous preacher, drowned in the
Humber ten years before, had grace and point.

# 19    *'In Legationem Domini Oliveri St John ad Provincias Foederatas'*

This Latin poem of eight elegiac couplets 'Upon the Embassy of Lord
Oliver St John to the United Provinces' is further evidence that
Marvell was already at Appleton House very early in 1651. Oliver St
John (1598–1673) was selected for the crucial Dutch mission in mid-

February of 1651 and he sailed for The Hague in mid-March with 250 men in his suite; he was Lord Chief Justice of the Court of Common Pleas. He came into Marvell's orbit in February 1651 because he was related to Lady Fairfax by marriage. She was born Anne Vere, fourth daughter and co-heiress of Sir Horace Vere, Lord Vere of Tilbury (1565–1635) and she married Thomas Fairfax on 20 June 1637. Her elder sister Catherine was the wife of an older Oliver St John who died comparatively young, an uncle of this Oliver.

In his epigram Marvell's wit played on the two halves of the ambassador's name. 'Oliver' was linked to 'olive' and 'olive branch', which symbolised peace: 'St John' suggested war, in that it harked back to the sons of Zebedee, James and John, whom Christ called 'sons of thunder' in Mark III 17 and who, in Luke IX 54, wanted him to call down fire from heaven upon the inhospitable Samaritans. Did the Dutch, then, want peace or war? The 'Oliver' or the 'St John'?

Marvell's Latin was meant to gratify Lady Fairfax, but she may well have forwarded it to her kinsman. It was not printed until 1681.

## 20 'Epigramma in Duos montes Amosclivum et Bilboreum. Farfacio'

Probably this Latin epigram of twelve elegiac couplets 'On the Two mountains Almscliff and Bilbrough' was also written in the earlier part of Marvell's tutorship at Appleton House. It is addressed to Lord Fairfax, but ends with a smiling invitation to young Mary to try writing poetry.

Almscliff (or Amescliff) was five miles south of Harrogate. Bilbrough (or Billborow) stood twenty miles east of Almscliff and five miles north-west of Appleton House. The manor and rectory of Bilbrough belonged to Lord Fairfax; in fact, Lady Fairfax and he were later buried in Bilbrough Church. Their Appleton House was in the parish of Bolton Percy.

Because the Latin poem has an English successor, it will be helpful to give a prose translation of it here.

You see how the heights of Mount Almscliff and Mount Bilbrough partition the plain with mighty boundary-marks.

Almscliff stands untamed, with towering rocks all about: Bilbrough's genial head is garlanded by a tall ash. On Almscliff's rough nape there bristles a menacing crag: Bilbrough's smooth neck tosses a green mane. Almscliff supports the heavens on Atlantean crest: Bilbrough bends Herculean shoulders submissively. (1−8)

Bilbrough confines the view with a wood, as if by classical chariot-race starting-barriers, while Almscliff attracts the eye like a charioteer's goal. Almscliff rises up like a giant Pelion on Ossa: Bilbrough leads the dance, in the manner of a nymph on the summit of Pindus. (9−12)

Almscliff is lofty, sheer, rutty and steep: Bilbrough is sloping, mild, soft and pleasing. The two quite different dispositions are united under one lord and tremble as equals under Fairfax's sway. While he glides over his lands in triumphal car, in passing he grazes each mountain with level wheel. He can himself be both rough and mild, rough with opponents, mild to those who comply; so much so that anyone would think he had himself schooled his mountains and made one rough and one mild. (13−20)

Northern Pillars of Hercules they assuredly are, and the dark valley cleaves them as with a narrow sea in between. Bending thus forward, the two peaks have long been wondering, Mary, if they would not rather like to be a Parnassus of yours. (21−4)

Mount Parnassus, the classical haunt of the Muses, was often said to have two heights. Mary could only gain a Parnassus by loving the Muses and worshipping them, either by studying the classics or writing English poems of her own.

Marvell's picture of the two sides of Fairfax's nature, the rough and the mild, anticipated the later tribute of Fairfax's son-in-law, the second Duke of Buckingham, who wrote:

> Both sexes' virtues were in him combined;
> He had the fierceness of the manliest mind,
> And all the meekness too of womankind.

## 21   'Upon the Hill and Grove at Bill-borow' To the Lord Fairfax

For this poem Marvell chose to resume the stanza form that, we think, he had already used in 'The unfortunate Lover' and 'The Gallery'. Here his ten stanzas divide into four on 'the Hill' and six on 'the Grove'. Lord Fairfax only comes in with the grove, but the whole poem was devised as an offering to him and artistically its unity is complete. It is a manly and confident offering. Marvell was only eight years younger than Fairfax and had enough mettle to serve without fawning. Fairfax too was a Cambridge man who loved books and wrote poetry himself. His good opinion of 'Marvell the tutor' and 'Marvell the poet' were equally worth having.

### I

See how the arched Earth does here
Rise in a perfect Hemisphere!
The stiffest Compass could not strike
A Line more circular and like;
Nor softest Pensel draw a Brow                                5
So equal as this Hill does bow.
It seems as for a Model laid,
And that the World by it was made.

### II

Here learn ye Mountains more unjust,
Which to abrupter greatness thrust,                          10
That do with your hook-shoulder'd height
The Earth deform and Heaven fright,
For whose excrescence ill design'd,
Nature must a new Center find,
Learn here those humble steps to tread                       15
Which to securer Glory lead.

### III

See what a soft access and wide
Lyes open to its grassy side;
Nor with the rugged path deterrs
The feet of breathless Travellers.                        20
See then how courteous it ascends,
And all the way it rises bends;
Nor for it self the height does gain,
But only strives to raise the Plain.

### IV

Yet thus it all the field commands,                      25
And in unenvy'd Greatness stands,
Discerning further then the Cliff
Of Heaven-daring *Teneriff.*
How glad the weary Seamen hast
When they salute it from the Mast!                        30
By Night the Northern Star their way
Directs, and this no less by Day.

In stanza I 'archèd' and 'Compass' and 'Model' are all architectural
terms, but the architect's compass pencil becomes in line 5 a soft brush
used by an artist to paint his sitter's brow. (In Marvell's 'The last
Instructions to a Painter' the word 'pencil' always means 'brush' and
the word 'draw' always means 'paint'.) The architectural metaphor
returns in line 13 in 'ill-designed'.

In lines 4 and 6 'like' and 'equal' mean 'regular', while 'unjust'
means 'irregular' in line 9. It is the regularity of the hill's hemispheri-
cal outline that the verb 'bow' portrays in line 6. The hill is rainbow-
shaped. 'Bow' could be pronounced as 'beau' or 'bough'.

'Nature' in line 14 presides over the physical universe and 'center' is
the spherical earth's centre, whose exact location must be affected by
mountainous irregularities on the earth's surface. Line 13 means 'on
account of whose badly designed outgrowth'.

In stanza III 'its grassy side' (l.18) is the one which in the Latin verses
was a green mane on a horse's smooth neck, while the 'rugged path'
(l.19) was the way up at the opposite end. In lines 22–3 each 'it' refers
to the 'access' in line 17.

Throughout lines 21–6 the details are subtly personalised. Marvell is paving the way for the entry of Fairfax. His qualities are foreshadowed: his courtesy and unselfishness in the behaviour of the hill, his supremacy and authority in the view from the summit, which is the summit's own supreme view. In retrospect one can see that Marvell aimed thus to bridge the transition from hill to grove.

Bilbrough Hill was only 145 feet above sea-level whereas the world-famous Teneriffe in the Canaries rose almost 12,000 feet higher. The element of hyperbole here should not be overestimated, however. The human eye has limitations, and what the poet says in lines 29—32 is that *the mast-head look-out* on a northward sailing ship sights the hill from the Humber estuary and the jaded sailors then know they are almost home. It is likely that he is speaking from experience here. He had himself surely come home to Hull by sea. If so, it would give him especial pleasure to look seaward from Bilbrough Hill. In line 29 'hast' is 'haste', but in its old pronunciation 'harst'. Thus in 'The last Instructions to a Painter', lines 645—6, Marvell wrote:

> Captain, Lieutenant, Ensign, all make haste,
> E're in the Firy Furnace they be cast.

Stanza V, without the least abruptness, introduces 'the Grove'.

### V

> Upon its crest this Mountain grave
> A Plump of aged Trees does wave.
> No hostile hand durst ere invade          35
> With impious Steel the sacred Shade.
> For something alwaies did appear
> Of the *great Master's* terrour there:
> And Men could hear his Armour still
> Ratling through all the Grove and Hill.          40

### VI

> Fear of the *Master*, and respect
> Of the great *Nymph* did it protect;
> *Vera* the *Nymph* that him inspir'd,
> To whom he often here retir'd,
> And on these Okes ingrav'd her Name;          45

Such Wounds alone these Woods became:
But ere he well the Barks could part
'Twas writ already in their Heart.

### VII

For they ('tis credible) have sense,
As We, of Love and Reverence,                    50
And underneath the Courser Rind
The *Genius* of the house do bind.
Hence they successes seem to know,
And in their *Lord's* advancement grow;
But in no Memory were seen                       55
As under this so streight and green.

### VIII

Yet now no further strive to shoot,
Contented if they fix their Root.
Nor to the wind's uncertain gust,
Their prudent Heads too far intrust.             60
Onely sometimes a flutt'ring Breez
Discourses with the breathing Trees;
Which in their modest Whispers name
Those Acts that swell'd the Cheek of Fame.

### IX

Much other Groves, say they, then these          65
And other Hills him once did please.
Through Groves of Pikes he thunder'd then,
And Mountains rais'd of dying Men.
For all the *Civick Garlands* due
To him our Branches are but few.                 70
Nor are our Trunks enow to bear
The *Trophees* of one fertile Year.

### X

'Tis true, yee Trees, nor ever spoke
More certain *Oracles* in Oak.
But Peace, (if you his favour prize)              75
That Courage its own Praises flies.

Therefore to your obscurer Seats
From his own Brightness he retreats:
Nor he the Hills without the Groves,
Nor Height but with Retirement loves.            80

In stanza V at line 34 the 1681 Folio read 'A plum of aged Trees does wave'. It also had 'frght' without a vowel in line 12 and 'furthe' without a final consonant in line 27. Cooke corrected these in 1726 to 'fright' and 'farther' (though 'further' would have been best), and he changed 'Plum' to 'Plume'; crests on the tops of helmets from Homeric times onwards contained tall feathers or plumes; heraldry displayed them; Marvell's own coat of arms did. Cooke made the change without knowing that Marvell had written 'An Horatian Ode' and in its lines 97–8 had asked:

What may not then our *Isle* presume
While Victory his Crest does plume!

The reading 'Plump' was first suggested by Margoliouth in his first Oxford edition of the poems (1927), but it was no wild conjecture; he found it in the actual description of Bilbrough itself in Francis Drake's *Eboracum* (1736). 'The town standeth upon a rising Ground, or small hill to look at, yet a plump of trees upon it may be seen at forty miles distance; and, one way, if I am rightly informed, was before the old trees was cut down, the *landmark* for the entrance of ships into the *Humber*.' So by Dr Drake's day the trees that were 'aged' in 1651 had been replaced by a 'plump' or clump of young ones which could even so be seen forty miles off, though not from the mouth of the Humber. The reading 'Plump' in line 34 cannot be far wrong, but one may still wonder if 'Plum' was not an accepted form of the same word in 1651 and after. The hand of the corrector in 'Thompson's second MS. book' added three punctuation marks to the 1681 Folio and corrected as much as Cooke in the text, but it left 'Plum' alone. It makes a nice noise.

In stanzas V and VI the tenses from 'durst' onwards are past. When treating the past, Marvell often used the spice of hyperbole. He does so here. 'The hallowed grove of oaks was protected always from the forester's axe by the prestige of the present Lord Fairfax and its romantic associations with his courtship of Anne Vere!' The truth is that Thomas Fairfax had only become third Baron Fairfax of Cameron in the Peerage of Scotland on the death of Lord Ferdinando, his father, in 1648 and that he had married Anne Vere as recently as 1637, when he was 25; but their courtship was carried on at Denton in Yorkshire. Compared to the aged oaks he was a sapling. However, he is the 'great Master' in lines 38, 41 and she is the 'great Nymph Vera' in lines 42-3.

In stanza VII the tenses become present and the hyperbole subsides. Here the oaks have grown up with the House of Fairfax and they enshrine the 'Genius' or tutelary god of that House in each generation; but 'in no Memory', that is 'in the memory of no-one living', were seen so straight and green as 'under this Lord Fairfax'. But this soberer statement is dizzied by the new claim that trees have a quasi-human consciousness and power of communication, and that this is 'credible'. So it is, in the sense that Marvell himself believed it. It is part and parcel of the view of Nature which he expands in 'Upon Appleton House', but it was a mythological view; he met it first as a boy learning Greek.

And so in the second half of stanza VIII the oak leaves converse with the breeze and pay tribute to the military prowess of this Lord Fairfax. The gilded full-length figure of Fame, with cheeks puffed out and a long trumpet held to its lips, sometimes topped the canopy of sepulchral monuments then; Fame trumpeting the dead man's praises to the world.

In stanza IX every word except 'say they' in line 65 is spoken by the oak trees. 'Much other Groves . . . and . . . Hills' matches 'Far other Worlds, and other Seas' in 'The Garden', line 46. It may echo Milton's 'other Groves, and other streams' in 'Lycidas' (1638), line 174; this was a poem that the admiring Marvell remembered again and again. The 'Civick Garlands' were oak leaves, but soldiers only earned them originally by saving a comrade's life. 'One fertile year' means a year rich in triumphs, each meriting a trophy. Though 'trophies' had a separate history that began with the ancient Greeks, it seems likely that the garlands are the trophies here.

Stanza X brings the poem to a fine rhetorical close. It concludes, but does not recapitulate. Enough new material has been kept in reserve. The Oracle of Zeus at Dodona (in the modern Albania), the earliest oracle in Greece, was a sacred grove of oaks round a shrine. Certainly at one stage those who consulted the Oracle had the answer whispered to them by the telling rustle of oak leaves, which their receptive ears took in as words. This was what coloured Marvell's personal conviction that trees could speak, and it was to this that he was leading when he made the Bilbrough Grove 'sacred' in line 36 and said that the Trees were 'breathing' in line 62, uttered 'Whispers' in line 63 and 'spoke' in stanza IX. 'What they spoke was never more accurately or definitely spoken by the Dodona oaks', he was saying in lines 73–4.

The word 'peace' has a double purport in line 75. It is the old Shakespearian call for silence, but it also reminds us that Fairfax the man of war has become Fairfax the man of peace. Only cowards fly from the enemy, which Fairfax never did, but 'That Courage' (of Fairfax's) flies from other men's praises of him. Again, generals do not like to 'retreat' but, being so modest, Fairfax retreats from the limelight of national politics to the obscurity of the Bilbrough oaks.

The final couplet completes this line of thought, but it also takes us back to the title and brings the poem full circle. 'Neither does Lord Fairfax like hills without groves nor does he like "Height but with Retirement".' A pregnant phrase, this last! Bilbrough Hill was high and 'retired' in the sense of 'remote'. But let no-one forget that, after five years as the Parliament's victorious Commander-in-Chief, Fairfax had just been given charge of the Scottish campaign when in June 1650 he insisted on retiring from that height and from the Council of State and going into seclusion in Appleton House.

Marvell would not have based his climax on this fact if the retirement had not been quite recent. The novelty of such self-abnegation by a professional soldier at the age of thirty-seven, though extraordinary, would soon wear off. For that reason I believe this poem to belong to the first half of 1651.

# 22 'The Mower's Song'

## I

My Mind was once the true survey
Of all these Medows fresh and gay;
And in the greenness of the Grass
Did see its Hopes as in a Glass;
When *Juliana* came, and She                                   5
What I do to the Grass, does to my Thoughts and Me.

## II

But these, while I with Sorrow pine,
Grew more luxuriant still and fine;
That not one Blade of Grass you spy'd,
But had a Flower on either side;                    10
When *Juliana* came, and She
What I do to the Grass, does to my Thoughts and Me.

## III

Unthankful Medows, could you so
A fellowship so true forego,
And in your gawdy May-games meet,                   15
While I lay trodden under feet?
When *Juliana* came, and She
What I do to the Grass, does to my Thoughts and Me.

## IV

But what you in Compassion ought,
Shall now by my Revenge be wrought:                 20
And Flow'rs, and Grass, and I and all,
Will in one common Ruine fall.
For *Juliana* comes, and She
What I do to the Grass, does to my Thoughts and Me.

## V

And thus, ye Meadows, which have been               25
Companions of my thoughts more green,
Shall now the Heraldry become
With which I shall adorn my Tomb;
For *Juliana* comes, and She
What I do to the Grass, does to my Thoughts and Me.   30

This is the only poem of Marvell's to have a refrain; but then it is the only one written before 1657 with 'Song' in its title. Refrains help musicians in the setting or singing of a song. The two lines of the refrain here seem designed to match the action of mowing. To the words 'When *Juliana* came, and She' (later, 'For *Juliana* comes, and She') the Mower draws the scythe back across his body to the right.

He shuffles his feet into position and then cuts his next swathe to the words 'What I do to the Grass, does to my Thoughts and Me'. The twelve monosyllables are as flat and shorn of modulation and cadence as the poet could make them. And they never change.

In the three Oxford editions of Marvell's poems Margoliouth's explanation of the word 'survey' in line 1 reads: 'metaphor from a written survey of an estate'. Kermode's footnote in *The Selected Poetry of Marvell* (Signet Classics, 1967), p.104, says: 'account, as might be given by a surveyor'. But manorial surveys were *written* by lawyers. They took each freehold or copyhold tenant in turn and defined every field in his tenure by approximate acreage and field name and with reference to what exactly bounded it or abutted on it to the north, south, east and west; the same wordy definitions went into leases. It was not this piecemeal writing that Marvell had in mind, though he knew all about it, having owned and sold Cambridgeshire land. No, the metaphor here is from a 'true survey'. This was an accurately measured, artistically coloured estate map, made to scale by a skilled surveyor. The Mower had *a picture of meadows* in mind. As a 'true survey' delineated green meadows, so his mind was fresh and gay once like them; and the colour of the grass seemed then a reflection of his own optimistic thinking, 'green' being the traditional colour of 'hope', as Kermode rightly notes (*ibid.*).

In stanza II 'these' are 'these Medows' and the time remains past; in writing 'while I . . . pine', Marvell was once again imitating the Latin use of the present tense with *dum* (while) in past time. In line 8 'still' means 'always', and lines 9 and 10 mean 'With the result that one saw no blade of grass without a flower on its right and its left'.

In stanza III, still in past time, the Mower upbraids the meadows for enjoying their usual May games and not sorrowing, as gratitude and friendship required, in sympathy with him. The repeated 'so' is not the blemish that it might seem; in line 13 it is stressed and slow and means 'in that way', but in line 14 it is unstressed and quick. The adjective 'gaudy' or 'gawdy', like the noun 'gaudy', meant 'festival' then (Latin *gaudium*, joy).

In stanza IV 'ought' was the old-fashioned form of 'owed'. What his old friends the meadows *owed* him out of pity, but did not pay, he will exact now in murderous revenge. The mood in this stanza is lethal. The stressed words in line 21 are highlighted by the four unstressed 'and's. The tense changes to the future at this point and the first line of the refrain to 'For *Juliana* comes, and She'.

So it remains in stanza V. After the imminent death the funeral will come, and the tomb, and then FINIS. So ended 'An Elegy upon the Death of my Lord Francis Villiers'. 'The unfortunate Lover' ended so. No doubt, with the Mower we should be less literal; even if the patrician language is the same, it is a pauper's grave that he will have in the meadow, in among the dead grass. As Professor Edward W. Taylor neatly observed on p.154 of *Nature and Art in Renaissance Literature* (Columbia University Press, 1964): 'For the Mower all flesh is grass, all grass flesh'.

# 23  'The Mower to the Glo-Worms'

### I

Ye living Lamps, by whose dear light
The Nightingale does sit so late,
And studying all the Summer-night,
Her matchless Songs does meditate;

### II

Ye Country Comets, that portend                    5
No War, nor Princes funeral,
Shining unto no higher end
Then to presage the Grasses fall;

### III

Ye Glo-Worms, whose officious Flame
To wandring Mowers shows the way,              10
That in the Night have lost their aim,
And after foolish Fires do stray;

### IV

Your courteous Lights in vain you wast,
Since *Juliana* here is come,
For She my Mind hath so displac'd                15
That I shall never find my home.

This delicate miniature, devised on a glow-worm scale, consists of one sentence. The main clause is held back until the start of the last stanza. The three stanzas before that are parallel apostrophes ('Ye living Lamps', 'Ye Country Comets', 'Ye Glo-Worms'), each followed by three-and-a-half lines of relative clause. The title guides us through those three stanzas, but it leaves the poet room to surprise us in the fourth.

Nightingales often bring the best out of poets; and certainly here stanza I makes a musical sound. Its sense too goes deeper than might appear. One needs to ask who in Marvell's day sat up late at night in summertime, studying by the light of a lamp and composing superlative songs, while the rest of the world slept. Who but a scholar-poet such as Marvell himself? Milton's 'Il Penseroso' (1645) sought an isolation like that.

> Or let my Lamp at midnight hour
> Be seen in som high lonely Towr.

The solitary nightingale, then, in stanza I emulates the English poet; emulates Marvell himself. The nightingale has a fixed perch. She sits late. By the live glow-worm lamps she improvises matchless songs of her own all the night. The wit lies in the fact that, just as the lamp was necessary for the midnight poet, so the 'dear light' provided by the glow-worms is made to seem necessary for the nightingale here. The glow-worms are the true heroes.

In stanza II the phrase 'Country Comets' combines two ideas. On the one hand, there was the widely-held superstition that comets 'portended' or 'presaged' some national disaster, like the outbreak of war or the death of a sovereign. On the other hand, natural historians from Pliny onwards had observed that glow-worms came and went with the hay harvest. To bring together the great and the small in this way enhances the glow-worms' importance. In line 6 Marvell intended no assonance in 'War, nor'; for him 'far' and 'star' rhymed with 'war', but 'nor' did not.

The 'Grass's fall' in line 8 brought the glow-worms nearer the Mower. In stanza III they coincide, except that 'the Mowers' are plural. In line 9 'officious' means 'serviceable', 'helpful'. The 'Flame' is a help to mowers who have worked till they cannot see any more and who then, stumbling home in the dark, lose their way through following Jack-o'-lanterns *alias* will-o'-the-wisps *alias* 'foolish Fires' (a literal rendering of the Latin *fatui ignes* or *ignes fatui*).

Stanza IV begins with idioms that are not so much English as French. 'Since' in line 14 is a temporal conjunction and the present tenses of 'waste' and 'is come' should be taken as past: 'You have been wasting your hospitable lights to no purpose, ever since Juliana came on the scene'. Juliana was Latin for Gillian, a plebeian name then, often shortened to Jill. The title had said nothing of her, the nymph of 'The Mower's Song'. Only now is the love affair unveiled.

Some of Marvell's lyrics travel full circle and finish where they began. This one follows a straight line that starts a long way from the Mower and ends when it reaches him and reveals his plight. It is beautifully contrived.

It is also very English. Hay was an essential part of the English economy and the hay harvest a crucial stage in the farmer's year. Marvell saw two such harvests at Appleton House and he was the first English poet to extend the pastoral tradition by giving the shepherd-ess Gillian a lover, Damon, who was not a shepherd and must not therefore succeed. She wanted no mixed marriage.

## 24    'Damon the Mower'

The eleven eight-lined stanzas make this the longest of the Appleton Mower poems. It is also the most theatrical, though staged in the open air. Stanza I introduces the characters and sets the scene.

I

> Heark how the Mower *Damon* Sung,
> With love of *Juliana* stung!
> While ev'ry thing did seem to paint
> The Scene more fit for his complaint.
> Like her fair Eyes the day was fair;          5
> But scorching like his am'rous Care.
> Sharp like his Sythe his Sorrow was,
> And wither'd like his Hopes the Grass.

The tedium and inertia of a sweltering day are conveyed by the four short similes, all beginning with 'like', and by the fivefold repetition of 'his'. In line 5 'fair' means 'beautiful', as it will do in line 33.

The eight stanzas that follow are spoken (or sung) by Damon himself. His hands are busy scything and to sing is his sole means of emulating the age-old shepherds' pipes.

## II

Oh what unusual Heats are here,
Which thus our Sun-burn'd Meadows sear!                              10
The Grass-hopper its pipe gives ore;
And hamstring'd Frogs can dance no more.
But in the brook the green Frog wades;
And Grass-hoppers seek out the shades.
Only the Snake, that kept within,                                   15
Now glitters in its second skin.

## III

This heat the Sun could never raise,
Nor Dog-star so inflame's the dayes.
It from an higher Beauty grow'th,
Which burns the Fields and Mower both:                              20
Which mads the Dog, and makes the Sun
Hotter then his own *Phaeton*.
Not *July* causeth these Extremes,
But *Juliana's* scorching beams.

## IV

Tell me where I may pass the Fires                                  25
Of the hot day, or hot desires.
To what cool Cave shall I descend,
Or to what gelid Fountain bend?
Alas! I look for Ease in vain,
When Remedies themselves complain.                                 30
No moisture but my Tears do rest,
Nor Cold but in her Icy Breast.

## V

How long wilt Thou, fair Shepheardess,
Esteem me, and my Presents less?
To Thee the harmless Snake I bring,                                 35

Disarmed of its teeth and sting.
To Thee *Chameleons* changing-hue,
And Oak leaves tipt with hony-dew.
Yet Thou ungrateful hast not sought
Nor what they are, nor who them brought.          40

### VI

I am the Mower *Damon*, known
Through all the Meadows I have mown.
On me the Morn her dew distills
Before her darling Daffadils.
And, if at Noon my toil me heat,          45
The Sun himself licks off my Sweat.
While, going home, the Ev'ning sweet
In cowslip-water bathes my feet.

### VII

What, though the piping Shepherd stock
The plains with an unnumbrèd Flock,          50
This Sithe of mine discovers wide
More ground then all his Sheep do hide.
With this the golden fleece I shear
Of all these Closes ev'ry Year.
And though in Wooll more poor then they,          55
Yet am I richer far in Hay.

### VIII

Nor am I so deform'd to sight,
If in my Sithe I looked right;
In which I see my Picture done,
As in a crescent Moon the Sun.          60
The deathless Fairyes take me oft
To lead them in their Danses soft;
And, when I tune my self to sing,
About me they contract their Ring.

### IX

How happy might I still have mow'd,          65
Had not Love here his Thistles sow'd!

But now I all the day complain,
Joyning my Labour to my Pain;
And with my Sythe cut down the Grass,
Yet still my Grief is where it was:                    70
But, when the Iron blunter grows,
Sighing I whet my Sythe and Woes.

In stanza III the text has benefited from the Bodleian volume (MS.
Eng. poet. d. 49) which the Library acquired in 1945. This is a copy of
the expurgated 1681 Folio with manuscript corrections and additions
in late seventeenth- or early eighteenth-century hands. Margoliouth
in 1952 had 'little doubt' that it was the manuscript book which
Thompson said reached him in 1776, when his collected edition of
Marvell was already in the press. It is commonly called therefore
'Thompson's second MS. book', or in shorthand T2. In 'Damon the
Mower' the 1681 Folio printed lines 21–2: 'Which made the Dog,
and makes the Sun /Hotter then his own Phaeton'. The corrector in T2
inked out the 'e' of 'made' and inked in an 's' giving 'mads'. This
surely was what Marvell wrote. The 'dog days' came in July and
August and took their name from the dog-star Sirius. They were the
hottest days in the year and coincided with, if they did not actually
cause, madness in dogs. The old reading 'made', though un-
questioned from 1681 to 1945, had two distinct flaws. First, its past
tense was odd in the month of July. Second, the syntax involved a
telescoping of 'Which . . . makes the Sun /Hotter then (than) his own
Phaeton' and 'Which made the Dog . . . /Hotter then his own
Phaeton'; but though Helios the Greek sun-god was Phaeton's father,
Sirius was no relation at all.

In spite of their apparent simplicity Damon's eight stanzas are
designed with consummate skill. Several times a phrase or idea that
seemed over and done with is later resumed. In line 9, for instance,
most first-time readers will take the phrase 'unusual Heats' at its face
value and not ask why 'unusual' or why plural 'Heats'. But in lines
17–24 those who do ask these questions are answered. To the July
heat of the dog-star and sun the scorching heat of Juliana's higher
beauty has been added. This sends the dog-star mad (just as heat
affects four-footed dogs) and makes the Sun 'hotter than his own
Phaeton'. It is a moot point whether Phaeton is object or subject.
Phaeton *was* in the myth very hot; Juliana's heat might be making the
sun hotter still. But Marvell is surely concerned with this world's
surface and the temperature here. Juliana's 'scorching beams' make

the sun *now* hotter *here* than Phaeton made the world long ago, when the horses of the sun ran away with him. The wit in lines 23–4 depends on our pronouncing the month as it scans, *Júlie*, like the first half of *Juliána*. This was the customary pronunciation. Herrick's 'Júly-flowers' or 'Gélli-flowers' were Perdita's 'gíllyvors' in *The Winter's Tale*.

A long stretch of interweaving begins in lines 10–14. In the meadows now 'sunburned' and 'seared', instead of good green grass there are left green frogs and grass-hoppers; the stresses in lines 13 and 14 fall on 'Green' and 'Grass', not on 'Frog' or 'hop'. Unable in this heat to 'dance' and 'pipe' or chirp any more, the frogs cool their lamed back-legs in the brook and the silent grass-hoppers go off to find shade. The picture seems complete at this point, but it does not end here. In lines 27–8 the Mower takes up the thread when, in much more rhetorical language, he asks:

> To what cool Cave shall I descend,
> Or to what gelid Fountain bend?

For by 'bend' he means 'travel'; 'gelid Fountain' means 'chilly brook'; and the best shade is in a 'cool Cave'. Thus in 'Clorinda and Damon', lines 9, 11 and 12, the enticing Clorinda inquires:

> Seest thou that unfrequented Cave?
> In whose cool bosom we may lye
> Safe from the Sun.

But in 'Damon the Mower' Juliana's heat has invaded the caves and dried up the brooks. What were the only 'Remedies' are remedies no more; they too 'complain' now. No coldness any longer remains except in her heart, no moisture except in his eyes.

The main concern of stanza V is Juliana's coldness. But the reader is surely invited to smile at the Mower's bucolic presents: the innocuous snakes, the colour-changing chameleons, the sticky oak-leaf boughs, all culled from his meadows. Shepherds had given shepherdesses courting-presents in poetry before, but no Mower had. Again the reader can smile at the pun in '(h)armless Snake . . . Disarmed', though the humourless Damon will not see it. He sees only Juliana's neglect.

> Yet Thou ungrateful hast not sought
> Nor what they are, nor who them brought.

The construction of this sentence, and its double negative, imitate classical Greek.

If it was not the gifts, then, that put her off, two other possible explanations remain. Either she does not know him, not having yet looked his way, or she thinks all mowers beneath her and has deliberately averted her eyes. In effect, stanza VI is the poet's reply to the first possibility and stanza VII to the second.

In VI Damon's dignity and spirit rebuke the amused reader as well as advancing his suit. 'If Juliana does not know him, his Meadows do. If she does not favour him, then she should, for the early morn does, the noon day sun does, the late evening does.' It is an eloquent stanza, strategically placed at the centre of the poem. The first four lines are among the most musical that Marvell ever wrote.

> I am the Mower *Damon*, known
> Through all the Meadows I have mown.
> On me the Morn her dew distills
> Before her darling Daffadils.

The fivefold initial 'm' is exactly balanced by the fivefold initial 'd', those being the two consonants of the title 'Damon the Mower', re-arranged as 'the Mower Damon' here. The long 'i' (twice) and long 'o' (three times) in the first couplet have a force that contrasts with the delicacy of the second couplet's short 'i', which comes four times, including the rhymes.

The third couplet is earthier. The dog and sun have perhaps exchanged roles when 'the Sun himself *licks off* my sweat'; 'het' is the pronunciation of the rhyming word 'heat'. The melody and tenderness return in the fourth couplet and bring with them wit; 'bathes in cowslip-water' has wit.

> While, going home, the Ev'ning sweet
> In cowslip-water bathes my feet.

The ladies in those days bottled the juice of cowslips and used it as a skin-lotion on their feet. The sweet lady Evening 'bathes' the home-going Mower's bare feet in the dew on the heads of the cowslips. The wild daffodils and cowslips take the poem back to April and May.

In VII Damon, like a good debater, answers an imaginary objector, perhaps Juliana herself, and champions his under-prized calling against the over-prized shepherd's. 'Piping' and 'plains', with their plosives, register pugnacious contempt.

> What, though the piping Shepherd stock
> The plains with an unnumbrèd Flock,
> This Sithe of mine discovers wíde
> More ground then all his Sheep do hide.
> With this the golden fleece I shear
> Of all these Closes ev'ry Year.

'Discovers wide' means 'uncovers widely'. The Jason myth is cleverly used. Damon steals the shepherd's thunder by 'shearing', not 'mowing', his 'golden fleece', not his 'yellow hay'. A 'close' (pronounced like the adjective) was an enclosed field. Hay had indeed a high market value, but Damon conveniently forgets to include the carcass value of sheep.

Stanza VIII starts with a literal translation of the Latin shepherd Corydon's '*Nec sum adeo informis*' in the Second Eclogue of Virgil, line 25: 'Nor am I so deform'd-to-sight'. It is brilliantly adapted here. In Virgil Corydon stood on the edge of the shore and looked down at his reflection in a calm sea. Damon sees, not just his reflection, but his 'Picture done' – that is, his portrait painted by an artist – in the curved steel of his scythe. And, since the angle and shape of the blade make him think of a crescent moon, he must be holding the scythe upside down, getting ready to sharpen it. 'He sees his portrait in the downward curve of the blade as he has often seen the sun in a crescent moon.' The moon has, of course, no light save what comes from the sun. It is a highly intelligent image and yet seems a piece of observation within this Mower's scope.

Mention of the moon leads on to fairies, and 'deathless' will lead on to death. Just as the morn and noon and evening favoured Damon in stanza VI, so now he is the fairies' favourite. They like him to lead their dances and they like to hear him sing. The eager circle around him comes closer at his mere trial notes; 'they contract their Ring' by shortening its radius. Stanzas VI and VIII both end with the end of a day.

Stanza IX, the last of the eight spoken by Damon, begins with the sighing of a rueful bachelor:

How happy might I still have mow'd,
Had not Love here his Thistles sow'd!

The sighing is heard in the cadence and vowels and not in the aitches
that start six of the words. Marvell's pronunciation did not bother
about aspirates much; '*an higher* Beauty' in line 19 is one of many
indications of that in his prose and his verse. As thistles vex a mower's
bare feet, so love has vexed him here, adding pain to his labour. He
cuts down the grass still, but he cannot dislodge his grief. Even the act
of sharpening his scythe makes his woes keener.

Stanza X changes to narrative and the tenses are past, but Marvell
will not let the poem end tamely like that and in stanza XI wit and
paradox provide Damon with a dramatic speech. The art that
dictated a theatrical beginning dictates a theatrical close.

### X

While thus he threw his Elbow round,
Depopulating all the Ground,
And, with his whistling Sythe, does cut          75
Each stroke between the Earth and Root,
The edged Stele by careless chance
Did into his own Ankle glance;
And there among the Grass fell down,
By his own Sythe, the Mower mown.               80

### XI

Alas! said He, these hurts are slight
To those that dye by Loves despight.
With Shepherds-purse, and Clowns-all-heal,
The Blood I stanch, and Wound I seal.
Only for him no Cure is found,                  85
Whom *Julianas* Eyes do wound.
'Tis death alone that this must do:
For Death thou art a Mower too.

In line 79 'down' is to be pronounced 'doan'; in the same way
elsewhere he rhymed 'Throne' and 'crown'. There is an interesting
grammatical point in lines 73 – 5. The conjunction 'while' is followed
by 'threw' in the past tense and 'does' in the present, though the action
is past; the first is the English use, the second the Latin. In line 74 the

bulky Latin derivative '*Depopulating* all the Ground' exactly matches line 47 of 'The Garden', '*Annihilating* all that's made'. The Latin *depopulari* meant 'to lay waste', 'to pillage'. Marvell pictured a rather different sort of pillaging in the haymaking in 'Upon Appleton House', lines 423–4:

> The Women that with forks it fling,
> Do represent the Pillaging.

The art of scything lay in cutting really close to the gound. But any hidden unevenness was a danger to the artist's unprotected front foot. Thomas Johnson recorded such a scything accident in his enlarged edition (1633) of John Gerard's *Herbal* (1597). A mower in Kent cut his leg to the bone, but crawled to the herb *Stachys palustris*, which he then bound round the cut with his shirt. In a few minutes he was mowing again: in a few days the wound was healed. Because the clownish mower refused Johnson's medical help, in Gerard's *Herbal* Johnson called the plant 'Clownes wound-wort or All-heale' (p.1004). The same book elsewhere listed *Capsella bursa-pastoris* or 'Shepherds purse' (p.276) as stanching bleeding in any part of the body, whether drunk as a medicine or applied as a poultice.

Here it does look as if Damon used 'Shepherds purse' to stanch the bleeding and 'Clowns-all-heal' to seal the wound. He did not look for ease in vain: these remedies did not complain. But the really incurable condition is 'to be wounded by Juliana's eyes'. Sooner or later, that must prove mortal.

A lesser wit would have been content to end with that thought. But Marvell's last line invokes the traditional picture of Father Time as an ancient man with a scythe over his back. He transfers the image to Death: 'For, Death, thou art a Mower too.' He evidently liked the finality of this 'do – too' rhyme, for he used it again in 1667 to finish his lengthiest satire, 'The last Instructions to a Painter'.

> But this great work is for our Monarch fit,
> And henceforth *Charles* only to *Charles* shall sit.
> His Master-hand the ancients shall out-do,
> Himself the *Poet* and the *Painter* too.
>
> (ll.945–8)

# 25 'Ametas and Thestylis making Hay-Ropes'

This diminutive, quicksilver eclogue also belongs to the Appleton era. In the hayfield stanzas of 'Upon Appleton House' it was Thestylis who brought 'the mowing camp their Cates' in LI and she seems to stem from Virgil's Thestylis, who fed the reapers in his Second Eclogue. She comes again in this eclogue of Marvell's, but by way of Milton's 'L'Allegro', lines 86–90. There 'the neat-handed Phyllis' repairs to the cornfield 'with Thestylis to bind the sheaves':

> Or, if the earlier season lead,
> To the tann'd Haycock in the Mead.

It needed two people, two 'parties', to twist the ropes of hay that bound haycocks, without which they would 'disband' and not 'stand'. Normally two women would do this, but here Ametas has manoeuvred himself into partnering Thestylis at the end of the day. He has been courting her for some time. She has stayed non-committal and coy; but, unlike the more famous Coy Mistress, she does have a tongue in her head.

## I

### Ametas

> Think'st Thou that this Love can stand,
> Whilst Thou still dost say me nay?
> Love unpaid does soon disband:
> Love binds Love as Hay binds Hay.

## II

### Thestylis

> Think'st Thou that this Rope would twine          5
> If we both should turn one way?
> Where both parties so combine,
> Neither Love will twist nor Hay.

### III

#### *Ametas*

Thus you vain Excuses find,
Which your selves and us delay:                    10
And Love tyes a Woman's Mind
Looser then with Ropes of Hay.

### IV

#### *Thestylis*

What you cannot constant hope
Must be taken as you may.

### V

#### *Ametas*

Then let's both lay by our Rope,                    15
And go kiss within the Hay.

The metre is trochaic heptasyllabic throughout. Despite the five
Roman numerals the poem consists of four quatrains, all ending in
'Hay'. Out of ninety-eight words as many as eighty-five are
monosyllables, a high proportion matched only in some parts of 'The
Nymph complaining for the death of her Faun'. Simplicity was
Marvell's watchword in both.

Even so, the first quatrain here has a sophisticated pattern of sound.
In lines 1 – 2 'st' comes five times and 'th' comes four. In line 4 six of the
seven syllables are stressed, so urgently does Ametas plead. He takes
his argument from the work of the moment. Love unrequited
('unpaid') is a haycock unroped with hay and such love cannot
'stand', any more than such a haycock. She has refused him before
many times – in line 2 'still' means 'always'.

Thestylis ripostes teasingly by mimicking his syntax and capping
his metaphor. Neither mutual love nor a hayrope can be woven or
twined if he and she do not operate in contrary directions. This is
obviously true in twining hay; of a pair standing north and south, the
second partner must turn it westwards if the first turns it eastwards. In
love this may not be the man's view, but there is feminine wisdom in
it. Charmian might advise Shakespeare's Cleopatra: 'In each thing

give him way, cross him in nothing.' But Cleopatra knew better. 'Thou speakest like a fool, the way to lose him', she said. (*Antony and Cleopatra*, II, iii).

Frustrated, Ametas shifts his ground and in III inveighs against all women on behalf of all men. His pronouns are now plural. 'That way you women find empty excuses which delay yourselves and us men'. There is a textual crux here. The 1681 Folio printed 'your selve' and all three Oxford editions (1927, 1952, 1971) have kept that. In his modernised version in *The Selected Poetry of Marvell* (Signet Classics, 1967), p. 105, Kermode printed 'yourself'. But in T2 the eighteenth-century reviser changed the Folio's 'selve' to 'selves', a correction that the Oxford editors missed when they incorporated T2 in the *apparatus criticus* or text in 1971. Ametas goes on in lines 11–12 to attack the inconstancy of womankind; the haycock is tied fairly loosely by a hayrope, but a woman's mind is tied more loosely still by a man's love and that is entirely her fault.

Thestylis concedes the point. Her reply may sound enigmatic, but Ametas sees just what she means. 'Our inconstancy is your opportunity. You men must take when you can the love that you can't hope to be constant.' Thus encouraged, he jumps at his chance. To 'lay by' is to 'set aside' or 'store away'. In 'The Gallery', line 6, Marvell tells Clora that his old Arras-hangings 'by are laid'. So here Ametas says: 'Let's put our hayrope on one side and go kiss in the Hay.' He is punning on the word Hay. There is 'Hay' all around to kiss in, but haymakers ended every evening with the circular folk dance called 'the Hay' and that ended with the partners kissing. We shall see this in 'Upon Appleton House', stanza LIV, which finishes:

> When at their Dances End they kiss,
> Their new-made Hay not sweeter is.

Marvell's pun allows Ametas to register his returning good humour; it also clinches the wit of the eclogue in a memorable way.

# 26   'The Garden' (and 'Hortus' translated)

Of Marvell's longer lyrics 'The Garden' is probably the best-known and most enjoyed. It has wit and beauty, variety and depth. It is very original and adventurous. It is also very difficult.

A keen analyst will see that the nine stanzas divide into two sets of four, with a final singleton by way of a coda. It is no accident that only I, V and IX start with exclamations, or that IV and VIII alone delve into the past.

In stanza I the poet deprecates ambition, which drives men to distraction as they vie for hollow honours, crowns of leaves from this tree or that plant. The slight shade cast by an isolated tree or plant hints at a prudently passive life-style. The thick shades of congregated trees and flowers in the garden weave the only garlands worth having, 'garlands of repose'.

In II, III, IV he goes on to say that, far from being ambitious himself, he has long sought Innocence and Quiet, those inseparable sisters. He has looked for them for years in great cities. Now he has stumbled on them in the garden, where he ought always to have expected them to be. No society is half as civilised as this solitude: no women are as loving as these trees. Foolish lovers do not understand this, but the god of Love does; it is to the garden that Cupid comes to relax when not employed in affairs of the heart. Garden trees and plants were what the ancient gods loved on earth all along. The myths have misrepresented their aims.

I

How vainly men themselves amaze
To win the Palm, the Oke, or Bayes;
And their uncessant Labours see
Crown'd from some single Herb or Tree.
Whose short and narrow verged Shade          5
Does prudently their Toyles upbraid;
While all Flow'rs and all Trees do close
To weave the Garlands of Repose.

## II

Fair quiet, have I found thee here,
And Innocence thy Sister dear!        10
Mistaken long, I sought you then
In busie Companies of Men.
Your sacred Plants, if here below,
Only among the Plants will grow.
Society is all but rude,        15
To this delicious Solitude.

## III

No white nor red was ever seen
So am'rous as this lovely green.
Fond Lovers, cruel as their Flame,
Cut in these Trees their Mistress name.        20
Little, Alas, they know, or heed,
How far these Beauties Hers exceed!
Fair Trees! where s'eer your barkes I wound,
No Name shall but your own be found.

## IV

When we have run our Passions heat,        25
Love hither makes his best retreat.
The *Gods*, that mortal Beauty chase,
Still in a Tree did end their race.
*Apollo* hunted *Daphne* so,
Only that She might Laurel grow.        30
And *Pan* did after *Syrinx* speed,
Not as a Nymph, but for a Reed.

Stanza I is a single sentence, despite the heavy punctuation employed to slow the pace down. Thus the antecedent of 'Whose' in line 5 is 'Herb or Tree', more especially 'Tree'. The limited shadow cast by the isolated tree reproaches, from the standpoint of prudence, the professionals who overtax themselves in the sun. 'Narrow verged' is a compound adjective despite the lack of hyphen. It covers many square yards. In line 7 'close' means 'combine'.

A crown of palm leaves traditionally rewarded the warrior, a crown of oak leaves the citizen or athlete, a crown of laurel (bays) the poet. Marvell seeks no laurel here for himself. Crowns were also woven in classical times from grass or parsley, wild olive or pine, ivy or myrtle. 'Some single Herb or Tree' could be any one of these.

'Repose' in line 8 and 'quiet' in line 9 are synonyms and link the two stanzas. In '*Hortus*', the Latin version of the poem, 'the garlands of repose' are '*tranquillae serta Quietis*' and the sisters are '*Quies*' and '*Simplicitas*'. But 'repose' helps the rhyme.

The pairing of innocence and quiet is uncommon, but not unique. The famous verse in 'To Althea from Prison' may be its source:

> Stone Walls doe not a Prison make,
>   Nor Iron bars a Cage;
> Minds innocent and quiet take
>   That for an Hermitage.

Until Lovelace revised his popular song in 1647, that third line had been 'A spotless mind, and Innocent'. Marvell was involved in the publication of *Lucasta* and must have known of the change.

The sense of lines 13–16 is: 'If your heavenly plants grow at all here below, they only consent to grow among the plants of the garden. All society is merely barbarous, compared to this delicious solitude.' The *New English Dictionary* quotes 'Society is all but rude' under 'all but' in the sense of 'nearly'. But Marvell also wrote, in 'The Resolved Soul and Created Pleasure', line 36, 'The rest is all but Earth disguised', which quite clearly meant 'All the rest is merely earth disguised'. The same principle operates here.

It will be noticed that the twelve couplets in stanzas II, III, IV are uniformly end-stopped. In fact, every one is a sentence on its own. This produces the epigrammatic effect that Marvell needs. The tone of III and IV is facetious. A string of paradoxes follows the provoking wit of:

> Society is all but rude,
> To this delicious Solitude.

The world of culture proceeds on the assumption that society civilises mankind, while solitude breeds backwoodsmen and boors. Marvell stands that notion on its head. His experience was different.

The 'white' and 'red' of line 17 are the court beauty's white skin and red lips and cheeks, the lilies and roses of medieval romance. The 'green' is predominantly the colour of the leaves. It is Marvell's favourite colour, as Victoria Sackville-West pointed out in her *Andrew Marvell* (Faber, 1929), pp.35—8. As noun or adjective, 'green'figures twenty-five times in his lyrics alone; three times in this one.

Having deflated the ladies, he makes fun of the infatuated men. 'Fond' means 'foolish'. What sensible man would use his girl's name to deface the superior beauty of a tree? But 'fond Lovers' are heedless, ignorant and cruel; in a word, 'rude'. He will not follow their bad example.

All the same, he wishes us to know that he too has loved. 'When *we* have run *our* Passions heat' in line 25 proves that.

The word 'heat' provides the first pun in the poem (though the ambiguity—hunters have between them claimed seven kills in the first stanza alone). In Marvell's day gentlemen 'ran a heat' when they raced their horses against each other for practice; for purses they 'ran a course'. There was also the 'heat' engendered by the 'Passion' of love, the 'Flame' of line 19. Love too was hotly competitive. 'When we have run our Passions heat' plays on the two senses.

There is a second pun on 'race' in line 28, or so it would seem. There was the obvious 'race' on foot between the fleeing Daphne and the ardent pursuing god. But, as such races always ended in the metamorphosis of the maiden, which is what happened here, Daphne's barrenness was the end of their 'race' or family. 'It is your duty to give me grandchildren', Peneus, the father of Daphne, had told her in Ovid.

There is no pun or ambiguity, however, in 'retreat' in line 26, where the keyword is 'hither'. Freed for a time from active service, Cupid 'makes his best retreat' *to this garden*. He travels to it as unerringly and expeditiously as he can. The garden is not being called a retreat.

The Apollo—Daphne and Pan—Syrinx stories are told in that order by Ovid in *Metamorphoses*, Book I, with only the Jupiter—Io story in between. Marvell tells us in *The Rehearsal Transpros'd* (ed. Smith, Oxford University Press, 1971, p.38) that he read of Io and Jupiter 'at School'. So did every seventeenth-century schoolboy. In Ovid the gods Pan and Apollo chased Syrinx and Daphne to gratify their lust. Marvell's bold travesty of the truth is put forward with tongue in cheek.

His Latin version of 'The Garden' is complete so far as the first four stanzas are concerned. The thirty-two English octosyllabics compare with no fewer than forty-eight Latin hexameters. And in Edmund

Blunden's verse translation of the Latin (*Times Literary Supplement*, 12 August 1955) there are fifty-four decasyllabic lines. It cannot then surprise anyone that my prose version of '*Hortus*' below runs to 517 words and contains material not found in 'The Garden'.

O Mankind, what passion so agitates your hearts (frenzy, alas, for Palm and Laurel or a single Herb!) that one tree hardly crowns your unbridled labours and its scanty leaves do not wholly encircle your heads? While every kind of Flower and an entire Wood, interweaving at once, combine to make garlands of calm quiet. (ll. 1 – 6)

Kindly Quiet, I hold thee dear! And thee, Simplicity, full sister of Quiet! For that reason I spent those years searching for you in temples and cities and the tall palaces of kings, but in vain. Green plants and green shade had concealed you in the dim silences of gardens far away. (ll. 7 – 11)

Oh! if I may, leafy citizenesses, intrude on your retreats, wanderer that I am, weary and panting for a better life, then keep me as a new fellow-townsman of yours and, granting my prayer, co-opt me to your flowering realms. (ll. 12 – 15)

You Muses – and I call thee, Apollo, to witness that I speak true, for thou knowest – I delight not in herds of men, or the roars of the circus, or the bellows of the forum. No, what attract me are the sanctuaries of Spring, and dumb veneration, and solitary communion. (ll. 16 – 19)

What man is not enchanted by the beauty of a maiden's face? Yet, though that should surpass the snow in whiteness and be redder than the richest dye, your green vigour would excel it, in my view. Girls' hair could not compete with your foliage, nor girls' arms with your branches, nor could girls' voices match your tremulous whispering. (ll. 20 – 4)

Ah! how often have I seen lovers (who would credit it?) carving the name of their mistress in your more potent bark! They were not ashamed at their inscriptions scarring your sacred trunks! If ever I desecrate your stocks, no Neaera or Chloe or Faustina or Corynna shall be read there, but each tree's name shall be entered in its bark (*or* book). O my dear plane and cypress and poplar and elm! (ll. 25 – 31)

Here Love doffs his wings and strolls about on sandalled feet, laying aside his unstrung bow and whizzing arrows. He stands his torches upside down and has no more desire to be feared. Or else he lies stretched out full length and sleeps, head on quiver, deaf even to Venus, should she call. His empty dreams bring him no reminder of past escapades. (ll. 32—7)

The gods above rejoice at the Tyrant's loss of heat, and, though they have tried nymphs and goddesses so many times, they are better off now that each has his own pet tree. Jupiter is desperately enamoured of a long-lived oak and has left his wife Juno all alone; she was never so jealous of a rival before. No adulterous stains pollute the bed of Vulcan in Lemnos; Mars does not think of Venus, if he has his ash. Phoebus pressed hard on the tracks of the beautiful Daphne that she might turn into laurel; he sought nothing more. And as for goat-footed Pan's pursuit of the fleeing Syrinx, his sole object was to win a musical reed for his pipes. (ll. 38—48)

There are ten more Latin lines (49—58), but they match stanza IX and must wait. There is no Latin version of stanzas V to VIII. If Marvell wrote one, the 1681 Folio editors never had it. They printed instead '*Desunt multa*' (Much is missing). But these four stanzas are so English in character and content, so enthusiastic and fresh, that they never were translated *from Latin*. Of that one can feel sure.

### V

What wond'rous Life in this I lead!
Ripe Apples drop about my head;
The Luscious Clusters of the Vine      35
Upon my Mouth do crush their Wine;
The Nectaren, and curious Peach,
Into my hands themselves do reach;
Stumbling on Melons, as I pass,
Insnar'd with Flow'rs, I fall on Grass.      40

### VI

Mean while the Mind, from pleasure less,
Withdraws into its happiness:
The Mind, that Ocean where each kind
Does streight its own resemblance find;
Yet it creates, transcending these,      45
Far other Worlds, and other Seas;

Annihilating all that's made
To a green Thought in a green Shade.

## VII

Here at the Fountains sliding foot,
Or at some Fruit-trees mossy root,　　　　50
Casting the Bodies Vest aside,
My Soul into the boughs does glide:
There like a Bird it sits, and sings,
Then whets, and combs its silver Wings;
And, till prepar'd for longer flight,　　　55
Waves in its Plumes the various Light.

## VIII

Such was that happy Garden-state,
While Man there walk'd without a Mate:
After a Place so pure, and sweet,
What other Help could yet be meet!　　　60
But 'twas beyond a Mortal's share
To wander solitary there:
Two Paradises 'twere in one
To live in Paradise alone.

In line 33 Marvell meant 'lead' to be pronounced 'led', like the noun 'lead'. Elsewhere, he rhymed it with 'tread' in 'Upon the Hill and Grove at Bill-borow', lines 15–16, and he wrote in 'Upon Appleton House', lines 163–4,

> And your Example, if our Head,
> Will soon us to perfection lead.

This same line 33 contains the one textual crux in the poem. All editors printed 'in this' until Thompson for some reason unknown printed 'is this' in 1776: 'What wond'rous Life is this I lead!' Grosart copied Thompson in 1872, but the three Oxford editions of 1927, 1952 and 1971 have retained what was presumably the manuscript reading, 'in this', and it is retained here. Many critics, however, still prefer 'is this' and J. B. Leishman, in *The Art of Marvell's Poetry* (Hutchinson, 1966), p.295n., went so far as to say: 'I cannot imagine any really convincing defence of the appropriateness of "in this".'

Were it the first line of the poem, one might hesitate to challenge a Leishman so sure of his ground. But it is line 33 in a poem of seventy-two lines and it has to be viewed in its context in relation to the poem as a whole.

Marvell was a logical builder not given to abruptness or discontinuity of thought. 'In this' means 'in this garden'. It links stanza V to stanza IV, where 'hither' meant 'to this garden'. Take 'in this' away and there is no link between V and IV. Instead, one is left with what appears to be a new start.

A careful reading, moreover, will show that Marvell is, consciously or unconsciously, avoiding the use of the word 'garden' between the title and the entry of the Garden of Eden in line 57. Yet he characteristically keeps harping on the 'here' and 'now'. The persistent present tenses and first persons combine to register the 'now'. The 'here' is supplied by a locative sequence which stretches from 'here' in line 9, through 'this delicious Solitude' (line 16), 'this lovely green' (line 18), 'these Trees' (line 20), 'these Beauties' (line 22), 'hither' (line 26), 'in this' (line 33), to 'Here' in line 49. One concludes that the conservatism of the Oxford editors has been both 'appropriate' and right.

What makes the line so important is the fact that it introduces, not just stanza V (the delights of the body), but stanzas VI and VII (the delights of the mind and the soul). The opening couplet of VIII then looks back at all three and likens the solitary bliss of the poet in the Garden to Adam's happy life in the Garden of Eden before Eve was born.

> Such was that happy Garden-state,
> While Man there walk'd without a Mate.

The four stanzas, individually so different, are elaborately unified.

In V the poet is the innocent lord of creation as he wanders through the garden alone: innocent, because he is free, and the place is free, from all carnal desire – there are not even any animals about; lord, because he is so much superior to the trees and the plants. But he can still be the target of innocent love. Mature fruits play the feminine role. They welcome his approach and, within their physical limits, ply him with their individual charms; his senses are innocently gratified.

The fruits grow at methodically diminishing heights (apples high up, grapes lower down, nectarine and peach lower still, and then melons on the ground). The parts of his upright body to be visited come in a correspondingly descending order (his tall head, his mouth, hands, feet). The ripe apples at the end of their boughs dip down lovingly 'about' his head; they 'drop' in that sense, but they do not drop off – etymologically 'drop' is a cognate of 'droop'. The ripe grapes on the vine lean forward and kiss him hard on the mouth. The ripe nectarines and peaches ('curious' meaning 'fashioned with exquisite care') reach out from opposite sides, one towards his left hand, one towards his right, asking to be taken and held.

Under these intensely pleasurable influences, his mental concentration falters. He stumbles over the melons in his path. His ankles are caught and held by arching flowers. Thus snared, he falls forward on the grass. The melons, flowers and grass all wanted to have him to themselves; like the taller fruits, they consciously waylaid him. But such garden ambuscades are harmless; whereas in the world outside 'stumbles', 'snares' and 'falls' spell temptation, sin and death. There is a humorous anti-climax in the heavily stressed fourth and eighth syllables of the line 'Insnar'd with *Flów'rs*, I fall on *Gráss.*'

The sensuousness of the action is reinforced by the sound. Alliteration and assonance play their part: the 'w' and 'l' in line 33; the 'p' in 'Ripe Apples drop'; the juicy 'ush' in 'Luscious' and 'crush'; the 'm' in 'my Mouth' and 'Melons'; the hard 'c' in 'Clusters', 'curious' and 'crush'; the soft 's' in 'Stumbling', 'Insnar'd', 'pass' and 'Grass'. The phrasing is unusually steady and horizontal in pitch until the easy descent of the final 'fall on grass'. The melodic path of 'Ripe Apples drop about my head' confirms that the apples are not dropping vertically several feet to the ground. That would not help.

Stanza VI takes a step up the scale of values. 'From pleasure less', meaning (as Leishman rightly says) 'from the lesser pleasure of the senses', the mind withdraws 'to the greater pleasure of its own inner happiness'. The withdrawal began in line 39 (hence the 'Mean while' of line 41). Significantly 'the Mind' is not called 'my Mind'. The pleased body, now mindless, remains on the grass. 'Withdraws' is not a military metaphor, but a social. It is as though the lord leaves the high table on the dais in the thronged hall for the privacy of the quiet withdrawing-room.

The new paramountcy of 'the Mind' is asserted and hammered home by the repetition of the word in the triple-rhyming 'Mind–kind–find' of lines 43–4. Thus detached, it becomes the reader's mind as much as the poet's; the mind of man.

The 'Ocean' metaphor is born of the belief, old as Pliny, that each 'kind' of land creature has its counterpart or close 'resemblance' living in the sea. Similarly in the mind, Marvell argues, the image or idea matches the reality; they recognise each other straightaway ('streight' is an adverb).

'But this cognitive Mind is also creative', he goes on to say.

> Yet it creates, transcending these,
> Far other Worlds, and other Seas;

Here the key word is 'these'. It is not a pronoun looking back to 'kind' and 'resemblance', but an adjective looking forward to 'Worlds' and 'Seas'. There have to be 'these (real) Worlds and Seas' before there can be 'other (imaginary) Worlds and Seas'. By 'Worlds' he means 'lands'. 'Transcending' is not a philosophical or technical term, but a plain word for 'greatly surpassing'; so it is in 'Clorinda and Damon', line 21, where the god Pan spoke 'Words that transcend poor Shepherd's skill'. What the couplet maintains, then, is this: 'The mind creates imaginary lands and seas, which greatly surpass these real lands and seas and are very different from them.'

The next couplet brings the stanza to a magical close:

> Annihilating all that's made
> To a green Thought in a green Shade.

'Annihilating . . . To' means 'reducing . . . to the nothingness of'. The mighty Latin derivative is succeeded by eleven small Old English words. In that order the twelve make an eloquent blend. The magic is in the last line.

Since stanzas V and VI form one episode, it is likely that Marvell intended ' a green Thought in a green Shade' to epitomise the active mind of the abstracted thinker, physically passive in shadow on the grass, where line 40 left him. As M. C. Bradbrook and M. G. Lloyd Thomas wrote (op. cit., p.62): 'There must be a green shade, otherwise no green thought: that is, he only achieves the power of complete detachment through the instrumentality of that particular time and place.'

Between VI and VII there is an interval of time and a change of scene. And though in VII the poet resumes in the same present tense, he is in fact recalling separate ecstasies in different parts of the garden on various occasions in the recent past:

> Here at the Fountains sliding foot,
> Or at some Fruit-trees mossy root . . .

The sound of the second line closely imitates the first, notably in the 'f, t' of 'Fountains' and 'Fruit-trees'. In both lines the beats fall on syllables 1, 4, 6, 8, and in both the caesuras have stopped. In the next line the same pattern continues:

> Casting the Bodies Vest aside . . .

The three lines move with uniform ease in a hushed and reverent tone. We arrive on a new plane of human experience when the smooth fourth line completes the sentence:

> My Soul into the boughs does glide.

The first half-stanza beginning 'Here' is followed by a second half-stanza beginning 'There'. It lifts us to the highest pitch in the poem.

> There like a Bird it sits, and sings,
> Then whets, and combs its silver Wings;
> And, till prepar'd for longer flight,                                55
> Waves in its Plumes the various Light.

In VIII the tone changes completely and Marvell goes back to the past with his tongue in his cheek, as he had done in IV. There it was the mythical past of Ovid's *Metamorphoses*. Here it is the Biblical past of Genesis, the story of Adam and Eve.

It was on the sixth day of the Creation that God made man (Genesis, I 27). In II 8 God planted a garden in Eden 'and there He put the man whom He had formed'. In II 9 God caused every kind of tree 'that is pleasant to the sight and good for food' to grow there, and in the centre He put the tree of life and the tree of knowledge of good and evil. In II 10 the garden received the water of the river of Eden. In II 15 God put man into the garden 'to dress it and to keep it'. In II 16– 17 God gave the man leave to eat freely of every other tree, the tree of life included, but forbade him to eat of the tree of knowledge on pain of death the same day. In II 18 God said: 'It is not good that the man should be alone; I will make him an help meet for him.' ('Meet' meant 'suitable'.) In II 19 the man was named Adam. In II 21–2 God made woman out of a rib taken from Adam when asleep. In II 24 Adam took the woman to wife and proclaimed the institution of marriage. In III 20, after the Fall, Adam named his wife Eve. All this Marvell read in the King James's Bible of 1611.

The bachelor poet is not concerned in stanza VIII with the Fall, but with the idyllic bachelorhood of Adam in Eden when he too walked alone.

> Such was that happy Garden—state,
> While Man there walk'd without a Mate:
> After a Place so pure, and sweet,
> What other Help could yet be meet!      60

In the first line the suffix 'state' cannot be just a 'state of feeling or mind'; that would suit 'happy', but it would not suit 'Man there walk'd'. 'Garden—state' must also be a place. The word seems intended to convey the notion of Paradise, but at the same time to proclaim the re-arrival of wit. Possibly Marvell coined it on the analogy of a Greek 'city—state'; the 'Garden' of Eden and a sovereign, independent 'state'.

A thorough re-reading of stanzas V to VII will show that, in selecting the material, Marvell was quietly devising a solo Paradise of his own which in due course would stand comparison with the solo Paradise of Adam in VIII. Thus, in V to VII the trees are all fruit-trees and an apple-tree is specifically named; in legend, though not in the Bible, the fruits of the tree of knowledge were apples, of course. Then, in V the fruits are all ripe, in keeping with another tradition; as Donne said in his Sermon II, 'In paradise the fruits were ripe the first minute, and in heaven it is alwaies Autumne, God's mercies are ever in their maturity.' Again, in V to VII the poet keeps to the hours of daylight, but his introductory 'What wond'rous *Life* in this I lead!' applies even better to Adam's life in Eden all round the clock. In VII the 'Fountains sliding foot' will convey to modern readers an artificial jet fountain, fit for Versailles or Trafalgar Square, and a spray-saturated slippery approach. But elsewhere in Marvell a fountain is a natural watercourse, and as such it parallels the river of Eden here. Finally in line 51 'Casting the Bodies Vest aside' ('vest' meaning 'coating of flesh') suits the naked Adam even better than the garden-poet, inevitably clothed.

The romantic thrice-married Milton was to make a perfect love match out of Adam and Eve in *Paradise Lost*. The sceptical bachelor Marvell preferred to prick the bubble of romance. He used wit in III and IV to put solitude above society and the beauty of women below the beauty of trees. With equal relish he now paradoxically makes Eve's arrival in the 'Garden—state' spoil everything for Adam, even before the Temptation and the Fall. To be left alone, however, was more than Adam could expect.

> But 'twas beyond a Mortal's share
> To wander solitary there:
> Two Paradises 'twere in one
> To live in Paradise alone.

'Share' here means 'portion' and so paves the way for the neat arithmetic of the closing epigram. Unfortunately for the sound of this couplet we have stopped pronouncing 'one' as 'own', the sound it had still for Marvell; the sound which gave English the new words 'atone' and 'alone' out of 'at one' and 'all one'. We still use it in 'only', which was formerly 'onely'.

It is noteworthy that, for the sake of his argument, Marvell was ready to falsify Genesis as flagrantly as he had falsified *Metamorphoses* in stanza IV. Everybody would know then that in the Bible the Adam 'living alone' was no 'Mortal' at all. He could eat freely of the Tree of Life. He obeyed God and did not touch the forbidden fruit of the neighbouring Tree of Knowledge or risk death, whatever death was. Marvell followed the orthodox account in that poignant comment on the Civil Wars, a disaster to England, in 'Upon Appleton House', lines 321—2 and 327—8:

> Oh Thou, that dear and happy Isle
> The Garden of the World ere while
> . . .
> What luckless Apple did we tast,
> To make us Mortal, and Thee Wast?

So the travesty of Genesis was perpetrated as a piece of wit and was expected to be recognised as such. If it is not, we fail the poet and his cleverness is wasted on us.

And now the last part, the final stanza, arrives; but only after another interval of time and another change of scene. Paradise is forgotten. Adam was the only gardener there. Here in the sunshine, away from the canopy of trees, a professional artist has laid out the latest seventeenth-century garden novelty, a floral sun-dial.

## IX

How well the skilful Gardner drew                    65
Of flow'rs and herbes this Dial new;
Where from above the milder Sun
Does through a fragrant Zodiack run;
And, as it works, th'industrious Bee
Computes its time as well as we.                     70
How could such sweet and wholsome Hours
Be reckon'd but with herbs and flow'rs!

The English reader may miss the pun on clock 'time' and the flower 'thyme', then commonly also spelt 'time'. But the Latin version insists on it. For '*Hortus*' begins again at this point. The ten Latin lines (49–58) can be rendered thus:

Nor shalt thou depart without a poem of gratitude, O Maker of the Garden, who hast marked the increasing hours and the intervals of the day with short-stemmed plants and beauteous flowers. There the brighter sun strays through sweet-scented signs. Instead of braving the Bull and the unsheathed pincers of the Crab, it glides towards the safe shade of the violets and roses. And the busy bee, intent on its honeyed task, seems to measure its allotment of duty with the thyme that tells the hour. O the pleasant passage of time! O health-giving leisure! O hours worthy to be numbered with herbs and flowers!

The big discrepancy between the two poems here is the season. In '*Hortus*' we have 'the brighter Sun' ('*Sol candidior*'). It abandons its routine course toward Taurus (the Bull) and Cancer (the Crab) and glides down to the safer violets and roses of the dial. Roughly speaking, the sun is in Taurus in May and in Cancer in July. So in '*Hortus*' the season is Springtime, April. But in IX we read of 'the milder Sun', and, of course, the season must be Autumn to fit in with the ripe fruits of stanza V. The only flower specifically named is the thyme, which still blooms in September. Violets and roses have gone.

The details of the dial in both versions agree with the floral dial in Loggan's *Cantabrigia Illustrata* (1690), Plate XVI, 'Pembroke Hall'. It was well established in the north-east corner of the Master's garden when Loggan did the drawing in 1681. Briefly, this dial was composed of three concentric circles. In the outermost, seventeen daylight hours were numbered clearly with short herbs, and between them every half-hour was similarly marked with a bold decimal point. A great metal gnomon stood in the innermost circle. In the wide middle circle between, over thirty narrow lines of taller plants pointed radially at the hours and half-hours. The sun's shadow thrown by the gnomon indicated the time. The radial plants were a help when the shadow fell short.

In '*Hortus*' the half-hour points would be *intervalla diei*, 'the intervals of the day'; and the 'increasing hours' would be either 4 to 12 in the forenoon or 1 to 8 after that. The bees 'computing' the time would be working on the herbs of the numerals themselves.

> How could such sweet and wholsome Hours
> Be reckon'd but with herbs and flow'rs!

Marvell ended all his rhetorical questions with exclamation marks.

# 27   'Upon Appleton House', to my Lord Fairfax

Marvell had addressed 'Upon the Hill and Grove at Bill-borow' to *the* Lord Fairfax, but he addresses 'Upon Appleton House' to *my* Lord Fairfax. Time had deepened their intimacy.

Both poems are gifts to Lord Fairfax. He is freely complimented in both, but in the third person. Where the poet uses the second person, he speaks to his reader. Sometimes he and his reader become 'we' or 'us'. So the imperative 'expect' in line 1 is addressed to the reader, newly arrived on a first visit to Appleton House; and in line 775, when night falls and the poem ends, Marvell says to the reader 'Let's in'; that is, 'Let us go indoors'. For the reader is to stay the night. Thus it is essentially a hospitable house. And Marvell is proud to be there.

## THE HOUSE

### I

Within this sober Frame expect
Work of no Forrain *Architect*;
That unto Caves the Quarries drew,
And Forrests did to Pastures hew;
Who of his great Design in pain                    5
Did for a Model vault his Brain,
Whose Columnes should so high be rais'd
To arch the Brows that on them gaz'd.

### II

Why should of all things Man unrul'd
Such unproportion'd dwellings build?              10
The Beasts are by their Denns exprest:
And Birds contrive an equal Nest;
The low roof'd Tortoises do dwell
In cases fit of Tortoise-shell:
No Creature loves an empty space;                 15
Their Bodies measure out their Place.

### III

But He, superfluously spread,
Demands more room alive then dead.
And in his hollow Palace goes
Where Winds (as he) themselves may lose.          20
What need of all this Marble Crust
T'impark the wanton Mote of Dust,
That thinks by Breadth the World t'unite
Though the first Builders fail'd in Height?

### IV

But all things are composed here                  25
Like Nature, orderly and near:
In which we the Dimensions find
Of that more sober Age and Mind,
When larger sized Men did stoop

To enter at a narrow loop;                                   30
As practising, in doors so strait,
To strain themselves through *Heavens Gate*.


### V

And surely when the after Age
Shall hither come in *Pilgrimage*,
These sacred Places to adore,                                35
By *Vere* and *Fairfax* trod before,
Men will dispute how their Extent
Within such dwarfish Confines went:
And some will smile at this, as well
As *Romulus* his Bee-like Cell.                              40


### VI

*Humility* alone designs
Those short but admirable Lines,
By which, ungirt and unconstrain'd,
Things greater are in less contain'd.
Let others vainly strive t'immure                            45
The *Circle* in the *Quadrature*!
These *holy Mathematicks* can
In ev'ry Figure equal Man.


### VII

Yet thus the laden House does sweat,
And scarce indures the *Master* great:                       50
But where he comes the swelling Hall
Stirs, and the *Square* grows *Spherical*;
More by his *Magnitude* distrest,
Then he is by its straitness prest:
And too officiously it slights                               55
That in it self which him delights.


### VIII

So Honour better Lowness bears,
Then That unwonted Greatness wears.
Height with a certain Grace does bend,
But low Things clownishly ascend.                            60

And yet what needs there here Excuse,
Where ev'ry Thing does answer Use?
Where neatness nothing can condemn,
Nor Pride invent what to contemn?

IX

A Stately *Frontispice of Poor*                    65
Adorns without the open Door:
Nor less the Rooms within commends
Daily new *Furniture of Friends*.
The House was built upon the Place
Only as for *a Mark of Grace*;                    70
And for an *Inn* to entertain
Its *Lord* a while, but not remain.

X

Him *Bishops-Hill*, or *Denton* may,
Or *Bilbrough*, better hold then they:
But Nature here hath been so free                  75
As if she said leave this to me.
Art would more neatly have defac'd
What she had laid so sweetly wast;
In fragrant Gardens, shady Woods,
Deep Meadows, and transparent Floods.              80

XI

While with slow Eyes we these survey,
And on each pleasant footstep stay,
We opportunly may relate
The Progress of this Houses Fate.

Ben Jonson's poem 'To Penshurst', the Kent home of the Sidneys,
had likewise begun by praising the house for what it was not:

Thou art not, PENSHURST, built to envious show,
    Of touch, or marble; nor canst boast a row
Of polish'd pillars, or a roofe of gold;

and it ended in lines 99—102 by returning to the same theme:

> Now, PENSHURST, they that will proportion thee
>   With other edifices, when they see
> Those proud, ambitious heaps, and nothing else,
>   May say, their lords have built, but thy lord dwells.

Marvell's opening stanzas provide a leisurely start to a poem seven times the length of Ben Jonson's. Picture yourself with Marvell outside the unpretentious ('sober') south elevation of Appleton House. He tells you in stanza I not to expect a sumptuous continental interior, with lofty roof modelled on the architect's distended skull in the throes ('pain') of giving birth to his brain-child ('great design'), and with pillars built so high as to make all beholders open their eyes in astonishment till their brows form a similar arch. All three relative pronouns ('That', 'Who', 'Whose') have 'Architect' as antecedent; he designed and he built.

In line 12 'an equal Nest' is one moulded to the shape of the sitting bird (the 'hatching Throstle', for instance, that will come in line 532). In the compressed lines 21–2 the key syllables are 'park' and 'Mote': 'What need is there for this vast marble palace, with a roof ('Crust') the size of a park, to enclose a sinful mortal who was, and will be again, a mere speck ('Mote') of dust?' The 1681 Folio nonsensically printed 'Mose', but the pen of the corrector in Thompson's second MS. book changed this to 'Mote'. Margoliouth did not know that in 1927, when he gave 'Mote' a slight preference over Cooke's 1726 emendation 'Mole'.

The 'first Builders' in line 24 were the architects of the brick Tower of Babel in Genesis, XI 1–9. They planned to unite earth and sky. This man plans to girdle the globe! The 'loop' of line 30, like any loophole higher up in a wall, is 'strait' and 'narrow', the twin Biblical words in Matthew, VII 13–14: 'Enter ye in at the strait gate. Because strait is the gate, and narrow is the way, which leadeth unto life, and few there be that find it.' So 'Heavens Gate' in line 32 leads on to the religious metaphors that start stanza V: 'Pilgrimage', 'sacred Places', 'adore'. The poet sees people, centuries ahead, smiling at the great General's small Appleton House just as he had seen visitors smiling in Rome, a few years before, on the legendary site of its founder's straw 'cell'. The enlargement of 'Romulus's' to 'Romulus his' followed a fashion begun by the Tudors. Marvell had already written 'Charles his' in 'Tom May's Death', line 76; it helped to slow the pace down.

In the first half of stanza VI the present and the past are combined. The new Appleton House is built on the old sober scale, 'Those short but admirable Lines', which modest heroes like Romulus and Fairfax alone can design. The two men are both good examples of 'things greater contain'd in things less'.

The second half of VI combines geometry and architecture with wit. Equality is the new theme. In mathematics 'the Quadrature' was a square equal in area to a given circle. The vain efforts of mathematicians to square the circle were already a joke. 'Immure' was an architectural word.

> Let others vainly strive t'immure       45
> The *Circle* in the *Quadrature*!
> These *holy Mathematicks* can
> In ev'ry Figure equal Man.

The mathematics of Appleton House are 'holy' because the Fairfaxes live there; for the same reason they were 'these sacred Places' in line 35. Circle and square are only two geometrical figures. The chief stress in line 48 falls on the first syllable of 'ev'ry'. There lies the heart of the wit. For Appleton House can 'equal Man' in every geometrical figure (line, angle, rectangle, as well as circle and square). The verb 'equal' conveys the same notion as the adjective in 'equal Nest'; it means 'match' or 'fit'. But it also retains its strict mathematical sense. And 'Figure' too has a second sense of 'human figure', according to the posture of man (sitting, lying, standing, climbing the stairs etc.).

In stanza VII the opening 'Yet thus' means 'even as it is' and we return to the 'greater in less' theme. The house in lines 49–50 is a servant or beast of burden that carries its great master with difficulty and in so doing breaks out into a sweat. In lines 51–6 the poet concentrates on 'the Hall'. There is a difficulty here. In the 1927 Oxford edition (repeated in 1952 and 1971) Margoliouth explained 'the swelling Hall . . . grows Spherical' as referring to the cupola which Markham in his *Life of the Great Lord Fairfax* (1870) said surmounted the centre of the house. This explanation would work for the hall of an Oxford college with a cupola in its roof. But the two engravings made at the end of the 1650s by Daniel King (British Museum, Harley MS. 2073, f.126) of Appleton House show the cupola above the third storey and far removed from the ground floor.

This stanza must therefore be figurative. The Master loves the proportions of the hall as it is, but the self-conscious hall feels inadequate every time he comes in. 'It billows outwards and upwards. It grows spherical.' This can have no literal basis at all.

Stanza VIII seethes with abstract nouns, but is saved by eight athletic verbs. 'So' at the start means 'in the same way' and relates to lines 53—4:

> More by his *Magnitude* distrest,
> Then he is by its straitness prest.

Lines 57—8 mean: 'In the same way a man of rank endures a humble position better than a man of humble position assumes sudden rank'. 'That' in line 58 is 'Lowness'. In line 64 'invent' means 'find'.

Stanza IX is both graphic and well contrived. The word 'Frontispice' came straight from the medieval Latin *frontispicium* (full face view) and was first used as an architectural term; it means 'decorated entrance' here, but the entrance is metaphorically decorated with poor folk who know they will be fed. Grantees of monastic lands at the Dissolution were obliged to continue the old Almonry hospitality in any house that they built on the site. Here the door is open; the north door in the courtyard, no doubt. An elaborate chiasmus adorns lines 65—8. The order in the first couplet is straightforward: subject, verb, adverb, object. In the second couplet that order is reversed: object, adverb, verb, subject (with an extra adverb, 'daily', thrown in). 'Furniture' is the subject of 'commends' and 'Rooms' are its object. Relays of friends throng the downstair rooms every day. They 'furnish' the rooms. So the house entertains the rich and the poor.

In lines 69—72 the thought must relate to the General's own epigram (Bodleian MS. Fairfax 40) 'Upon the New-built House att Apleton'. Punctuated, and with three abbreviations expanded, it goes:

> Think not, O Man that dwells herein,
> This House as a stay, but as an Inne
> Which for Convenience fittly stands
> In way to one nott made with hands.
> But if a time here thou take Rest,
> Yett think Eternity's the Best.

It bears no date, but Margoliouth believed that the first Lord Fairfax, who died in 1640, had begun the new house in 1637 or 1638 and that it 'was finished about the time of the General's retirement in 1650'. Ralph Thoresby (1658—1725) recorded in his diary a visit to 'Nun-

Appleton' on 16 October 1712; he talked to old Robert Taite who 'saw the old house pulled down, and a stately new one erected by Thomas Lord Fairfax, the General', whose servant he was. The Sir Thomas Fairfax who died in 1599, or his father Sir William, built the 'old house' out of the nunnery stone soon after the Dissolution in 1542. The new house was built of brick.

It seems certain, then, that Marvell in 1651 − 52 had seen his Lord's epigram before he wrote stanza IX. He repeated 'an Inn'. He changed 'for Convenience' to 'for a Mark of Grace' (token of favour) and wrote 'a while' for 'a time'. The house was built to entertain its Lord a while, but not to remain.

In stanza X, line 74, 'they' are 'the Rooms' in Appleton House (line 67). The rooms may be bigger at Bishops-Hill, the Fairfax town-house in York, or at Denton or Bilbrough, his other country-houses, but the Appleton grounds are the best of the four and they are the products of Nature, not Art. In line 80 the 'Floods' are the river and streams, transparent and clear.

Stanza XI prepares the reader for the next phase, the nunnery history. Poet and reader shall stroll through the grounds and together by question and answer reconstruct 'the Progress of this Houses Fate'.

> A *Nunnery* first gave it birth. 85
> For *Virgin Buildings* oft brought forth.
> And all that Neighbour-Ruine shows
> The Quarries whence this dwelling rose.

Marvell deliberately telescopes the first and second Appleton Houses into one. The first was mainly of nunnery stone and probably had no cupola. Its replacement had a stone cupola, but was otherwise of brick. It is wrong to argue that Marvell only saw the first house. He was there after the rebuilding.

## ISABEL THWAITES
### (GREAT-GREAT-GRANDMOTHER OF THE GENERAL)

### XII

> Near to this gloomy Cloysters Gates
> There dwelt the blooming Virgin *Thwates*; 90
> Fair beyond Measure, and an Heir

Which might Deformity make fair.
And oft She spent the Summer Suns
Discoursing with the *Suttle Nunns*.
Whence in these Words one to her weav'd,                    95
(As 'twere by Chance) Thoughts long conceiv'd.

### XIII

'Within this holy leisure we
'Live innocently as you see.
'These Walls restrain the World without,
'But hedge our Liberty about.                              100
'These Bars inclose that wider Den
'Of those wild Creatures, called Men.
'The Cloyster outward shuts its Gates,
'And, from us, locks on them the Grates.

### XIV

'Here we, in shining Armour white,                         105
'Like *Virgin Amazons* do fight.
'And our chast *Lamps* we hourly trim,
'Lest the great *Bridegroom* find them dim.
'Our *Orient* Breaths perfumed are
'With incense of incessant Pray'r.                         110
'And Holy-water of our Tears
'Most strangly our Complexion clears.

### XV

'Not Tears of Grief; but such as those
'With which calm Pleasure overflows;
'Or Pity, when we look on you                              115
'That live without this happy Vow.
'How should we grieve that must be seen
'Each one a *Spouse*, and each a *Queen*;
'And can in *Heaven* hence behold
'Our brighter Robes and Crowns of Gold?                    120

### XVI

'When we have prayed all our Beads,
'Some One the holy *Legend* reads;

'While all the rest with Needles paint
'The Face and Graces of the *Saint*.
'But what the Linnen can't receive                    125
'They in their Lives do interweave.
'This Work the *Saints* best represents;
'That serves for *Altar's Ornaments*.

### XVII

'But much it to our work would add
'If here your hand, your Face we had:                    130
'By it we would *our Lady* touch;
'Yet thus She you resembles much.
'Some of your Features, as we sow'd,
'Through ev'ry *Shrine* should be bestow'd.
'And in one Beauty we would take                    135
'Enough a thousand *Saints* to make.

### XVIII

'And (for I dare not quench the Fire
'That me does for your good inspire)
' 'Twere Sacriledge a Man t'admit
'To holy things, for *Heaven* fit.                    140
'I see the *Angels* in a Crown
'On you the Lillies show'ring down:
'And round about you Glory breaks,
'That something more then humane speaks.

### XIX

'All Beauty, when at such a height,                    145
'Is so already consecrate.
'*Fairfax* I know; and long ere this
'Have mark'd the Youth, and what he is.
'But can he such a *Rival* seem
'For whom you *Heav'n* should disesteem?                    150
'Ah, no! and 'twould more Honour prove
'He your *Devoto* were, then *Love*.

## XX

'Here live beloved, and obey'd:
'Each one your Sister, each your Maid.
'And, if our Rule seem strictly pend,                    155
'The Rule it self to you shall bend.
'Our *Abbess* too, now far in Age,
'Doth your succession near presage.
'How soft the yoke on us would lye,
'Might such fair Hands as yours it tye!                   160

## XXI

'Your voice, the sweetest of the Quire,
'Shall draw *Heav'n* nearer, raise us higher.
'And your Example, if our Head,
'Will soon us to perfection lead.
'Those Virtues to us all so dear,                         165
'Will straight grow Sanctity when here:
'And that, once sprung, increase so fast
'Till Miracles it work at last.

## XXII

'Nor is our *Order* yet so nice,
'Delight to banish as a Vice.                             170
'Here Pleasure Piety doth meet;
'One perfecting the other Sweet.
'So through the mortal fruit we boyl
'The Sugars uncorrupting Oyl:
'And that which perisht while we pull,                    175
'Is thus preserved clear and full.

## XXIII

'For such indeed are all our Arts;
'Still handling Natures finest Parts.
'Flow'rs dress the Altars; for the Clothes,
'The Sea-born Amber we compose;                           180
'Balms for the griv'd we draw; and Pasts
'We mold, as Baits for curious tasts.
'What need is here of Man? unless
'These as sweet Sins we should confess.

## XXIV

'Each Night among us to your side     185
'Appoint a fresh and Virgin Bride;
'Whom if *our Lord* at midnight find,
'Yet Neither should be left behind.
'Where you may lye as chast in Bed,
'As Pearls together billeted.     190
'All Night embracing Arm in Arm,
'Like Chrystal pure with Cotton warm.

## XXV

'But what is this to all the store
'Of Joys you see, and may make more!
'Try but a while, if you be wise:     195
'The Tryal neither Costs, nor Tyes.
Now *Fairfax* seek her promis'd faith:
Religion that dispensed hath;
Which She hence forward does begin;
The *Nuns* smooth Tongue has suckt her in.     200

## XXVI

Oft, though he knew it was in vain,
Yet would he valiantly complain.
'Is this that *Sanctity* so great,
'An Art by which you finly'r cheat?
'Hypocrite Witches, hence *avant*,     205
'Who though in prison yet inchant!
'Death only can such Theeves make fast,
'As rob though in the Dungeon cast.

## XXVII

'Were there but, when this House was made,
'One Stone that a just Hand had laid,     210
'It must have fall'n upon her Head
'Who first Thee from thy Faith misled.
'And yet, how well soever ment,
'With them 'twould soon grow fraudulent:
'For like themselves they alter all,     215
'And vice infects the very Wall.

## XXVIII

'But sure those Buildings last not long,
'Founded by Folly, kept by Wrong.
'I know what Fruit their Gardens yield,
'When they it think by Night conceal'd.                    220
'Fly from their Vices. 'Tis thy state,
'Not Thee, that they would consecrate.
'Fly from their Ruine. How I fear
'Though guiltless lest thou perish there.

## XXIX

What should he do? He would respect                        225
Religion, but not Right neglect:
For first Religion taught him Right,
And dazled not but clear'd his sight.
Sometimes resolv'd his Sword he draws,
But reverenceth then the Laws:                             230
For Justice still that Courage led;
First from a Judge, then Souldier bred.

## XXX

Small Honour would be in the Storm.
The *Court* him grants the lawful Form;
Which licens'd either Peace or Force,                      235
To hinder the unjust Divorce.
Yet still the *Nuns* his Right debar'd,
Standing upon their holy Guard.
Ill-counsell'd Women, do you know
Whom you resist, or what you do?                           240

## XXXI

Is not this he whose Offspring fierce
Shall fight through all the *Universe*;
And with successive Valour try
*France*, *Poland*, either *Germany*;
Till one, as long since prophecy'd,                        245
His Horse through conquer'd *Britain* ride?
Yet, against Fate, his Spouse they kept;
And the great Race would intercept.

## XXXII

Some to the Breach against their Foes
Their *Wooden Saints* in vain oppose.          250
Another bolder stands at push
With their old *Holy-Water Brush*.
While the disjointed *Abbess* threads
The gingling Chain-shot of her *Beads*.
But their lowd'st Cannon were their Lungs;     255
And sharpest Weapons were their Tongues.

## XXXIII

But, waving these aside like Flyes,
Young *Fairfax* through the Wall does rise.
Then th'unfrequented Vault appear'd,
And superstitions vainly fear'd.               260
The *Relicks false* were set to view;
Only the Jewels there were true.
But truly bright and holy *Thwaites*
That weeping at the *Altar* waites.

## XXXIV

But the glad Youth away her bears,             265
And to the *Nuns* bequeaths her Tears:
Who guiltily their Prize bemoan,
Like Gipsies that a Child had stoln.
Thenceforth (as when th'Inchantment ends
The Castle vanishes or rends)                  270
The wasting Cloister with the rest
Was in one instant dispossest.

## XXXV

At the demolishing, this Seat
To *Fairfax* fell as by Escheat.
And what both *Nuns* and *Founders* will'd     275
'Tis likely better thus fulfill'd.
For if the *Virgin* prov'd not theirs,
The *Cloyster* yet remained hers.
Though many a *Nun* there made her Vow,
'Twas no *Religious House* till now.            280

The heroine of these stanzas, Isabel Thwaites, duly married her hero in 1518. He was William Fairfax of Steeton, 'First from a Judge, then Souldier bred' (l.232). His father was a Judge in the Court of Common Pleas. His mother was the daughter of George Manners, Lord Roos, a veteran soldier when he died in 1513 at the Siege of Tournai. The poet's finger moves up the family tree, first to the father, then across to the mother's side.

Isabel, an orphan, was sole heir to the Denton and Askwith estates and the York house Bishops-Hill. That much Marvell knew. He does not seem to have known that the Prioress of Appleton was Lady Anna Langton, her guardian and aunt. He brings the girl to the nunnery because she 'dwelt near' and he has her innocently chattering away with the nuns:

> And oft She spent the Summer Suns
> Discoursing with the *Suttle Nunns*.

He also makes his 'Abbess' an old lady, 'far in Age', in 1518. But, according to tradition, she was still Prioress twenty-four years later at the Dissolution in 1542. It was a White Ladies or Cistercian House; hence the 'shining Armour white' in line 105. Not knowing about Lady Anna, he gave his recruiting speech to a nameless nun.

It begins in stanza XIII with a burst of paradox. The nunnery walls give the nuns their freedom and imprison the rest of the world! Its iron bars cage 'those wild Creatures, called Men'; the gates and grilles close outwards, away from the nuns! The world is a prison: the nunnery is a free place!

There is likewise a paradoxical jest in the phrase 'Virgin Amazons' (l.106). As fierce Amazons, they will put up a fight in lines 249–56. As meek virgins, they trim their lamps here; but in Matthew, XXV 1–13, the five wise virgins kept their lamps full of oil and only trimmed them at midnight when the Son of God (the Bridegroom) so unexpectedly came. 'Hourly' in line 107 refers to the offices in Books of Hours, from 'Prime' to 'Compline'. That leads on to the 'incessant Pray'r' (rhyming with 'are', pronounced 'air') in line 112. A sweet breath and a clear complexion were precious gifts to a girl. Mary Fairfax will be complimented on both in line 304.

In stanza XV, amid much false coin, line 114 rings true. Marvell writes from experience when he speaks of such tears as those 'With which calm Pleasure overflows'. His own chief pleasure was communion with Nature, and what was 'calm' moved him most.

The word will come with the kingfisher at twilight in the ineffable
lines 669–72:

> The modest *Halcyon* comes in sight,
> Flying betwixt the Day and Night;  670
> And such an horror calm and dumb,
> *Admiring Nature* does benum.

Stanzas XVI and XVII make a pair. The speaker fits Isabel
flatteringly into the future nunnery day. When each nun had said her
*Paternoster* and *Aves* and *Gloria* fifteen times round, counting them off
on her rosary beads, the embroidery session began. While one nun
read a saint's life ('holy Legend') aloud, the others embroidered the
saint; they naturally sewed female saints. If the beautiful Isabel joined
them, they could work her features into every altar frontal. Her
beauty had not yet reached its peak, 'But even as you are (Yet thus)
Our Lady is very like you' (l.132).

Stanzas XVIII to XXI move faster, for good tactical reasons. They
deal with the delicate issue of Isabel's engagement to Fairfax. The
flying parenthesis at the outset, 'for I dare not quench the Fire /That
me does for your good inspire', is glib, but what follows is 'long-
conceiv'd':

> 'Twere Sacriledge a Man to admit
> To holy things, for *Heaven* fit.

And Isabel is one of those holy things. The subtle nun paints a picture
of Isabel, with the angels above showering her with white lilies in the
shape of a crown: Le Couronnement de la Vierge Isabel. Glory breaks
round her, a glory that proclaims her superhuman, a dazzling light.

> All Beauty, when at such a height,
> Is so already consecrate.

It is at this point of crisis that the name of Fairfax is broached:

> *Fairfax* I know; and long ere this
> Have mark'd the Youth, and what he is.
> But can he such a *Rival* seem
> For whom you *Heav'n* should disesteem?  150
> Ah, no! and 'twould more Honour prove
> He your *Devoto* were, then *Love*.

The compromise solution is here. Fairfax cannot be ignored, but with him as her '*Devoto*', not '*Love*', she can have him and Heaven too. He would adore her from afar and she would love God. This chaste, cloistered view is poles apart from the world's ideal of marriage.

But perhaps Isabel wants to satisfy ambition as well as honour. In their choice of a husband, many women have been ambitious. The subtle nun has thought of that too. The Abbess will not live much longer and is herself predicting the 'near succession' of Isabel. Miracle-working and canonisation will come in time. Could the world offer such glorious prospects as those?

The remainder of the speech, lines 169–96, glamorises the life of the privileged novice in the days to come. 'The Cistercians are not yet so fastidious or scrupulous as to outlaw delight. At Appleton pleasure and piety blend, the one sweet perfecting the other, as happens in the making of jam.' Fruit is mortal, like pleasure. When the nuns picked the fruit in the orchard, it died. (The present tense in 'while we pull' imitates the Latin; 'that which perish'd while we pull' would in Latin be *id quod periit dum carpimus*.) When the nuns boiled the fruit and the sugar, piety in the shape of sugar 'uncorrupted' the fruit and preserved it 'clear and full'. Corruption and mortality go together in the Bible. 'For this corruptible must put on incorruption, and this mortal must put on immortality. So when this corruption shall have put on incorruption, and this mortal shall have put on immortality, then shall be brought to pass the saying that is written, Death is swallowed up in victory.' (I Corinthians, XV 53–4).

As in the art of jam-making, so in the rest of the nunnery arts. There is no tension there between Nature and Art, in stanza XXIII this nun claims. The two coexist. The nuns gather flowers in the garden to decorate the altars. Ambergris, excreted by sperm whales at sea, is stored here to perfume the altarclothes. To treat the injured ('griev'd'), the nuns extract balsams from trees. They mould 'pastes', which may mean 'pasties' or 'pâtés', as extra refreshments ('Baits') between refectory meals for those with fine palates ('curious tasts'). Given all these communal blessings, what need can the nuns have of men? Except perhaps priests to hear the confessions of those who think they may have over-indulged!

There remains the imaginary objection: 'But I shall be lonely at night without a husband.' Stanza XXIV answers that. The nuns sleep two to a bed. Isabel can choose any nun she likes for her bedfellow; a different one every night, if she likes. There they will happily lie, free from danger.

> Whom if *our Lord* at midnight find,
> Yet Neither should be left behind.

The first line returns to the coming of the Bridegroom at midnight in the parable of the wise virgins in Matthew, XXV 1–13. The second line refers to Matthew, XXIV 40–1: 'There shall two men be working in the field: the one shall be taken and the other left. Two women shall be grinding at the mill: the one shall be taken and the other left.' In both chapters the moral is the same. 'Watch therefore: for ye know not what hour your Lord doth come.' (XXIV 42.) 'Watch therefore, for ye know neither the day nor the hour wherein the Son of man cometh.' (XXV 13). Moreover Luke, XVII 34, says: 'I tell you, in that night there shall be two men in one bed; the one shall be taken, and the other shall be left.'

There they will happily lie, then: 'quartered ("billeted") together in bed, chaste as pearls; their arms round each other lovingly; pure as glass ("Chrystal"); warmed by their cotton nightgowns'. Cotton and sugar were unknown to England in 1518, but in 1652 they were imported delights. Even so, say lines 193–4, 'this is nothing (compared) to the many other joys (which) you see and can add to'. Let her come and give the convent a free trial without obligation:

> The Tryal neither Costs, nor Tyes.

So ends the nun's hundred-line speech; the round number suggests controlled planning. Now Fairfax is told by the poet to act.

> Now *Fairfax* seek her promis'd faith:
> Religion that dispensed hath;
> Which She hence forward does begin;
> The *Nuns* smooth Tongue has suckt her in.　　200

An alarm bell rings in these lines. The nun's rhetoric has triumphed over Isabel's engagement. Lines 197–9 mean: 'Now go and claim her plighted word, Fairfax. For monastic authority ("Religion") has annulled that pledge, and your Isabel is beginning monastic life ("Religion") and is to be a nun from now on.' So the trial did tie!

Fairfax's 'complaint' in lines 203–24, the only other speech in the poem, must not be misunderstood. Like 'The Nymph complaining for the death of her Faun', the shocked Fairfax merely soliloquised. No one else heard him. It is the same in 'To his Coy Mistress' at the end of this book. If Marvell and his coy lady had all the space in the world, she could be amusing herself in India while he 'complained' in Hull:

> Thou by the *Indian Ganges* side                    5
> Should'st Rubies find: I by the Tide
> Of Humber would complain.

To 'complain' was to utter endless laments. So here the distraught young Fairfax could not stem words that he knew to be futile. Day after day he 'complained' to himself.

> Oft, though he knew it was in vain,
> Yet would he valiantly complain.

What we have, then, in lines 203—24 is the supposed gist of his fulminations and ravings, organised into art form. Homer did much the same thing when he made his heroes speak to their own 'brave hearts'.

Lines 203—8 are addressed to the nuns. Their convent is their prison, their dungeon. Their professions of sanctity are false. They are witches, who have cast spells on his girl. They must go. 'Hence! Avaunt!'

Stanzas XXVII and XXVIII are addressed to Isabel. The tone, though masterful, is kind. What has happened is not her fault. In XXVII the argument runs: 'If in the building of this convent one stone had been honestly laid to the glory of God, that stone would have fallen on the head of the nun who first seduced you from your engagement to me. But no! All these nuns are so fraudulent that the best-intended stone would have become perverted by now. Their vice infects even the wall.' In XXVIII Fairfax hints at one vice and specifies one fraud. The vice is secret fornication with men. Isabel's chastity is threatened, he thinks.

> I know what Fruit their Gardens yield,
> When they it think by Night conceal'd.                    220
> Fly from their Vices.

The fraud is more palpable and pertinent. They wish to lay their hands on her estate.

'Tis thy state,
Not Thee, that they would consecrate.

But the end of the nunnery is near, indeed the end of all the buildings 'Founded by Folly, kept by Wrong'; the monasteries will soon be destroyed.

The narrative is straightforward enough in ll.225–70. The central fact was probably true, that William Fairfax took the convent to court and obtained an order to recover his fiancée, if necessary by force. She must have come of age before the hearing and expressed her own consent. The sequel was probably true also, that Fairfax had to use force. Undoubtedly she was rescued and the marriage took place.

Marvell was in tune with the Puritan opinion of his day in treating the monastic system as something that should never have been. In 1637 Nathaniel Whiting wrote 4000 hilarious lines on the amours of nuns and monks in *The Pleasant History of Albino and Bellama* and in the 1650s he was a Puritan parson. We can be sure that Marvell's account of Nun Appleton, and not least the assault in lines 241–56, would have seemed 'pleasant history' too to the Puritan and Presbyterian Fairfaxes.

Though Sir William's antecedents had been judges, his descendants in the next four generations were soldiers. They are the 'Offspring fierce' of line 241. In line 244 'either Germany' means 'both Germanys, High and Low'. Of the 'prophecy'd . . . ride' in lines 245–6 no written trace has been found, but it clearly relates to a Fairfax, *one* of the 'offspring', and so the assumption must be that it was a family prophecy fulfilled by the Lord General himself, ubiquitous victor of the nation-wide Civil Wars.

In the auction that followed the Dissolution of the Monasteries and augmented the King's Revenues, a Fairfax secured the Appleton nunnery buildings and lands. Marvell says it was William and Isabel. 'Escheat' in line 274 was the process by which, if a tenant died heirless, his estate automatically came back to the lord of the manor. The Fairfaxes had no such lordship before the Dissolution. After it, they had. Presumably William and Isabel built the first Appleton House. Certainly Marvell must have been told that Sir Thomas, their warrior son, laid out the remarkable flower garden. The next stanza says so.

## THE FLOWER GARDEN

### XXXVI

From that blest Bed the *Heroe* came,
Whom *France* and *Poland* yet does fame:
Who, when retired here to Peace,
His warlike Studies could not cease;
But laid these Gardens out in sport          285
In the just Figure of a Fort;
And with five Bastions it did fence,
As aiming one for ev'ry Sense.

### XXXVII

When in the *East* the Morning Ray
Hangs out the Colours of the Day,          290
The Bee through these known Allies hums,
Beating the *Dian* with its *Drumms*.
Then Flow'rs their drowsie Eylids raise,
Their Silken Ensigns each displayes,
And dries its Pan yet dank with Dew,          295
And fills its Flask with Odours new.

### XXXVIII

These, as their *Governour* goes by,
In fragrant Vollyes they let fly;
And to salute their *Governess*
Again as great a charge they press:          300
None for the *Virgin Nymph*; for She
Seems with the Flow'rs a Flow'r to be.
And think so still! though not compare
With Breath so sweet, or Cheek so faire.

### XXXIX

Well shot ye Firemen! Oh how sweet,          305
And round your equal Fires do meet;
Whose shrill report no Ear can tell,
But Ecchoes to the Eye and smell.
See how the Flow'rs, as at *Parade*,

Under their *Colours* stand displaid:                310
Each *Regiment* in order grows,
That of the Tulip Pinke and Rose.

## XL

But when the vigilant *Patroul*
Of Stars walks round about the *Pole*,
Their Leaves, that to the stalks are curl'd,        315
Seem to their Staves the *Ensigns* furl'd.
Then in some Flow'rs beloved Hut
Each Bee as Sentinel is shut;
And sleeps so too: but, if once stir'd,
She runs you through, or askes *the Word*.          320

## XLI

Oh Thou, that dear and happy Isle
The Garden of the World ere while,
Thou *Paradise* of four Seas,
Which *Heaven* planted us to please,
But, to exclude the World, did guard                325
With watry if not flaming Sword;
What luckless Apple did we tast,
To make us Mortal, and Thee Wast?

## XLII

Unhappy! shall we never more
That sweet *Militia* restore,                        330
When Gardens only had their Towrs,
And all the Garrisons were Flowrs,
When Roses only Arms might bear,
And Men did rosie Garlands wear?
Tulips, in several Colours barr'd,                  335
Were then the *Switzers* of our *Guard*.

## XLIII

The *Gard'ner* had the *Souldiers* place,
And his more gentle Forts did trace.
The Nursery of all things green
Was then the only *Magazeen*.                        340

The *Winter Quarters* were the Stoves,
Where he the tender Plants removes.
But War all this doth overgrow:
We Ord'nance Plant and Powder sow.

### XLIV

And yet there walks one on the Sod                345
Who, had it pleased him and *God*,
Might once have made our Gardens spring
Fresh as his own and flourishing.
But he preferr'd to the *Cinque Ports*
These five imaginary Forts:                       350
And, in those half-dry Trenches, spann'd
Pow'r which the Ocean might command.

### XLV

For he did, with his utmost Skill,
*Ambition* weed, but *Conscience* till.
*Conscience*, that Heaven-nursed Plant,           355
Which most our Earthy Gardens want.
A prickling leaf it bears, and such
As that which shrinks at ev'ry touch;
But Flowrs eternal, and divine,
That in the Crowns of Saints do shine.            360

### XLVI

The sight does from these *Bastions* ply,
Th' invisible *Artilery*;
And at proud *Cawood Castle* seems
To point the *Batt'ry* of its Beams.
As if it quarrell'd in the Seat                   365
Th' Ambition of its *Prelate* great.
But ore the Meads below it plays
Or innocently seems to gaze.

'From that blest Bed the *Heroe* came' can only refer to a child of the marriage of William and Isabel Fairfax. Their heir was a distinguished soldier, Sir Thomas. So 'these Gardens' that Marvell walked in had been laid out by the Elizabethan Sir Thomas in the exact shape ('just Figure') of a fort, with five bastions for all-round defence.

A bastion was normally an irregular pentagon, with four strong walls angled outwards and an open fifth side or base in the line of the main works that it strengthened. It seems, then, that here the groundplan had a regular pentagon at its centre and a bastion based on each side. The alleys ('Allies') in line 291 would be internal walks of grass or cobble-stones that stretched to the tip of each bastion. The gardener 'paraded' lines of pinks and tulips and roses either side of each alley or he massed them in 'regiments' alone.

What of 'those half-dry Trenches' in line 351? They seem part of the original plan. They are outside 'these Gardens', outside 'these five imaginary Forts'; some way outside, probably. The poet is inside the gardens and can point to 'those Trenches' beyond. They may have been two or more circles, crossed only by an entry near the house. Something was needed to keep out cattle, but magic may also have dictated a combination of pentagon and double circle around. The pentagon embodied the favourable number 'five', and a double circle was the recognised way of fending off evil spirits. At Appleton there was the possibly hostile influence of the suppressed nunnery; its ruins stood near and its best stone had been taken to build the first Appleton House. Marvell is oblivious of magic, but it does not follow that a century earlier no such influences entered into the design of the old soldier's garden-fort.

In lines 289–320 Marvell covers a May day and night in the flower garden in terms of life in a garrison fort. When Dawn hoists coloured flags in the eastern sky, the humming bees go down the lines beating reveille ('the Dian'). The flowers wake and open their petals and dry out the dew and refurbish their 'odours'. Metaphorically, they unfurl silk ensigns, dry the pan of their musket-locks and replenish their gunpowder-flasks. When Lord Fairfax comes, they fire a salute of sweet scents. Later they pay the same compliment to Lady Fairfax. But they 'press no charge' for young Mary when she arrives, because they think her a flower like themselves. The poet agrees with them to a certain extent. 'Go on thinking so always!' he tells them, 'though you are not equal ("compare") with such sweet breath as hers is, or with cheek so fair as hers.'

The word 'compare' began life as the Latin adjective *compar*, meaning 'co-equal'. Livy used *compar* more than most authors, and when Dr John Bellenden in the sixteenth century translated Livy into broad Scots for King James the Fifth, he wrote 'compare' for *compar*; the example given by the *Oxford English Dictionary* and the *New English Dictionary* is (with spelling anglicised) 'though they were not

compare with you in lineage and blood'. Marvell too is following the
Latin use of *compar*. He is saying in effect: 'though you are not
compare with her in sweetness of breath or fairness of cheek'. This
explanation is far more natural than the one usually given, that
'compare' is an intransitive verb and 'not compare' is short for 'do not
compare', meaning 'do not challenge comparison' (Margoliouth) or
'do not invite comparison' (Kermode) or 'do not vie' (Donno). The
last word to leave out of any such prohibition is 'do'. This clause
comes between two energetic commands, 'think so still!' and 'Well
shot ye Firemen!' A prohibition, so placed, could hardly begin with
'though' or end without an exclamation mark!

In line 305 the 'Firemen' are the flower-musketeers. The scents that
they discharge are 'sweet'. Their 'Fires' are 'round' and 'equal', not
ragged and unequal; they are being praised for the perfect unanimity
of their ceremonial shooting. In lines 307–8 'report' is the object of
'tell' and the subject of 'Ecchoes'; the shrill report of their figurative
volley is too high-pitched for the ear to detect, but it has repercussions
for the eye and the nose. Marvell now summons the eye to admire the
varicoloured flowers in their military formations. They stand in full
view all the day.

But in stanza XL night comes and the stars carry out their foot-
patrol in the northern sky. The flower leaves curl up against the stalks
and look like stored ensigns fastened to staves. The flowers themselves
shut their petals. Bees began the day and bees end it.

> Then in some Flow'rs beloved Hut
> Each Bee as Sentinel is shut;
> And sleeps so too: but, if once stir'd,
> She runs you through, or askes *the Word*.          320

That is how the 1681 Folio printed the last line. But Cooke in 1726
changed 'or' to 'nor'. Kermode in 1967 and Donno in 1972 followed
Cooke. Kermode added, on p.126 of his *Selected Poetry of Marvell*
(Signet Classics, 1967), that 'if the 1681 reading is right, *or* must mean
*ere* – "before asking the password".' But in that subordinate sense
Marvell's verb would have been the conjunctive 'ask', not the
indicative 'askes'. The straightforward 1681 line is witty and
Marvellian. The bee's instinctive reaction comes first; she stings you.
In soldiering language, she 'runs you through'. But sentries are
trained to challenge and then ask for the password. One can only
laugh at the idea of a bee's buzz being thought to do this. The jest

comes at the end of a stanza-group. By italicising *'the Word'* Marvell
asks his reader to deliver drolly what is intended as a Parthian shot.

For lines 321–60 form a new group. In them, Britain is one great
God-given island-garden, a paradise guarded by sea on all its four
sides ('four' is scanned with two syllables in line 323), but a Paradise
now unaccountably lost through internal dissension and recourse to
arms.

> What luckless Apple did we tast
> To make us Mortal, and Thee Wast?

The question is brilliantly put. And the two brilliant stanzas that
follow begin with a further question. Is the loss utterly irretrievable?

> Unhappy! shall we never more
> That sweet *Militia* restore?

The actual historical militia was a Local Defence Volunteer Force.
'That sweet *Militia*' (scanned with four syllables) is a figurative phrase
for the sweet English garden-state that obtained before the apple was
tasted. The only towers then were garden towers of clipped yew.
Flowers were the only garrisons. The only arms were the thorns on
roses. Men wore garlands of roses; not oak and not palm. The
'Switzer' tulips of red and yellow were the only uniformed guards.
(Parkinson included this very tulip in his *Terrestris Paradisus* and
Marvell saw the red-and-yellow-uniformed Swiss Guards in the
Vatican when he was in Rome.) The only forts were star-shaped
gardens like the Appleton one. There was the nursery garden to
supply plants to the flower-beds, but no magazine to supply
gunpowder to troops. Hot-houses were the only winter quarters. It
was peaceful. It was ideal.

> But War all this doth overgrow:
> We Ord'nance Plant and Powder sow.

The 'Ordinance' was heavy artillery. That was its spelling at first.

Stanzas XLIV and XLV refer to Marvell's Lord Fairfax, though
not by name. In line 347 'once' means 'one day in the future'. We use
it only of the past, but in 1640 William Habington could write to his
future wife in 'To Castara, inquiring why I loved her', line 15: 'And
'mongst the dead thou once must lie'. So in lines 345–8 Marvell is

saying: 'And yet that man is living who might have one day (had it pleased him and God) restored peace to the land and made Britain's garden flourish and be as fresh as his own at Appleton House.'

> But he preferr'd to the *Cinque Ports*
> These five imaginary Forts:                           350
> And, in those half-dry Trenches, spann'd
> Pow'r which the Ocean might command.

Mrs E. E. Duncan-Jones explained this passage in a letter to the *Times Literary Supplement* of 11 November 1955 which cannot be faulted. When Fairfax resigned his Generalship in June 1650, he ceased to attend the Council of State. The next year he was not re-elected. On 19 February 1650 an Act of Parliament had assigned to the Council collectively 'all powers appertaining to the Lord High Admiral and Warden of the Cinque Ports'. As one of the Council from February to June, Fairfax had a share in those offices. When he voluntarily quitted the Council, he gave up both. He preferred 'these five imaginary Forts' to the wardenship of the Cinque Ports. He confined ('spann'd') 'in those half-dry Trenches' power which, as Lord High Admiral, could be commanding the Ocean. 'Those . . . trenches' were also half-wet.

He gave up the Generalship on grounds of conscience. He could not in conscience attack Scots on their side of the border; he was a Scottish peer after all. Marvell cleverly works the Puritan conscience into his gardening metaphor. He makes it a plant grown in Heaven's nursery garden ('that Heaven-nursed Plant'), a plant which our gardens on earth most lack ('want'). The familiar 'pricks' of conscience he transfers to the plant:

> A prickling leaf it bears, and such
> As that which shrinks at ev'ry touch.

This is Marvell's second reference to what Sylvester's *Du Bartas* (1606) terms the 'Shame-faced' plant and Gerard's *Herbal* (1633) called 'Herba Mimosa or the Mocking herbe'. He had already written in 'An Elegy upon the Death of my Lord Francis Villiers' (1648) of Chlora, the dead man's love:

> And like the Modest Plant at every touch
> Shrunk in her leaves and feard it was too much.

So conscience shrinks here, but it bears immortal and divine flowers which shine in the crowns of saints. Fairfax will have his reward hereafter.

That thought ends the five-stanza digression into national affairs. It began abruptly and its end may appear abrupt too. But what happens is that for stanza XLVI Marvell moves to the side of the flower garden which overlooks the river meadows. In line 361 'these Bastions' are not all five, but the two from which cannon fire could be brought to bear on Cawood Castle, two miles to the south-east. Cawood was a seat of the Archbishops of York. In 1643, however, Parliament had abolished all bishoprics and confiscated their revenues. This was a measure with which the Puritan Fairfax and Presbyterian Lady Fairfax would whole-heartedly have agreed; they were against church government by bishops on principle. The poet's *animus* against the 'Prelate great' is not personal, Archbishop John Williams had only been translated from Lincoln to York in 1641 and within a few months had withdrawn to North Wales, where he died in 1650. When Marvell was at Appleton House, no Archbishop of York was alive.

If we give due weight to the stresses, lines 361–6 mean: 'No cannons fire from these bastions. But the eye shoots frequent looks, the artillery that cannot be seen. In particular, the eye appears to aim its beam at proud Cawood Castle and batter that; as if it took strong exception to the worldliness of an Archbishop who owned so pretentious a seat.' The tone in the second couplet is aggressive:

> And at proud *Cawood Castle* seems
> To point the *Batt'ry* of its Beams.

The harsh double hard 'c' of Cawood Castle is reinforced with the 'p' and 'b' plosives. The 'k' sound is repeated in 'quarrel'd' and the 'p' in 'Prelate' in the two lines that follow. A smiling urbanity, however, returns at the end:

> But ore the Meads below it plays,
> Or innocently seems to gaze.

There may be a pun in 'plays': (1) 'strikes repeatedly' (of shot); (2) 'moves capriciously' (of eyesight). There is no pun in 'gaze', which speaks only of eyesight. In Thompson's second notebook, however, the same hand that changed 'gates' in line 43 of 'To his Coy Mistress'

to 'grates' turned 'gaze' here to 'graze'. Such a reading might mean
(1) 'skim superficially' (of shot); (2) 'feed like cattle' (of eyesight).
Presumably the T2 corrector had this in mind. Whether he had any
manuscript authority, though, one cannot say. Either way, the
couplet provides a good transition to the River Meadows, the poem's
next phase.

## THE RIVER MEADOWS
### (BEFORE THE FLOOD)

### XLVII

And now to the Abbyss I pass
Of that unfathomable Grass,                          370
Where Men like Grashoppers appear,
But Grashoppers are Gyants there:
They, in there squeaking Laugh, contemn
Us as we walk more low then them:
And, from the Precipices tall                        375
Of the green spires, to us do call.

### XLVIII

To see Men through this Meadow Dive,
We wonder how they rise alive.
As, under Water, none does know
Whether he fall through it or go.                    380
But, as the Marriners that sound,
And show upon their Lead the Ground,
They bring up Flow'rs so to be seen,
And prove they've at the Bottom been.

### XLIX

No Scene that turns with Engines strange            385
Does oftner then these Meadows change.
For when the Sun the Grass hath vext,
The tawny Mowers enter next;
Who seem like *Israelites* to be,
Walking on foot through a green Sea.                 390
To them the Grassy Deeps divide,
And crowd a Lane to either Side.

## L

With whistling Sithe, and Elbow strong,
These Massacre the Grass along:
While one, unknowing, carves the *Rail*,                                  395
Whose yet unfeather'd Quils her fail.
The Edge all bloody from its Breast
He draws, and does his stroke detest;
Fearing the Flesh untimely mow'd
To him a Fate as black forebode.                                         400

## LI

But bloody *Thestylis*, that waites
To bring the mowing Camp their Cates,
Greedy as Kites has trust it up,
And forthwith means on it to sup:
When on another quick She lights,                                        405
And cryes, he call'd us *Israelites*;
But now, to make his saying true,
Rails rain for Quails, for Manna Dew.

## LII

Unhappy Birds! What does it boot
To build below the Grasses Root;
When Lowness is unsafe as Hight,                                         410
And Chance o'retakes what scapeth spight?
And now your Orphan Parents Call
Sounds your untimely Funeral.
Death-Trumpets creak in such a Note,                                     415
And'tis the *Sourdine* in their Throat.

## LIII

Or sooner hatch or higher build:
The Mower now commands the Field;
In whose new Traverse seemeth wrought
A Camp of Battail newly fought:                                          420
Where, as the Meads with Hay, the Plain
Lyes quilted ore with Bodies slain:
The Women that with forks it fling,
Do represent the Pillaging.

### LIV

And now the careless Victors play,                    425
Dancing the Triumphs of the Hay;
Where every Mowers wholesome Heat
Smells like an *Alexanders sweat*.
Their Females fragrant as the Mead
Which they in *Fairy Circles* tread:                   430
When at their Dances End they kiss,
Their new-made Hay not sweeter is.

### LV

When after this 'tis piled in Cocks,
Like a calm Sea it shews the Rocks:
We wondring in the River near                          435
How Boats among them safely steer.
Or, like the *Desert Memphis Sand*,
Short *Pyramids* of Hay do stand.
And such the *Roman Camps* do rise
In Hills for Soldiers Obsequies.                       440

### LVI

This *Scene* again withdrawing brings
A new and empty Face of things;
A levell'd space, as smooth and plain,
As Clothes for *Lilly* strecht to stain.
The World when first created sure                      445
Was such a Table rase and pure.
Or rather such is the *Toril*
Ere the Bulls enter at Madril.

### LVII

For to this naked equal Flat,
Which *Levellers* take Pattern at,                     450
The Villagers in common chase
Their Cattle, which it closer rase;
And what below the Sith increast
Is pincht yet nearer by the Beast.
Such, in the painted World, appear'd                   455
*Davenant* with th' Universal Heard.

## LVIII

They seem within the polisht Grass
A Landskip drawn in Looking-Glass.
And shrunk in the huge Pasture show
As Spots, so shap'd, on Faces do.                    460
Such Fleas, ere they approach the Eye,
In Multiplying Glasses lye.
They feed so wide, so slowly move,
As *Constellations* do above.

## THE RIVER MEADOWS
### (IN FLOOD)

### LIX

Then, to conclude these pleasant Acts,               465
*Denton* sets ope its *Cataracts*;
And makes the Meadow truly be
(What it but seem'd before) a Sea.
For, jealous of its *Lords* long stay,
It try's t'invite him thus away.                     470
The River in it self is drown'd,
And Isles th'astonisht Cattle round.

### LX

Let others tell the *Paradox*,
How Eels now bellow in the Ox;
How Horses at their Tails to kick,                   475
Turn'd as they hang to Leeches quick;
How Boats can over Bridges sail;
And Fishes do the Stables scale.
How *Salmons* trespassing are found;
And Pikes are taken in the Pound.                    480

### LXI

But I, retiring from the Flood,
Take Sanctuary in the Wood.

The two opening stanzas, XLVII and XLVIII, show Marvell at his best, sensuous and intelligent, exuberant and relaxed. The first takes him down to the meadows. The initial emphasis is on the syllable 'grass', with its sibilant ending. The eye views with pleasure the unbroken greenness below: the intellect apprehends it in nautical terms that culminate in the 'green Sea' of line 390.

> And now to the Abbyss I pass
> Of that unfathomable Grass,                               370
> Where Men like Grashoppers appear,
> But Grashoppers are Gyants there:

The true music depends on keeping the aspirate and stress of modern pronunciation out of 'hopp'. The seventeenth-century rule was to accent the first syllable only in compound nouns, whatever their length. In stating this rule, Ben Jonson's *English Grammar* (1640) gave the extreme examples of 'ténnis-court-keeper' and 'chímney-sweeper'. Compared with them, 'grássuper' was easy to say. Marvell stretches a point in scanning it each time 'Gráshoppér'.

He took his grasshopper–giant combination from Numbers, XIII 33: 'And there we saw the giants, the sons of Anak, which come of the giants: and we were in our own sight as grasshoppers, and so we were in their sight.' The spies' report curdled the blood of the Israelites there. Here Marvell drolly plays with perspective. To him at the top of the slope the men in the distance at the bottom are the size of grasshoppers. Down there (he knows, because he has been there) scores of squeaking grasshoppers perch on the tips of the grass spires, gigantic in height. He can talk of them, then, deriding and mocking himself and his companion on the walk down for being so much nearer the ground (and looking nearer than they are);

> They, in there squeaking Laugh, contemn
> Us as we walk more low then them:
> And, from the Precipices tall                               375
> Of the green spires, to us do call.

By the time XLVIII starts, the walkers have reached the foot of the slope. What had been 'that unfathomable Grass' in the distance is now 'this Meadow' near at hand. The men in it are life-size.

To see Men through this Meadow Dive,
We wonder how they rise alive.
As, under Water, none does know
Whether he fall through it or go. 380
But, as the Marriners that sound,
And show upon their Lead the Ground,
They bring up Flow'rs so to be seen,
And prove they've at the Bottom been.

The men dive *through* the grass, not *into* it. But, as happens in deep water, no-one immersed in such deep grass can tell if he is falling downwards or advancing forwards, 'Whether he fall through it or go'. So it seems to the watcher a perilous journey that they make and something of a miracle that their heads re-appear above the grass from time to time.

However, they do survive and they come up with wild flowers in their hands and so prove that they did reach the bottom, like sailors who have earth on their lead and so prove they have plumbed the full depth of the sea. This latter idea Marvell put to hilarious use in the opening lines of *The Character of Holland*, a satire written shortly after he finished his two years at Appleton House.

> *Holland*, that scarce deserves the name of *Land*,
> As but th'Off-scouring of the *British Sand*;
> And so much Earth as was contributed
> By *English Pilots* when they heav'd the Lead . . .

Stanza XLIX begins with a metaphor which will grow in importance when repeated in lines 419, 441, 465. It is designed to make the River Meadow stanzas cohere.

> No Scene that turns with Engines strange 385
> Does oftner then these Meadows change.
> For when the Sun the Grass hath vext,
> The tawny Mowers enter next . . .

This word 'Scene' covers scenery and stage. The guests at the aristocratic masques of the 1630s were regaled with exciting scenery. Changes of scene were engineered by devices for rotating the stage. But since novelty was half the attraction, no old scene was ever brought back. Scene-changes were therefore few. In Milton's *Comus*

(1634) there were two. Marvell's River Meadows in these fourteen stanzas change scene five times. The cycle of operations is thus combined into, as it were, a single dramatic performance.

The first scene-change in lines 387–8 takes place some time after noon, when the sun has 'vexed' the green grass spires. Implicit in 'the tawny Mowers enter next' is some such stage direction as 'Enter a numerous troop of sunburnt mowers in single file'.

The simile that follows is sophisticated, but in its elementary form of Israelites walking through the Red Sea it derives from Exodus, XIV 21–2: 'Moses stretched out his hand over the sea . . . and the waters were divided. And the children of Israel went into the midst of the sea upon the dry ground: and the waters were a wall unto them on their right hand, and on their left.' Lines 391–2 adapt this account to the mowers:

> To them the Grassy Deeps divide,
> And crowd a Lane to either side.

That is, the grasses push to right and left to leave a narrow path for the mowers. Just so, a street crowd would open to let a horseman through. The sophisticated image of the 'green Sea', however, in the couplet before –

> Who seem like *Israelites* to be,
> Walking on foot through a green Sea

– may well have occurred to the poet after reading Wisdom, XIX 7: 'Where water stood before, dry land appeared; and out of the Red sea a way without impediment; and out of the violent stream a green field.' (The same chapter had 'quails' in verse 12.)

In stanza L the mowers start scything. They will be at their scything all day. One couplet is enough to establish the sight and the sound:

> With whistling Sithe, and Elbow strong,
> These Massacre the Grass along:

The key word is 'Massacre'. It both adds to the generally sibilant sound and, more important, introduces the theme of 'Battail and Murther and sodain Death', as the old Litany put it. The adverb 'along' plays its part; it means 'at full length' and is not unconnected with death. Seven years later Marvell repeated it, and repeated the rhyme 'strong', in 'A Poem upon the Death of O.C.', lines 251–2. He had seen Cromwell dead.

> That port which so majestique was and strong,
> Loose and depriv'd of vigour, stretch'd along.

Even so, in the Appleton meadows, the semi-human grass is massacred and lies dead. All flesh is grass. The hapless 'Rail' or corncrake shares at once the same fate. The mower 'detests' what he has done and fears for his own future safety, for he too is young.

No such scruples afflict the village maiden who has her great moment in the next stanza.

> But bloody *Thestylis*, that waites
> To bring the mowing Camp their Cates,
> Greedy as Kites has trust it up,
> And forthwith means on it to sup:
> When on another quick She lights,                    405
> And cryes, he call'd us *Israelites*;
> But now, to make his saying true,
> Rails rain for Quails, for Manna Dew.

She is the same cottager who teased Ametas to such good effect in 'Ametas and Thestylis making Hay-Ropes'. As the cateress who waits on the mowers, she is doubtless meant to recall the Thestylis in Virgil's Second Eclogue who brought garlic and wild thyme to the reapers. Marvell paints a deft portrait of her; it brightens the poem as well as advancing the theme. Bloody and greedy, she seizes the victim and trusses it up to cook for her supper. Lucky, she then chances ('lights') on another one that is alive ('quick') and kills it. Breezy and loud, she scores off the poet by capping his allusion to Exodus, XIV, with another from the same Book. In Exodus, XVI 12–15, Moses promised the Israelites: 'At even ye shall eat flesh, and in the morning ye shall be filled with bread.' His saying came true. 'At even the quails came up and covered the camp', and in the morning Manna rained down for their bread. Thestylis pretends that Marvell is a second Moses, for whom rails rain instead of quails and evening dew instead of morning manna. And Marvell, her creator, pretends that he is composing aloud on the spot and so can have been overheard!

After any death one must expect mourning and funeral; sometimes an inquest as well. All three are duly forthcoming in stanza LII. To avoid such casualties in the future, the verdict is that rails must alter their nesting habits. In the meantime the air echoes with the distress calls of the 'orphaned' parents (*orphanos* being Greek for 'bereaved'). Their notes are harsh and grating at the best of times; hence the later name 'corncrake' ('crake', 'croak' and 'creak' being onomatopoeic and clearly akin). The 'sourdine' was a trumpet, but it was also the mute inserted in the trumpet at funerals in church. The two senses are used here in turn:

> Death-Trumpets creak in such a Note,
> And 'tis the *Sourdine* in their Throat.

A second change of scene comes in stanza LIII. The field has a 'new Traverse'. This was the name for a stage curtain in masques. It could be painted or worked ('wrought'). The stanza introduces a different day. The meadows are mowed and resemble a battle-field after the fighting is done. 'Camp of Battail' translates the French *champ de bataille*. The mowers have won.

> The Mower now commands the Field;
> In whose new Traverse seemeth wrought
> A Camp of Battail newly fought:    420
> Where, as the Meads with Hay, the Plain
> Lyes quilted ore with Bodies slain:

The 'Massacre' of the grass that the warrior-mowers began in line 394 is completed in line 422 in the same metaphor of 'Bodies slain'. The word 'quilted' is admirably chosen. The scythed grass lies in long parallel lines with bare field between. In the same way, lines of padding stand out on a quilt from the unpadded stitched linen between.

In the calm after any battle civilian predators would be seen pillaging corpses and littering the ground with their rejects. Similarly dispersed over a mown hayfield, women with pitchforks lift the hay up and scatter it to help it to dry. All this is compressed into one vivid couplet:

> The Women that with forks it fling,
> Do represent the Pillaging.

After a Roman victory came the Roman triumph. So here in

stanza LIV. Against the same imaginary backcloth the mowers and their womenfolk dance the old country dance known as 'the Hay', a circular dance to tabor and pipe. Lines 426 and 432 make the obvious pun on 'Hay'. So did Ametas in the last line of 'Ametas and Thestylis making Hay-Ropes'. Both poems have the couples kissing at the end of the dance. Plutarch's 'Life of Alexander the Great' observed (in Sir Thomas North's Elizabethan translation) that 'his body had so sweete a smell of it selfe, that all the apparell he wore next unto his body took thereof a passing delightful savour, as it had been perfumed'. Marvell is skilfully off-setting the aristocratic reader's distaste for malodorous peasants. Nothing must mar his Arcadian romance.

Stanza LV incorporates a third change of scene, unobtrusively made on a subsequent day. The hay has been raked into haycocks and they have been bound with hay-ropes. They stand at wide invervals. The poet and his companion regard the new aspect from a boat on the river ('we wondering' imitates the Latin ablative absolute, *nobis mirantibus*). Three similes suggest themselves: rocks protruding from a calm sea; squat pyramids in the Egyptian desert; Roman *tumuli* or burial mounds (so reviving the battlefield image).

> This *Scene* again withdrawing brings
> A new and empty Face of things.

The Latin noun *facies* meant (1) human face (2) aspect, appearance. So 'Face' means 'aspect' here. The fourth change of scene now occurs. The hay has been carted. There only remains:

> A levell'd space, as smooth and plain,
> As Clothes for *Lilly* strecht to stain.

The 'Clothes' were 'canvases', stretched for 'Lilly' to paint on. He was the Dutchman, Peter Lely, who came to England in 1641 as a young man and was knighted by Charles II after the Restoration. According to George Vertue (1684–1756) he painted a portrait of Marvell.

From the clean canvas the poet's mind proceeds to the 'Table rase' (Latin *tabula rasa*); that is 'erased tablet' or 'clean writing surface'.

> The World when first created sure
> Was such a Table rase and pure.

'Sure' is an adverb. On the third day of the Creation God made the

dry land, called Earth, and then said 'Let the earth bring forth grass';
so there must have been a moment, Marvell argues, when the Earth
was 'rase and pure', and, with the meadows in their present bare state,
that moment seems to have returned. Then he thinks of a better
illustration, the bare bull-ring ('Toril') at Madrid ('Madril'); better
for him, because it leads on to the entry of cattle.

> Or rather such is the *Toril*
> Ere the Bulls enter at *Madril*.
>
> For to this naked equal Flat,
> Which *Levellers* take Pattern at,                    450
> The Villagers in common chase
> Their Cattle, which it closer rase;

Villagers in English manors had a right to pasture their cows on
the lord's demesne when his hay had been harvested. It was a right
which they were not slow to exercise at Appleton: 'to this bare
plain . . . they drive ('chase') their cattle in common and the cows
shave it closer.'

As for 'Levellers', that was the nickname bestowed on the green-
ribbon-wearing party of radical democrats which flourished in
1646—9. (See Joseph Frank, *The Levellers*, Harvard University Press,
1955.) They preached the total abolition of rank and caused army
mutinies on the Parliament side; Lord Fairfax himself suppressed one
in 1649. Marvell is not being very serious in suggesting that 'this
naked equal Flat' was the Leveller's model ('Pattern'), but his use of
'levell'd' in line 443 and 'Levellers' here may well echo the title of
Prynne's anti-Leveller pamphlet *The Levellers Levell'd to the Very
Ground* (1648).

The next couplet is decidedly flippant. It referred to the Poet
Laureate's *Gondibert* (1651), which had been out for less than a
year.

> Such, in the painted World, appear'd
> *Davenant* with th' Universal Heard.

In Book II, Canto vi of his epic, Sir William Davenant described the
Temple of Praise at the House of Astragon. Its windowless walls were
covered like the Sistine Chapel with paintings. They began with a set
of panels on the Creation of the World; hence 'the painted World'. At

stanza 60 Davenant reached the Sixth Day, when God decreed the creation of cattle and other beasts and of Man:

60

Then strait an universal Herd appears;
  First gazing on each other in the shade;
Wondring with levell'd Eies, and lifted Ears,
  Then play, whilst yet their Tyrant is unmade.

61

And Man, the Painter now presents to view;
  Haughty without, and busy still within;
Whom, when his Furr'd and Horned Subjects knew,
  Their sport is ended, and their fears begin.

So the cows and their owners in the Appleton meadow are compared to tyrant Man and his oppressed cattle in the *Gondibert* painting, but Davenant himself is substituted for Adam. Marvell may be laughing at the mere thought of bringing Davenant in. But he may be laughing at the creation stanzas in Davenant, and he may even have noticed Davenant's weakness for the word 'universal'. In Book II alone it comes four more times:

(a) 'And give all grief one universal face' (iii, 14)
(b) 'Here the check'd Sun his universal Face' (vi, 16)
(c) 'Vertue to serve the Universal State' (vii, 53)
(d) 'The Universal Crown I would not weare' (viii, 43)

However, Marvell does go on to use the word seriously himself here in line 741: 'Whence, for some universal good, . . . '.

In stanza LVIII Marvell's imaginative wit supplies four more comparisons. Compressed as they are, they take a lot of understanding. The first says of the cows in the meadow:

They seem within the polisht Grass
A Landskip drawn in Looking-Glass.

In 1927 Margoliouth's explanation was: 'The reflection in the mirror appears to the eye to be smaller than the landscape.' In 1967 Kermode's note read: 'A landscape shown in a painting as reflected in a looking glass and thus reduced in size.' Neither scholar was on the right track. Marvell has no article before 'Looking-Glass'. He is using a generic term to signify *either* plate glass *or* glass silvered (for use as a mirror); both meanings were current in 1650. The key word in the couplet is 'polisht'. The light on the myriad blades of short grass makes them shine, and the shine seems a polish. That polish suggested the rhyming word 'Glass'; a flat field, with cows widely dispersed, polished like plate glass. And so: 'The cows in the polished grass seem a landscape picture painted in plate glass.' It does not matter if technically such painting cannot be done. He says 'seem'. He says 'polisht Grass'. The *New English Dictionary* quotes from a publication of 1703: 'These looking-glass plates are ground smooth and flat and Polished.'

The second couplet continues, after an artificial full stop, with 'Cows' still the subject:

> And shrunk in the huge Pasture show
> As Spots, so shap'd, on Faces do.

In the old pronunciation, which we still use in 'don't', 'show' and 'do' rhymed. The pasture here does no shrinking; it remains 'huge'. But the cows are dwarfed by the hugeness, 'shrunk' to the likeness of spots of the same shape ('so shaped') on human faces; not a very pleasing thought! In the next couplet it is the spots' turn to shrink.

> Such Fleas, ere they approach the Eye,
> In Multiplying Glasses lye.

'Such' is an adverb meaning 'similarly'. The name 'multiplying glass' came a generation before 'magnifying glass', but both names meant the same thing. Marvell is thinking of a light microscope which is raised to the eye. Spaced out between ordinary glass panels below, the dead fleas are seen first in their true size by the naked eye. J. B. Leishman makes the interesting suggestion, in *The Art of Marvell's Poetry* (Hutchinson, 1966), p.222n., that Marvell had read a passage in James Howell's *Familiar Letters* (1650): 'You look upon me . . . through a multiplying glass, which makes the object appear far bigger than it is in real dimension; such glasses as anatomists use in the dissection of bodies, which can make a flea look like a cow . . . ' Here the 'cow like a flea' wittily reverses Howell, Leishman suggests. One may add that Davenant wrote in his *Preface to Gondibert* of 'the

Eye of Envie (which enlarges objects like a multiplying glass) and makes Statesmen seem immense as Whales' (p.55).

So far the comparisons have been contemporary and distinctly fantastic. In the fourth Marvell changes the tone, recovers his gravity and slows the pace down. 'They' are the cows:

> They feed so wide, so slowly move,
> As *Constellations* do above.

It makes a beautiful ending to this particular phase. The meadow is quietly eliminated and day and night are rolled into one.

Stanza LIX makes the strangest scene-change, the fifth of the five. The meadows are flooded. The entertaining scenes are now called 'pleasant Acts':

> Then, to conclude these pleasant Acts,                    465
> *Denton* sets ope its *Cataracts*;
> And makes the Meadow truly be
> (What it but seem'd before) a Sea.
> For, jealous of its *Lords* long stay,
> It try's t'invite him thus away.                          470

Fairfax was lord of Denton as well as Appleton. Before the recent rebuilding of Appleton, Denton was the chief Fairfax house, and had been since 1518. These were the Fairfaxes of Denton. Presumably Marvell had been to the place. It stood thirty miles upstream on the left bank of the River Wharfe and boasted a set of small waterfalls, but even in flood they were never by any means 'Cataracts'. The Wharfe rises in the wettest part of the Pennines, which in winter are covered in snow. In consequence the river often overflows its banks at Appleton in the spring; but never in the summer. The conclusion is therefore unmistakable, and future stanzas will bear it out, that between LVIII and LIX seven or eight months elapse. This should overcome any reluctance to allow intervals of time between some of the previous 'scenes' or 'acts'. Starting in May at line 289, by line 650 we shall have seen the year round. We nearly do so in the River Meadows section alone. It *seemed* a sea in lines 369–84 (last May or June). It *is* a sea now (this March or April).

> The River in it self is drown'd,
> And Isles th'astonisht Cattle round.

Washing round them, it turns them into islands. They would naturally tend to group on raised ground.

The poet too must make for dry land. He does so in comical mood. Stanza LX adopts the Ciceronian device of detailing what is to be left out.

> Let others tell the *Paradox*,
> How Eels now bellow in the Ox;

The cattle bellow in gastric discomfort after gulping eels down with draughts of flood water. Ergo, it is the eels that bellow.

> How Horses at their Tails do kick,
> Turn'd as they hang to Leeches quick;

The hairs in the horsetail under water turn to live ('quick') leeches, which fasten on the horse and make it lash out. This was not so incredible in days when they believed that isolated horsepond creatures were engendered by the action of water on stray horse-hairs.

> How Boats    can over Bridges sail;
> And Fishes    do the Stables scale.

Given deep enough flood water, such strange things might happen. The calculated balance between this couplet and the next helps to make it all seem rational.

> How *Salmons*    trespassing are found;
> And Pikes    are taken in the Pound.

Every village had its walled enclosure, its pound, for the impounding of stray cattle.

Stanza LXI makes the transition from drowning meadows to watertight wood:

> But I, retiring from the Flood,
> Take Sanctuary in the Wood;
> And, while it lasts, my self imbark
> In this yet green, yet growing Ark;
> Where the first Carpenter might best        485

Fit Timber for his Keel have Prest.
And where all Creatures might have shares,
Although in Armies, not in Paires.

'Let others tell the *Paradox* . . . but I . . . Take Sanctuary in the Wood'. For the first time in the poem Marvell seeks safety in solitude. He retires on his own for the duration of the flood. The wood is to be his sanctuary and his live Noah's Ark. The trees are good enough ('Fit Timber') to have been pressed into service by Noah. Creatures are there in hosts ('Armies'), not in pairs as in the Ark.

Marvell's whole being expanded in solitude. It did so in his poem 'The Garden'. It does so here in 'The Wood' (though he did not use that title).

### THE WOOD

### LXII

The double Wood of ancient Stocks
Link'd in so thick, an Union locks,     490
It like two Pedigrees appears,
On one hand *Fairfax*, th'other *Veres*:
Of whom though many fell in War,
Yet more to Heaven shooting are:
And, as they Natures Cradle deckt,     495
Will in green Age her Hearse expect.

### LXIII

When first the Eye this Forrest sees
It seems indeed as *Wood* not *Trees*:
As if their Neighbourhood so old
To one great Trunk them all did mold.     500
There the huge Bulk takes place, as ment
To thrust up a *Fifth Element*;
And stretches still so closely wedg'd
As if the Night within were hedg'd.

### LXIV

Dark all without it knits; within     505
It opens passable and thin;

And in as loose an order grows,
As the *Corinthean Porticoes*.
The arching Boughs unite between
The Columnes of the Temple green;                    510
And underneath the winged Quires
Echo about their tuned Fires.


### LXV

The *Nightingale* does here make choice
To sing the Tryals of her Voice.
Low Shrubs she sits in, and adorns                   515
With Musick high the squatted Thorns.
But highest Oakes stoop down to hear,
And listning Elders prick the Ear.
The Thorn, lest it should hurt her, draws
Within the Skin its shrunken claws.                  520


### LXVI

But I have for my Musick found
A Sadder, yet more pleasing Sound:
The *Stock-doves*, whose fair necks are grac'd
With Nuptial Rings their Ensigns chast;
Yet always, for some Cause unknown,                  525
Sad pair unto the Elms they moan.
O why should such a Couple mourn,
That in so equal Flames do burn!


### LXVII

Then as I careless on the Bed
Of gelid *Straw-berryes* do tread,                   530
And through the Hazles thick espy
The hatching *Throstle's* shining Eye,
The *Heron* from the Ashes top,
The eldest of its young lets drop,
As if it Stork-like did pretend                      535
That *Tribute* to *its Lord* to send.

## LXVII

But most the *Hewel's* wonders are,
Who here has the *Holt-felsters* care.
He walks still upright from the Root,
Meas'ring the Timber with his Foot;                         540
And all the way, to keep it clean,
Doth from the Bark the Wood-moths glean.
He, with his Beak, examines well
Which fit to stand and which to fell.

## LXIX

The good he numbers up, and hacks;                          545
As if he mark'd them with the Ax.
But where he, tinkling with his Beak,
Does find the hollow Oak to speak,
That for his building he designs,
And through the tainted Side he mines.                      550
Who could have thought the *tallest Oak*
Should fall by such a *feeble Stroke*!

## LXX

Nor would it, had the Tree not fed
A *Traitor-worm*, within it bred.
(As first our *Flesh* corrupt within                        555
Tempts impotent and bashful *Sin*.)
And yet that *Worm* triumphs not long
But serves to feed the *Hewels young*.
While the Oake seems to fall content,
Viewing the Treason's Punishment.                           560

## LXXI

Thus I, *easie Philosopher*,
Among the *Birds* and *Trees* confer:
And little now to make me, wants
Or of the *Fowles*, or of the *Plants*.
Give me but Wings as they, and I                            565
Streight floting on the Air shall fly:
Or turn me but, and you shall see
I was but an inverted Tree.

### LXXII

Already I begin to call
In their most learn'd Original:                                    570
And where I Language want, my Signs
The Bird upon the Bough divines;
And more attentive there doth sit
Then if She were with Lime-twigs knit.
No Leaf does tremble in the Wind                                   575
Which I returning cannot find.

### LXXIII

Out of these scatter'd *Sibyls* Leaves
Strange *Prophecies* my Phancy weaves:
And in one History consumes,
Like *Mexique Paintings*, all the *Plumes*.                       580
What *Rome, Greece, Palestine*, ere said
I in this light *Mosaick* read.
Thrice happy he who, not mistook,
Hath read in *Natures mystick Book*.

### LXXIV

And see how Chance's better Wit                                   585
Could with a Mask my studies hit!
The Oak-Leaves me embroyder all,
Between which Caterpillars crawl:
And Ivy, with familar trails,
Me licks, and clasps, and curles, and hales.                      590
Under this *antick Cope* I move
Like some great *Prelate of the Grove*,

### LXXV

Then, languishing with ease, I toss
On Pallets swoln of Velvet Moss;
While the Wind, cooling through the Boughs,                        595
Flatters with Air my panting Brows.
Thanks for my Rest ye *Mossy Banks*,
And unto you *cool Zephyr's* Thanks,
Who, as my Hair, my Thoughts too shed,
And winnow from the Chaff my Head.                                600

LXXVI

How safe, methinks, and strong, behind
These Trees have I incamp'd my Mind;
Where Beauty, aiming at the Heart,
Bends in some Tree its useless Dart;
And where the World no certain Shot          605
Can make, or me it toucheth not.
But I on it securely play,
And gaul its Horsemen all the Day.

LXXVII

Bind me ye *Woodbines* in your twines,
Curle me about ye gadding *Vines*,          610
And Oh so close your Circles lace,
That I may never leave this Place:
But, lest your Fetters prove too weak,
Ere I your Silken Bondage break,
Do you, *O Brambles*, chain me too,          615
And courteous *Briars* nail me through.

LXXVIII

Here in the Morning tye my Chain,
Where the two Woods have made a Lane;
While, like a *Guard* on either side,
The Trees before their *Lord* divide;          620
This, like a long and equal Thread,
Betwixt two *Labyrinths* does lead.
But, where the Floods did lately drown,
There at the Ev'ning stake me down.

From the first and last stanzas we learn that there were two parallel
Appleton woods, with a long 'Lane' or 'ride' between, but that they
joined at the end. In LXXVIII the emphasis is on the lane, a
processional route for Lord Fairfax, with Trees posted at intervals,
like guardsmen, to right and to left. In LXII the emphasis is on the
junction. The 'Union' that 'locks' the two woods is an image of
wedlock; the long pedigrees of Fairfax and Vere, like the woods, run
parallel till united at last in the marriage of Thomas and Anne. 'In the
forest trees and the family trees there were many that had fallen in war

and many that were still living and aiming at Heaven.' The image is beautifully worked out.

Both woods in both stanzas are dense. In LXXVIII they are Cretan labyrinths, between which the narrow lane leads, like the thread that Ariadne gave Theseus to preserve him. In LXII the full-grown trees are 'Link'd in so thick'.

Stanzas LXIII and LXIV contrast the outside of the massed forest with the inside. A newcomer, reversing the proverb, cannot at first see the trees for the wood. Their nearness ('Neighbourhood') unifies them and makes them seem one 'huge Bulk'· stemming from one 'great Trunk'. This is the sort of fantastic 'vegetable' which in 'To his Coy Mistress' would in time grow 'vaster than Empires'. It seems here intent on vying with earth, air, fire and water to become a fifth element called 'tree'.

> And stretches still so closely wedg'd
> As if the Night within were hedg'd.

The caesuras come after 'still' (meaning 'always') and 'Night', each time at the halfway mark. The effect is antiphonal and balanced. Every foot is a perfect iambus.

The next stanza begins with a spondee, which modern pronunciation has somewhat spoilt.

> Dark all without it knits; within
> It opens passable and thin;

Ben Jonson's *English Grammar* told foreigners that the 'a' in 'all' 'obtaineth the full French sound, and is utter'd with the mouth and throat wide open'd, the tongue bent back from the teeth', as in 'balm' and 'calm'. So Marvell intended an assonantal spondee 'Dark arl'. That he was consciously manipulating sound is proved by the repeated short 'i' in six of the next seven syllables; five come in succession.

'Passable and thin' refers to the sparse undergrowth, the opposite of 'impassable and thick'. The next couplet refers to the spacing of the trees: the forest grows in 'loose order' or 'open order', the military phrase for 'arrangement at wide intervals', the opposite of 'close order'.

And in as loose an order grows,
As the *Corinthean Porticoes*.

The simile relates to Roman architecture, not Greek, and it only
points to the wide spacing of the Corinthian columns in the front of
Roman temples in general. The Greeks had used the Corinthian
order much less than the Doric and Ionic. They had known of the
arch, but hardly used it at all. The Romans, however, gloried in the
use of the arch and much preferred the Corinthian order. They built
their arches below the entablature, and spaced the columns wider
apart than the Greeks.

The arching Boughs unite between
The Columnes of the Temple green;

The eleven words are continuous and unbroken, a sequence designed
to suggest the inter-arched trees, a rare sequence in Marvell. The
temple metaphor has passed on from the '*Porticoes*'. We are now
inside this green temple listening to music:

And underneath   the winged Quires
Echo about   their tuned Fires.

The caesuras have come back. We must pause after 'underneath' and
'about' or the adverbs might seem prepositions. The bird-choirs
broadcast melodious love-songs ('Fires' being 'flames'). This was no
novel metaphor. The rapid progress of collegiate singing in
Elizabethan England had soon led her poets to compare birdsong in
forests to choristers 'in quires and places where they sing', as their
Prayer Book put it. Who could forget the fourth line in Shakespeare's
Sonnet 73?

That time of year thou mayst in me behold,
When yellow leaves, or none, or few, do hang
Upon those boughs that shake against the cold,
Bare ruin'd choirs where late the sweet birds sang.

That was autumn. This is spring and the birds are singing. They
occupy the next eight stanzas, the nightingale first. She is an artist, but
an empiricist; she chooses this place 'to sing the trials of her voice'.

> Low Shrubs she sits in, and adorns
> With Musick high the squatted Thorns.

The couplet is cunningly devised. The prose order 'in low Shrubs', 'with high Music', is re-arranged to form a chiasmus: adjective, noun, preposition ('Low Shrubs . . . in'); preposition, noun, adjective ('With Musick high'). 'Low' and 'high' will always seem antonyms, but they are not in fact antonyms here; the singer is low in relation to the ground and the song is *high* in importance and merit. Milton did much the same thing in the cathedral setting of 'Il Penseroso', lines 161−3:

> There let the pealing Organ blow,
> To the full-voic'd Quire below,
> In Service high, and Anthems cleer . . .

Marvell, however, goes on to use 'highest' in relation to the ground:

> But highest Oakes stoop down to hear,
> And listning Elders prick the Ear.

He is being doubly playful. Not only do the three trees adopt listening postures − the hawthorn 'squatted', the oaks 'stooping down', the elders like animals 'pricking the ear' − but there is a pun on 'Elders'; (1) trees; (2) persons of greater age. The hawthorn, as the bird's host, goes further and considerately retracts its thorns.

But in the daytime the nightingale solo has rivals and in stanza LXVI the poet prefers the stockdove duet, 'a Sadder, yet more pleasing Sound'. The mutual love of the stockdoves represents perfect marriage. On their beautiful necks they wear wedding rings, the insignia ('Ensigns') of marital chastity. They live in the elms. The poetical association of the dove with the elm dates back to Virgil's First Eclogue, line 58, '*nec gemere aeria cessabit turtur ab ulmo*' ('and the turtledove will not cease moaning from the high elm'). The same level cooing sound is in the line 'Sad pair unto the Elms they moan', and elsewhere in the stanza. But the moaning is inexplicable to human minds.

> O why should such a Couple mourn,
> That in so equal Flames do burn?

In LXVII Marvell travels from birds' song to birds' nests. To reach one in a hazel thicket, he 'treads careless on a bed of gelid strawberries'. He can afford to be careless, of course, about where he treads. In April the strawberry plants have not started to fruit; like the ground, they are 'gelid' (cold). But 'careless' is meant to convey his complete relaxation, without a care in the world. In the same spirit he will call himself 'easie Philosopher' soon; 'a naturalist at ease', that is.

The first half of this stanza has long been admired. The Wiltshire poet-parson William Lisle Bowles quoted it in his introduction to an edition of Pope in 1806. He went out of his way to praise Marvell for doing something that Pope could not.

> Sometimes Marvell observes little circumstances of rural nature with the eye and feeling of a true poet:
>
> > Then as I careless on a bed
> > Of gelid strawberries do tread,
> > And through the hazels thick espy
> > The hatching throstle's shining eye.
>
> The last circumstance is new, highly poetical, and could only have been described by one who was a real lover of nature, and a witness of her beauties in her most solitary retirement. It is the observation of such circumstances which can alone form an accurate descriptive rural poet. In this province of his art Pope therefore must evidently fail, as he could not describe what his physical infirmities prevented his observing.

A whole generation later this passage goaded Mark Pattison in Oxford to write: 'Familiarity with "the hatching throstle's shining eye" only proves that Bowles and Marvell had both been schoolboys and addicted to birdsnesting' (*Essays*, ed. H. Nettleship, 1889).

However, Bowles and Marvell had more in common than that, and the throstle couplet has continued to be a great favourite. Certainly it is well observed. But two other qualities also commend it. As musical sound, it repays close study; every 'th', for instance, seems a hazel obstruction – and 'th' comes five times. Then the awe of the naturalist-poet is transmitted to the reader; the motionless profile of the hen-thrush that ends in the one 'shining eye' seems so vivid that instinctively the trespasser on its mysteries draws back, whatever his age.

And yet those four lines are structurally quite incidental, a subordinate clause on the way to the main clause:

> The *Heron* from the Ashes top,
> The eldest of its young lets drop,

and those six lines of orthodox iambics are dramatically subordinate in turn to the star couplet, which is the last:

> As if it Stork-like did pretend
> That *Tribute* to *its Lord* to send.

Here the iambic rhythm is disrupted and a spondee in each line reinforces the wit: 'Stórk-líke' embodies the story that storks left one young bird behind in the rooftop nest as a leaving present to their host; '*Tríbúte*' turns the sacrificial offering into a manorial due. All these matters are 'wonders',

> But most the *Hewel's* wonders are,
> Who here has the *Holt-felsters* care.

This 'Hewel' or 'Hew-hole' is the green woodpecker and three stanzas are given to him. He is male and he does the woodcutter's work ('Holt-felsters care'). He is human, almost. He walks upright. He measures the timber in feet. He inspects every tree. He asks himself which is fit to stand and which fit to fell. He numbers the good. A bad one he fells. Thus far he is the complete holt-feller. Then for a moment in line 548 he becomes an ancient Greek who consults the oracle of Zeus in the grove of oaks at Dodona and 'finds the hollow oak to speak'. Then he changes his role and becomes a siege engineer. For with the word 'mines' in line 550 the image changes to the siege of a walled town. The sappers survey the walls to find a weak spot. There they dig a mine. They blow a hole in the wall and the besiegers pour through. The town falls. The woodpecker has taken all these steps. His success is a wonder of nature.

> Who could have thought the *tallest Oak*
> Should fall by such a *feeble Stroke*!
>
> Nor would it, had the Tree not fed
> A *Traitor-worm*, within it bred.

> (As first our *Flesh* corrupt within
> Tempts impotent and bashful *Sin*.)

The siege simile is thus extended and (parenthetically) deepened into Christian theology. As the fall of a town is hastened by treachery in the garrison, or one breach would not have been fatal, so the oak has to be 'tainted' with woodworm or the hewel would not attack it. And here lies a theological paradox, 'Flesh tempts Sin'. Our mortal flesh, corrupt since the Fall and so worm-eaten, 'tempts Sin', who without such encouragement would be too powerless and shy to seek an entrance. But the traitor-worms are executed and fed to the young and the oak is appeased and accepts its 'fall'.

It is in the light of this stanza chiefly that the poet says 'Thus' ('in these ways'):

> Thus I, *easie Philosopher*,
> Among the *Birds* and *Trees* confer:

He has advanced from the role of detached observer and become the intimate companion of the birds and the trees. He is only one short step away from becoming a bird or a tree, and the reader is wittily invited to complete his metamorphosis either way.

> Give me but Wings as they, and I
> Streight floting on the Air shall fly:
> Or turn me but, and you shall see
> I was but an inverted Tree.

This latter notion derived from Plato's *Timaeus*, 90A, where the philosopher visualised man as a heavenly plant whose roots were his head and whose branches were his arms and legs. 'Only stand me on my head', Marvell tells us, 'and you'll recognise that all this time I've been a frustrated, upside-down tree.'

Lines 569–76 register his accomplishments as a near-bird and lines 577–84 as a near-tree.

> Already I begin to call
> In their most learn'd Original:

The noun 'Original' means 'initial vocabulary' and harks back to the fifth day of Creation when God made the birds and saw that

everything was good. The initial vocabulary of bird-calls was either
(a) perfect, 'most learn'd', the truly erudite tongue, pure and
unadulterated by later accretions, or (b) that most often learnt.
Where his knowledge fails him, he makes 'signs' and is understood by
the bird on the bough, which pays him the most rapt attention, more
rapt than if she were glued there by lime. And as to the leaves:

> No Leaf does tremble in the Wind
> Which I returning cannot find.

Bird-like, among the high branches, he has learnt every individual
leaf. 'Not one trembles in the wind which I can't recognise next time I
come'. He 'comes' at tree-top level on wings.

For stanza LXXIII, however, he is back on the firm ground.

> Out of these scatter'd *Sibyls* Leaves
> Strange *Prophecies* my Phancy weaves:
> And in one History consumes,
> Like *Mexique Paintings*, all the *Plumes*.          580

'My Phancy' is 'my Imagination'. It plays with the leaves in a literate
way. The Cumaean Sibyl wrote her prophecies on dead leaves and
dropped them to the client below. That was one kind of 'scattering'.
These green leaves on the trees are 'scatter'd' in the sense that they
cover a wide area overhead; in the next couplet they make a 'light
Mosaick'. In imagination Marvell is a modern client of the Sibyl and
he pieces together her strange utterances inscribed on the under side of
high leaves. Like the bird, he 'divines'. He uses up ('consumes') all
their messages to form a single printed narrative ('one History'), in
the same way as Mexicans with scissors and paste made gorgeous
pictures with thousands of feathers in his own day.

The forest has become his library of books, just as Shakespeare's
Duke Senior found 'tongues in trees, books in the running brooks and
sermons in stones' in the Forest of Arden. Here he can read all the
wisdom of the western world's literature in these leaves.

> What *Rome, Greece, Palestine*, ere said
> Ĩ in this light *Mosaick* read.

In the tessellated canopy of spring leaves he does his reading; for
'read', though pronounced 'red' to rhyme with 'said', is as present in

tense as 'does lead', which in lines 621–2 rhymes with 'Thread'. He reads all the wisdom ever ('ere') uttered by the ancients in Latin, Greek and Hebrew, including the 'heavy Mosaick', those five books of Moses that formed the Pentateuch.

> Thrice happy he who, not mistook,
> Hath read in *Natures mystick Book.*

In that couplet the forest learning is perfectly summed up. This way lies true happiness. In the perfection of the couplet as pure sound, 'mistook' plays a noteworthy part. For though 'not mistook' means no more than 'unerringly', the two halves of 'mistook' anticipate the beginning and the end of its countervailing rhyme, *'mystick Book'*.

Nor does the academic metaphor end there. It opens the next stanza, LXXIV:

> And see how Chance's better Wit
> Could with a Mask my studies hit!

That is 'see how the superior intelligence of chance was able to provide me with a masquing-habit that matches my studies'. Chance dresses him without his stir, in a suitably haphazard way. Embroidery, which should come last, comes first; the oakleaves keep their caterpillars; the ivy, intimate and feminine and possessive, then mantles him and takes him in hand. The four verbs of line 590 carry the stresses and are vastly energetic, the labial 'l' being the highest common factor. She 'licks' him, and 'clasps' him, and 'curles' him, and 'hales' him. At the end he is ivy-mantled and dressed. What ivy does to a tree in a decade, she has done to him in a trice. So habited, he fancies himself processing up the nave like a sylvan archbishop in an antique prelatical cope:

> Under this *antick Cope* I move
> Like some great *Prelate of the Grove,*

'Move' is the first of five successive stressed syllables and between them they show him advancing grandly as he plays his hierarchical part. He had used 'Prelate great' in line 366 to describe the Archbishop of York. It retains its rank here.

The 1681 Folio ended stanza LXXIV with a comma which we

have retained, though it flouts the syntax. Stanza LXXV does follow
hard on its heels.

> Under this *antick Cope* I move
> Like some great *Prelate of the Grove*,
>
> Then, languishing with ease, I toss
> On Pallets swoln of Velvet Moss;
> While the Wind, cooling through the Boughs,       595
> Flatters with Air my panting Brows.

'Pallets swoln' are 'convex Beds'. They are plural because of their
forest profusion; 'tossing' moves him from this bed to that. 'Flatters' is
a strange verb. One takes it to mean 'gratifies'. Its advantage over
'flutters' lies in the sound. For not only does the short 'at' pair with the
short 'ant' of 'panting' in this line (though no brows, strictly speaking,
can pant), but it also leads on to the triple 'ank' of 'Thanks . . .
Banks . . . Thanks' in the next couplet:

> Thanks for my Rest ye *Mossy Banks*,
> And unto you *cool Zephyr's* Thanks,

in which we hear the voice of the gratified guest and are glad when he
goes on:

> Who, as my Hair, my Thoughts too shed,
> And winnow from the Chaff my Head.

The verb 'shed' means 'vigorously part'. His thoughts are a natural
mixture of light chaff and good grain. The 'winnowing' metaphor
seems to promise pure grain in the stanzas ahead.

This change comes at once. Stanza LXXVI links the wood to the
rest of the poem by reviving the Civil War metaphor. Of the inner
forest the poet has now made a fortress, a camp. Here his mind is
secure from beautiful women and affairs of the heart, secure also from
worldly ambition and toil. This stanza agrees well with the start of
'The Garden' and '*Hortus*'. But here he counter-attacks the world:

> But I on it securely play,
> And gaul its Horsemen all the Day.

'Play' means 'fire my weapons', and 'gaul' means 'vex, harass, annoy';
'gall' pronounced and spelt 'gaul' does not make an internal rhyme
with 'arl', as 'all' was pronounced.

Stanzas LXXVII and LXXVIII complete this section most sen-
suously and romantically. The time has come to leave the wood. The
poet knows he must go, but longs not to. In LXXVII he urges the
wood to keep him there by force for ever. In LXXVIII he does go,
but reluctantly. In his going, he twice more asks to be detained.

### LXXVII

Bind me ye *Woodbines* in your twines,
Curle me about ye gadding *Vines*,                        610
And Oh so close your Circles lace,
That I may never leave this Place:
But, lest your Fetters prove too weak,
Ere I your Silken Bondage break,
Do you, *O Brambles*, chain me too,                      615
And courteous *Briars* nail me through.

### LXXVIII

Here in the Morning tye my Chain,
Where the two Woods have made a Lane;
While, like a *Guard* on either side,
The Trees before their *Lord* divide;                    620
This, like a long and equal Thread,
Betwixt two *Labyrinths* does lead.
But, where the Floods did lately drown,
There at the Ev'ning stake me down.

In lines 609—10 the three rhymes 'bines, twines, Vines' are reinforced
with 'Bind'; the broken rhythm suggests the lax looping movement
involved in trussing him up. In lines 611—12 the loops are exquisitely
tightened. We sense this through the repeated long 'o' in the 'Óh só
clóse' and its breathless sibilants, which continue into 'Circles lace';
the verb, of course, is 'lace'. In lines 613—16 the consonant 'b' takes
over and the stanza ends as forcibly as it began.

As a stanza, though, it has suffered since William Empson
misinterpreted it so confidently in *Some Versions of Pastoral* (London,
1935, 1966). He spoke of 'an acceptance of Nature more masochist

than passive' and said that in it Marvell 'becomes Christ with both the
nails and the thorns'. Other critics have contentedly followed this
line. However, in his Oxford third edition (1971) notes Legouis has
rebelled. 'That the allusion to the crucifixion discovered here by
William Empson in 1932 [*sic*] should have become an article of faith
for a line of critics raises my astonishment. That Marvell should
disclose here masochistic tendencies I find no easier to believe: the
"Briars" are "courteous" and so is he' (p.290). This refutation was
needed.


## THE RIVER
### (AFTER THE FLOOD)

### LXXIX

For now the Waves are fal'n and dry'd,                    625
And now the Meadows fresher dy'd;
Whose Grass, with moister colour dasht,
Seems as green Silks but newly washt.
No *Serpent* new nor *Crocodile*
Remains behind our little *Nile*;                    630
Unless it self you will mistake,
Among these Meads the only Snake.

### LXXX

See in what wanton harmless folds
It ev'ry where the Meadow holds;
And its yet muddy back doth lick,                    635
Till as a *Chrystal Mirrour* slick;
Where all things gaze themselves, and doubt
If they be in it or without.
And for his shade which therein shines,
*Narcissus* like, the *Sun* too pines.                    640

### LXXXI

Oh what a Pleasure 'tis to hedge
My Temples here with heavy sedge;
Abandoning my lazy Side,
Stretcht as a Bank unto the Tide;

Or to suspend my sliding Foot     645
On th'Osiers undermined Root,
And in its Branches tough to hang,
While at my Lines the Fishes twang!

## LXXXII

But now away my Hooks, my Quills,
And Angles, idle Utensils.     650
The *young Maria* walks to night:
Hide trifling Youth thy Pleasures slight.
'Twere shame that such judicious Eyes
Should with such Toyes a Man surprize;
*She* that already is the *Law*     655
Of all her *Sex*, her *Ages Aw*.

## LXXXIII

See how loose Nature, in respect
To her, it self doth recollect;
And every thing so whisht and fine,
Starts forth with to its *Bonne Mine*.     660
The *Sun* himself, of *Her* aware,
Seems to descend with greater Care;
And lest *She* see him go to Bed,
In blushing Clouds conceales his Head.

## LXXXIV

So when the Shadows laid asleep     665
From underneath these Banks do creep,
And on the River as it flows
With *Eben Shuts* begin to close;
The modest *Halcyon* comes in sight,
Flying betwixt the Day and Night;     670
And such an horror calm and dumb,
*Admiring Nature* does benum.

## LXXXV

The viscous Air, wheres'ere She fly,
Follows and sucks her Azure dy;
The gellying Stream compacts below,     675

If it might fix her shadow so;
The stupid Fishes hang, as plain
As *Flies* in *Chrystal* overt'ane,
And Men the silent *Scene* assist,
Charm'd with the *Saphir-winged Mist*.                680


## MARY FAIRFAX

### LXXXVI

*Maria* such, and so doth hush
The *World*, and through the *Ev'ning* rush.
No new-born *Comet* such a Train
Draws through the Skie, nor Star new-slain.
For streight those giddy Rockets fail,                685
Which from the putrid Earth exhale,
But by her *Flames*, in *Heaven* try'd,
*Nature* is wholly *vitrifi'd*.


### LXXXVII

'Tis *She* that to these Gardens gave
That wondrous Beauty which they have;                690
*She* streightness on the Woods bestows;
To *Her* the Meadow sweetness owes;
Nothing could make the River be
So Chrystal-pure but only *She*;
*She* yet more Pure, Sweet, Streight, and Fair,        695
Then Gardens, Woods, Meads, Rivers are.


### LXXXVIII

Therefore what first *She* on them spent,
They gratefully again present.
The Meadow Carpets where to tread;
The Garden Flow'rs to Crown *Her* Head;                700
And for a Glass the limpid Brook,
Where *She* may all *her* Beautyes look;
But, since *She* would not have them seen,
The Wood about *her* draws a Skreen.

## LXXXIX

For *She*, to higher Beauties rais'd,                    705
Disdains to be for lesser prais'd.
*She* counts her Beauty to converse
In all the Languages as *hers*;
Nor yet in those *her self* imployes
But for the *Wisdome*, not the *Noyse*;         710
Nor yet that *Wisdome* would affect,
But as 'tis *Heavens Dialect*.

## XC

*Blest Nymph*! that couldst so soon prevent
Those *Trains* by Youth against thee meant;
Tears (watry Shot that pierce the Mind;)          715
And *Sighs* (Loves Cannon charg'd with Wind;)
*True Praise* (That breaks through all defence;)
And *feign'd complying Innocence*;
But knowing where this *Ambush* lay,
She scap'd the safe, but roughest Way.            720

## XCI

This 'tis to have been from the first
In a *Domestick Heaven* nurst,
Under the *Discipline* severe
Of *Fairfax*, and the starry *Vere*;
Where not one object can come nigh               725
But pure, and spotless as the Eye;
And *Goodness* doth it self intail
On *Females*, if there want a *Male*.

## XCII

Go now fond Sex that on your Face
Do all your useless Study place,                      730
Nor once at Vice your Brows dare knit
Lest the smooth Forehead wrinkled sit:
Yet your own Face shall at you grin,
Thorough the Black-bag of your Skin;
When *knowledge* only could have fill'd       735
And *Virtue* all those *Furrows* till'd.

### XCIII

Hence *She* with Graces more divine
Supplies beyond her *Sex* the *Line*;
And, like a *sprig of Misleto*,
On the *Fairfacian Oak* does grow;                    740
Whence, for some universal good,
The *Priest* shall cut the sacred Bud;
While her *glad Parents* most rejoice,
And make their *Destiny* their *Choice*.

### XCIV

Mean time ye Fields, Springs, Bushes, Flow'rs,         745
Where yet She leads her studious Hours,
(Till Fate her worthily translates,
And find a *Fairfax* for our *Thwaites*)
Employ the means you have by Her,
And in your kind your selves preferr;                  750
That, as all *Virgins* She preceds,
So you all *Woods, Streams, Gardens, Meads*.

### XCV

For you *Thessalian Tempe's Seat*
Shall now be scorn'd as obsolete;
*Aranjuez*, as less, disdain'd;                        755
The *Bel-Retiro* as constrain'd;
But name not the *Idalian Grove*,
For 'twas the Seat of wanton Love;
Much less the Dead's *Elysian Fields*,
Yet nor to them your Beauty yields.                    760

### XCVI

'Tis not, what once it was, the *World*;
But a rude heap together hurl'd;
All negligently overthrown,
Gulfes, Deserts, Precipices, Stone.
Your lesser *World* contains the same.                 765
But in more decent Order tame;
*You Heaven's Center, Nature's Lap,*
*And Paradice's Only Map.*

In lines 629–30 Marvell turns to good account the belief that in ancient Egypt crocodiles and serpents were bred direct from Nile mud. Thus in *Antony and Cleopatra*, II, vii, drunken Lepidus, who has never been to Egypt, tells Enobarbus, just back from there: 'Your serpent of Egypt is bred now of your mud by the operation of your sun; so is your crocodile.' Marvell may have had Shakespeare in mind. And when he likens the Wharfe to a snake in line 632, he may be influenced by Ben Jonson's 'Painted meads Through which a serpent river leads' in the epode *To Sir Robert Wroth*, lines 17–18.

He is his own master, however, when he develops the snake–river image in lines 633–6:

> See in what wanton harmless folds
> It ev'ry where the Meadow holds;
> And its yet muddy back doth lick,                    635
> Till as a *Chrystal Mirrour* slick;

'Slick' was the old form of 'sleek'. 'Its back' is the snake–river's own back. The folds are 'wanton' because they suggest a male amorous embrace; they are 'harmless folds' for that very reason – a snake's folds are the constrictor's normal means of attack. When the river is clean and transparent again, it mirrors everything near and it mirrors the overhead sun. In line 639 'shade' means 'shadow', but in the sense of 'reflected image'. Narcissus pined for his shade in the water; he mistook it for another mortal. The sun here does the same.

> And for his shade which therein shines,
> *Narcissus* like, the *Sun* too pines.

Beside this clear river in lines 641–4 the poet lies on one hip doing nothing, aware of the sedge's weight on his head, 'Stretcht as a Bank unto the Tide;' for the river was tidal at Appleton. Or in lines 645–8 he fishes from willow branches over deep water, using two or more rods at once. The verb 'twang' is facetious, but intelligible; the fishes that take the bait jerk his lines straight with a resonant twang. The exclamation mark that follows completes the sentence which began 'Oh what a Pleasure 'tis to hedge'. The 'sliding Foot' phrase in line 645 figures also in line 49 of 'The Garden' and is one of several factors common to both poems and suggesting a common date. Here the exposed root of the willow ('Osier') literally arrests his 'sliding Foot' and perhaps gives him a step up into the tree.

But fishing is an idle sport, he goes on. Hooks, floats ('Quills'), rods and lines ('Angles') are but 'Toyes'. Mary Fairfax must not find her young tutor so frivolously employed. Stanza LXXXII serves to close the gap between their ages. In actual fact he was thirty-one in the spring of 1652 and she not quite fourteen. For the moment he makes himself a boyish man and he makes her already an accepted model for her sex and time:

> *She* that already is the *Law*
> Of all her *Sex*, her *Ages Aw*.

In stanza LXXXIII, as Mrs Duncan-Jones has said, Marvell takes hints from Milton's 'Nativity Ode'. There 'wanton Nature' had prepared herself for the December-night birth of Jesus: 'Nature *in aw to him* Had doff't her gawdy trim' (32−3); 'It was no season then for her To *wanton* with the Sun her lusty Paramour' (35−6); 'The Windes with wonder *whist*, Smoothly the waters kist' (64−5); 'So when the *Sun in bed* Curtain'd *with cloudy red*, Pillows his chin upon an Orient wave' (229−31). Here 'loose Nature' prepares herself for young Maria's walk, 'in respect to her'; and 'whisht' here is only another form of 'whist', meaning 'hushed', while the sun goes 'to Bed' behind 'blushing Clouds'.

The French '*Bonne Mine*' (pleasant look) in line 660 is a nice Marvellian touch and comes well from the French tutor's mouth; '*Bonne*' is disyllabic as in French. 'Eben Shuts' in line 668 are English 'Black ebony shutters', an indoor image.

The lovely halcyon simile in lines 665−80 looks forward and back. In the matter of modest behaviour it looks back to the setting sun; 'So' in line 665 means 'with the same modesty as the Sun'. In the matter of breathtaking, magical beauty and speed it looks forward to Mary Fairfax; '*Maria* such, and so doth hush /The *World*, and through the *Ev'ning* rush' means 'Mary is like the halcyon and in the same way hushes the world etc.' The simile bridges 'The River' phase and the phase which promotes Mary Fairfax, two very different themes.

In the simile the bird is at once the English river-bank kingfisher, whose blue plumage and runaway speed had often awed Marvell, and the classical Greek marine halcyon which, according to myth, bred only in a floating sea-nest at the time of the winter solstice, when it charmed wind and wave to an absolute stillness. He had already combined the two birds in 'The Gallery' seascape, lines 35−6:

> The Halcyons, calming all that's nigh,
> Betwixt the Air and Water fly.

It flies 'betwixt the Day and Night' here, the modest bird of twilight, avoiding the world and making no noise.

> And such an horror calm and dumb,
> *Admiring Nature* does benum.

Marvell used '*horror*' in Latin to mean 'religious awe'. In '*Hortus*', lines 18–19, he explained what Nature meant to him: '*me Penetralia veris, Horroresque trahunt muti, et Consortia sola*' ('What attract me are the sanctuaries of Spring, and dumb veneration, and solitary communion'). He uses 'horror' in English here of the kingfisher herself, because she inspires a religious awe. She shocks 'admiring Nature' to a numbness. This was not mere hyperbole. It expressed what Marvell actually felt, just as his account of solitary communion in 'The Wood', that sanctuary of Spring, was perfectly genuine. We can see that it was this natural reverence, this childlike capacity for awe, which, coupled with a sharp eye and long memory, made him the true nature poet that he was.

Stanza LXXXV maintains this high standard. The 'azure dye' of the flying bird impregnates the glutinous ('viscous') air in its slipstream and the resulting impression is a 'Saphir-winged Mist'. All else that was moving becomes static. The river ceases to flow; it compacts to a jelly in hopes of retaining the bird's shadow. The stupefied ('stupid') fish cease to swim; the eye sees them hanging, like flies caught in glass when molten. What men there are there (and they include Marvell) stand enchanted and dumb.

An unusual feature of this stanza is that fewer than half the syllables are monosyllabic words. The rhetorical effect is achieved, not just by order and balance, but by the many disyllabic adjectives: '*viscous* Air', '*Azure* dy', '*gellying* Stream', '*stupid* Fishes', '*silent* Scene', '*Saphir-winged* Mist'.

It is a short step from the 'Saphir-winged Mist' to the next stanza's 'new-born Comet' and its balancing 'Star new-slain', which introduce Mary Fairfax. All now is courtly flattery and ingenious hyperbole. The kingfisher may benumb Nature,

> But by her *Flames*, in *Heaven* try'd,
> *Nature* is wholly *vitrifi'd*.

Either (a) Nature is melted into the same liquid that cooled into the incorruptible crystalline sphere which at the Creation suspended the fixed stars; or (b) her flames have the heat that makes glass, and she has the same effect on Nature.

In stanza LXXXVII Marvell starts to finish his poem. He gathers up his four outdoor strands in due order: gardens, woods, meadows, river. Back in lines 79–80 they were:

> . . . fragrant Gardens, shady Woods,
> Deep Meadows, and transparent Floods.

Their virtues are all ascribed now to young Mary:

> 'Tis *She* that to these Gardens gave
> That wondrous Beauty which they have;                690
> *She* streightness on the Woods bestows;
> To *Her* the Meadow sweetness owes;
> Nothing could make the River be
> So Chrystal-pure but only *She*;
> *She* yet more Pure, Sweet, Streight, and Fair,      695
> Then Gardens, Woods, Meads, Rivers are.

Once again 'are' is to be pronounced 'air'. Once again the poet arranges a perfect chiasmus. The nouns in line 696 are in the order of the rest of the stanza, but the adjectives in line 695 are exactly reversed.

The order is changed in LXXXVIII. The meadow gives Mary carpets; the garden gives her flowers for her head; the limpid brook gives her a looking-glass; the wood screens her all round. She is her own age here. And he in LXXXIX is his. As her tutor, he holds out the highest ideals in language study. Beauty is as beauty does. Her beauty is to speak beautiful Italian and French, to care for wise thought even more than for sound, and to cultivate wisdom as the language of heaven. What better way to lead her along those lines than by praising her for following them?

Stanzas XC and XCI praise her and her parents on more mundane grounds. She is praised for being alive to the dangers of young men and avoiding them. They are praised for bringing her up pure and good, the two Puritan ideals. Obviously Lady Fairfax had most to do with this. She is the 'starry Vere' of line 724; the Vere arms had a gold star (*estoile or*) in the first quarter of the shield.

Mary was the only surviving child. A second daughter died in infancy and there was no son. Lines 727–8 make the best of this disappointment; the girl has grown up in a 'Domestick Heaven', where

> . . . Goodness doth it self intail
> On *Females*, if there want a *Male*.

'Goodness bequeathes itself inalienably to daughters, if there is no son.' It stays in a good family. Mary can never part from goodness, any more than she can sell an entailed estate.

Stanza XCII satirises the generality of foolish ('fond') females, who are not pure and not good. They study only their faces in mirrors and never read printed books; they keep their varnished foreheads smooth and unwrinkled by never frowning at vice. On this cosmetic point James Winny, in *Andrew Marvell* (Hutchinson, 1962), p.143, nicely quotes Lady Wishfort in Congreve's *The Way of the World* (1700): 'Your ladyship has frown'd a little too rashly, indeed madam. There are some cracks discernible in the white varnish.' But the penalty, Marvell warns them, will one day have to be paid:

> Yet your own Face shall at you grin,
> Thorough the Black-bag of your Skin.

The 'Black-bag' was literally the woman's black mask worn at masquerades. Here it is metaphorically the ravaged face after years of heavy making-up. The horrible reflection in the mirror will register a hideous smile; a sad end, when a lifetime of knowledge and virtue could have kept the face wholesome, as will happen with Mary Fairfax.

Stanza XCIII looks ahead to her marriage. She with her knowledge and virtue assures the continuity of her lineage or line, more than women are normally asked to ('beyond her Sex'). Her parents' destiny depends on what husband they choose. The 'Priest' in line 742 is more Latin than English. The new Presbyterian England had abandoned the word, but the grove of Diana Nemorensis outside ancient Rome was served by a priest who had qualified for office by plucking the golden mistletoe bough. Even so whoever officiates at Mary's marriage will separate her from the main Fairfax oak, a mistletoe 'sprig' because young, a mistletoe '*Bud*'. In the event, what did she do? She married George Villiers, Duke of Buckingham, in

1657, aged nineteen, after her banns had been called twice in London for a marriage to the Earl of Chesterfield and she had defied everyone and rejected the match.

Stanza XCIV deals with the 'mean time' before she is 'translated' (transferred) to her future husband's home; before Fate 'find a *Fairfax* for our *Thwaites*'. The parenthetical lines 747—8 are structurally important. The word 'Fate' was last used in line 84 when Marvell embarked on relating 'The Progress of this House's Fate'. At great length in lines 85—280 he told the Thwaites—Fairfax story and this he is at pains to recall as he nears the end of his poem and seeks to assert the unity of the whole. Mary now is the key heiress, not the Isabel Thwaites of 1518, and she (it is hoped) will find a husband like William Fairfax.

That functional parenthesis apart, lines 737—68 gather together the Nun Appleton spots most personal to Mary and exalt them to a new pitch of perfection and in them re-centre the world. The three stanzas are designed as the rhetorical climax of the poem.

The sequence in line 752, '*Woods, Streams, Gardens, Meads*', deliberately reverses the sequence in stanza LXXXVIII, '*Meadow*', '*Garden*', '*Brook*', '*Wood*'. In line 745 however, the order is varied in the corresponding sub-species, 'Fields, Springs, Bushes, Flow'rs'. The metaphor is courtly. The parts that she patronises in 'her studious Hours', the places where she reads her books out of doors, are told to exploit her patronage and use it to rise to the top of their own *genus* or kind. They are to take the same steps by which men climb at court through the favour of the great. Now the grounds of Appleton House shall be world famous and the old world favourites neglected and scorned. The Vale of Tempe, the classical Greek beauty spot below Mount Olympus, shall now be dismissed as a thing of the past. The Aranjuez Gardens, laid out by the Tagus for Philip the Second of Spain, shall be reckoned contemptibly small and Buen Retiro, the Spanish royal seat near 'Madril', contemptibly artificial ('constrain'd'). Nor are the Appleton grounds matched in beauty by the Idalian Grove of Venus in Cyprus or the Elysian Fields of the Dead. But they must not be mentioned — the first was too lewd and the second too unlucky!

Stanza XCVI follows straight on. 'The World is not what once it was'. But what does that mean?

> 'Tis not, what once it was, the *World*;
> But a rude heap together hurl'd;

> All negligently overthrown,
> Gulfes, Deserts, Precipices, Stone.
> Your lesser *World* contains the same,    765
> But in a more decent Order tame;

Three explanations of the first couplet have been advanced. H. E. Toliver takes 'But' in line 762 as an adverb meaning 'only' and in *Marvell's Ironic Vision* (Yale University Press, 1965), p.129, notes: 'This stanza means, I think, that the world is now changed for the better (no longer being "but" a rude heap) through incorporation in Mary's world which is better still.' In 1726 Cooke must have thought much the same, for he printed:

> 'Tis not, as once appear'd, the World,
> A Heap confus'd together hurl'd; . . .

What authority he had for this, one cannot say. He was only aged twenty-two, an ex-pupil of Hugh Hutchin at Felsted but not a university man. The 1681 Folio text was reinstated in 1776 by Thompson, having already (unknown to Thompson) been hand-written into T2. Every editor has kept to it since. And in it the line 762 'But' is far better taken as a conjunction.

The second explanation is that of Margoliouth in the three Oxford editions: 'the world is no longer the world; since you created a new standard, it becomes by comparison a rude heap'. This fits the two previous stanzas, but it waters down line 761: 'The World is no longer *what it once was*.' That must take us back to the past and, once started, where do we stop? In the beginning God created the world and God saw that it was all good. What spoilt it was man's sin. Already in lines 321−8 Marvell has referred to the Fall. Addressing the island of Britain as 'Thou Paradise of four Seas', he has asked her, in reference to the Civil Wars:

> What luckless Apple did we tast
> To make us Mortal, and Thee Wast?

One therefore prefers the third explanation, that 'The World is not *what it was before the Fall*'. God made it out of chaos and sinful man has 'negligently overthrown' it and turned it back towards chaos. Frank Kermode noted this in his Signet Classic *Marvell* (1967), p.141: ' 'Tis . . . world: referring to the disorder of a fallen world, to be compared with the order and balance of the microcosm, or little world, of Mary Fairfax, which reflects the state of the world before paradise was lost.' This adds what Margoliouth missed. But the microcosm is the little world of Appleton House and has been since line 752. It now receives the crowning encomium:

> *You Heaven's Center, Nature's Lap,*
> *And Paradice's only Map.*

This is the only couplet of Marvell's that is italicised throughout. If that was indicated in his MS., obviously he meant it to be his grand climax, sonorous and slow.

It is not, however, the end of the poem. He wanted to end on the note on which he began, a quiet note of intimate wit. His beginning must be in his end. It took him one stanza to do this.


## THE EPILOGUE

### XCVII

> But now the *Salmon-fishers* moist
> Their *Leathern Boats* begin to hoist;                    770
> And, like *Antipodes* in Shoes,
> Have shod their *Heads* in their *Canoos.*
> How *Tortoise like*, but not so slow,
> These rational *Amphibii* go!
> Let's in: for the dark *Hemisphere*                        775
> Does now like one of them appear.

The fishers turn their leather coracles over and hoist them on to their heads. So hatted, they put Marvell in mind of the Cambridge song 'Square Cap', a favourite when Fairfax and he were at Trinity together. In verse 3 the leather-capped lawyer defended his faculty's headgear:

> The Antipodes wear their shoes on their heads,
> And why may not we in their imitation?

The Antipodes were *people* on the other side of the world before they were *places*. In 1398 John Trevisa wrote: 'Yond in Ethiopia ben the

Antipodes, men that have theyr feet against our feet.' The author of
'Square Cap', John Cleveland, saw them differently; they walked
upside down on the under side of the globe and so their heads needed
shoeing! Marvell's wit, taking over from Cleveland, races forward
with characteristic resource. The fishermen, coracle-roofed, bring
back the tortoises of lines 13 – 14.

> The low-roof'd Tortoises do dwell
> In cases fit of Tortoise-shell.

The Tortoise is an amphibian without a brain and moves slowly, but

> How *Tortoise like*, but not so slow,
> These rational *Amphibii* go!

And finally, wanting the descent of darkness to drive himself and his
reader indoors and so end his poem, he came by the brilliant idea of
likening the dome of the dark sky above him to the coracle on the
fisherman's head;

> Let's in: for the dark *Hemisphere*
> Does now like one of them appear.

No poet knew better than Marvell how to end a stanza or a poem.


# 28   'Musicks Empire'


This poem was first printed in the 1681 Folio. In 1716 it was one of
nine reprinted by Tonson in *Miscellany Poems*. In 1726 it reappeared
in Thomas Cooke's edition of Marvell.

It is a rhetorical poem, with undertones of drama. It may have been
composed against time. Some say that it was written for Cromwell,
but this is not a view which I share. Others say it was written for
Fairfax. New evidence below will strengthen their case.

### I

First was the World as one great Cymbal made,
Where Jarring Windes to infant Nature plaid.
All Musick was a solitary sound,
To hollow Rocks and murm'ring Fountains bound.

### II

*Jubal* first made the wilder Notes agree;                    5
And *Jubal* tun'd Musick's first Jubilee:
He call'd the *Ecchoes* from their sullen Cell,
And built the Organs City where they dwell.

### III

Each sought a consort in that lovely place;
And Virgin Trebles wed the manly Base.                    10
From whence the Progeny of numbers new
Into harmonious Colonies withdrew.

### IV

Some to the Lute, some to the Viol went,
And others chose the Cornet eloquent.
These practising the Wind, and those the Wire,            15
To sing Mens Triumphs, or in Heavens quire.

### V

Then Musick, the Mosaique of the Air,
Did of all these a solemn noise prepare:
With which She gain'd the Empire of the Ear,
Including all between the Earth and Sphear.                20

### VI

Victorious sounds! yet here your Homage do
Unto a gentler Conqueror then you;
Who though He flies the Musick of his praise,
Would with you Heavens Hallelujahs raise.

In the first twenty lines Marvell traces the development of musical sounds against a background of developing civilisation. He identifies five phases.

When the world began, winds made discords by clashing on the flat circle of earth. Music was confined to hollow rocks and murmuring streams, but the sounds were unconnected. This was Nature's phase. Man made no contribution (lines 1—4).

In the second phase, however, Man took over from Nature. Leaders of men drew followers into communal living and the city was born. In the same way Jubal, the Hebrew father of music, brought notes together and made them agree; with unison melodies he celebrated the first Hebrew festival of music, helped by his invention of the organ. He also attracted the hitherto unsociable echoes and they came to live with the organ notes (lines 5—8).

The third phase was one of consolidation. Organ tunes multiplied and the range of their notes was extended, in the same way that the population grows in a city (lines 9—10).

The fourth phase was the vigorous one. As an overcrowded city results in the more enterprising of the younger citizens seeking fresh outlets and establishing colonies overseas, so the musical notes and echoes migrated and colonised new instruments; stringed viols and woodwind. Harmony was the result. Voices joined in. This new music acclaimed men's triumphs on earth and God's merits in heaven (lines 11—16).

Then came the fifth phase, the climax. As colonies end by combining with the mother-country in an empire, so all the instruments and their notes were combined under music herself into one great orchestral symphony of sound, in the same way that tesserae are combined in a tessellated mosaic. With the transcendently harmonious, polyphonal sound, music gained the empire of the ear and included in her subjects all living beings above the earth and under the canopy of heaven (lines 17—20).

Thus the 'Music's Empire' of the title came about and there Music in 1652 reigned, still in mid-air. But now in the last stanza, lines 21—4, the victorious sounds of the air are told that they owe homage on Earth 'here' (*videlicet* at Appleton House) to General Fairfax, an even gentler conqueror. 'He is a modest man, who is embarrassed by praise' (the main theme of music). This point had been made by Marvell before. In 'Upon the Hill and Grove at Bill-borow', lines 75—8, he had silenced the trees of the grove, when they were praising Fairfax:

> But Peace, (if you his favour prize)          75
> That Courage its own Praises flies.
> Therefore to your obscurer Seats
> From his own Brightness he retreats.

On the other hand, Fairfax was a religious man, ever ready to praise God, and 'Musicks Empire' ends on this note. 'With you (the musical sounds which rule the air) he wishes to raise Hallelujahs in Heaven.' Hallelujah is Hebrew for 'Praise the Lord'.

There should be no doubt that the final lines do refer to Fairfax, though the only proof adduced so far has been the parallel just cited; all editors, from Margoliouth in 1927 onwards, have noted it. But a second proof, and this is new, involves Davenant's *Gondibert*. This was published in 1651 while Marvell was at Appleton House. He read it there or he could not have quoted it in lines 455–6 of 'Upon Appleton House'.

> Such, in the painted World, appear'd
> *Davenant* with th' Universal Heard.

Davenant had begun his stanza 60 of Book II, Canto vi, with the line: 'Then strait an universal Herd appears.' He was describing a wall-painting of the Creation in the Temple of Astragon.

Twenty stanzas later, however, Davenant described another picture near by, of an assembly singing to an orchestral accompaniment.

> 80
>
> Yet Musick here, shew'd all her Art's high worth:
>     Whilst Virgin-Trebles seem'd, with bashfull grace,
> To call the bolder marry'd Tenor forth:
>     Whose Manly Voyce challeng'd the Giant Base.

> 81
>
> To these the swift soft Instruments reply;
>     Whisp'ring for help to those whom winds inspire;
> Whose lowder Notes, to Neighb'ring Forrests flie,
>     And summon Nature's Voluntary Quire.

Since Marvell had read this, we can see where the 'Virgin Trebles' and 'manly Base' in his stanza III came from, though he put them to a different use.

It is also a fact that Davenant had a weakness for the word 'sullen'; in prose and in verse he used it a dozen times in the *Gondibert* quarto, always in the sense of 'morose and unsociable'. Marvell's 'sullen Cell' in line 7 means just that sort of rustic dwelling.

Finally, there is the obvious point that 'Musicks Empire' used a stanza form unique in Marvell and differing only from what Davenant described as 'my interwoven stanza of four' in the re-arranged unwoven couplets.

The presence of equivocations and puns is one indication that *Musicks Empire* was written to be declaimed and not sung. 'Jubal' and 'Jubilee' in line 6 are akin to 'Musick' and 'Mosaic' in line 17; the French spelling 'Mosaique' makes no difference to the sound. 'Sought' and 'consort' in line 9 make a third pair and 'consort' is also a pun, meaning (1) 'spouse' and (2) 'musical ensemble'. The other pun is on 'numbers' in line 11; the word means (1) 'groups of notes' and (2) 'digits'.

The most difficult line is the sixteenth. Editors with one accord have taken 'Heavens quire' to be 'choir of Heaven', and indeed 'choir' can be only a noun. Such a sense unbalances a line that has five syllables each side of the caesura, and the result is most un-Marvellian. As a noun 'quire' should have begun with a capital, like the 'Nature's Quire' of Davenant above. But the Tudors and Stuarts used 'quire' as a verb meaning 'sing'. In *The Merchant of Venice*, V, i, in Lorenzo's great speech on music, Shakespeare wrote:

> There's not the smallest orb that thou behold'st
> But in his motion like an angel sings,
> Still quiring to the young-eyed Cherubins.

I therefore take 'quire' to be a verb here and I amplify the line thus: 'To sing Men's Triumphs (on earth), or in Heaven's (Triumphs) (to) quire'. The resulting chiasmus is as Marvellian as the resulting balance. One should add that this balanced thought is echoed in lines 23–4 by the musick of the conquering general's praise on Earth and the Hallelujahs in Heaven.

Milton's *Comus* (1634) ended with the Song in which the Earl and Countess of Bridgewater in Ludlow Castle had their children presented to them, as they sat on their thrones in the audience. It is possible that 'Musicks Empire' was declaimed in the great hall of Appleton House on a musical occasion, and addressed at the end to the General. It has a theatrical ring.

# 29 'A Dialogue between Thyrsis and Dorinda' (the later version)

This revised version of the pre-1643 pastoral, with a re-written second half, was set to music by John Gamble and printed in his *Ayres and Dialogues for one, two and three voices* in 1659. It was printed as a poem in its own right in 1663, when it was one of several 'Ingenious Poems' included in an enlarged reprint of Samuel Rowland's 1609 book, *A Crew of Kind London Gossips*. That 1663 version coincides with the Cambridge University Library's Additional MS. 79, ff.19 and 19b, which is dated 1653. In our chronological order we have therefore placed 'the later version' at the beginning of that year. Perhaps it should be earlier.

The pastoral was set to music again by Matthew Locke (1630–77) and his setting was printed in 1675 in the elder John Playford's *Choice Ayres, Songs and Dialogues*. None of these publications in Marvell's lifetime vouchsafed the name of the author.

The text printed here is that of all three editions (1927, 1952, 1971) of Margoliouth's *Poems and Letters of Andrew Marvell*, save for two verbal changes specified below.

| | |
|---|---|
| *Dorinda*: | When Death, shall snatch us from these Kids, |
| | And shut up our divided Lids, |
| | Tell me *Thyrsis*, prethee do, |
| | Whither thou and I must go. |
| *Thyrsis*: | To the Elizium: |
| *Dorinda*: |                Oh, where is't? 5 |
| *Thyrsis*: | A Chast Soul, can never mis't. |
| *Dorinda*: | I know no way, but one, our home; |
| | Is our cell Elizium? |
| *Thyrsis*: | Cast thine Eye to yonder Skie, |

|            | There the milky way doth lye;           | 10 |
|            | 'Tis a sure but rugged way,             |    |
|            | That leads to Everlasting day.          |    |
| *Dorinda*: | There Birds may nest, but how can I,    |    |
|            | That have no wings and cannot fly?      |    |
| *Thyrsis*: | Do not sigh (fair Nimph) for fire       | 15 |
|            | Hath no wings, yet doth aspire          |    |
|            | Till it hit, against the pole,          |    |
|            | Heaven's the Center of the Soul.        |    |
| *Dorinda*: | But in Elizium how do they              |    |
|            | Pass Eternity away?                     | 20 |
| *Thyrsis*: | Oh, ther's, neither hope nor fear       |    |
|            | Ther's no Wolf, no Fox, nor Bear.       |    |
|            | No need of Dog to fetch our stray,      |    |
|            | Our Lightfoot we may give away;         |    |
|            | No Oat-pipe's needfull, there thine Ears| 25 |
|            | May feast with Musick of the Spheres.   |    |
| *Dorinda*: | Oh sweet! Oh sweet! How I my future state|   |
|            | By silent thinking, Antidate:           |    |
|            | I prethee let us spend our time to come |    |
|            | In talking of *Elizium*.                | 30 |
| *Thyrsis*: | Then I'le go on: There, sheep are full  |    |
|            | Of sweetest grass, and softest wooll;   |    |
|            | There, birds sing Consorts, garlands grow,|  |
|            | Cool winds do whisper, springs do flow. |    |
|            | There, alwayes is, a rising Sun,        | 35 |
|            | And day is ever, but begun.             |    |
|            | Shepheards there, bear equal sway,      |    |
|            | And every Nimph's a Queen of *May*.     |    |
| *Dorinda*: | Ah me, ah me.                           |    |
| *Thyrsis*: |             *Dorinda*, why do'st Cry?    |    |
| *Dorinda*: | I'm sick, I'm sick, and fain would dye: | 40 |
|            | Convince me now, that this is true;     |    |
|            | By bidding, with mee, all adieu.        |    |
| *Thyrsis*: | I cannot live, without thee, I          |    |
|            | Will for thee, much more with thee dye. |    |
| *Chorus*:  | Then let us give *Carillo* charge o'th Sheep,| 45 |
|            | And thou and I'le pick poppies and them steep|  |
|            | In wine, and drink on't even till we weep,|  |
|            | So shall we smoothly pass away in sleep. |   |

In the text above I have differed from Margoliouth and Legouis in retaining the 1681 Folio's 'snatch' in line 1 and 'Cast' in line 9; since Lawes and the 1681 Folio are agreed on these readings, I prefer them to 'part' and to 'Turn'.

The early version in Lawes was lively and simple. Dorinda asked innocent questions and Thyrsis gave indulgent replies. As dialogue it lacked any drama. The ball went forward and back eight times in thirty-four lines. The metre varied between trochaic heptasyllabics and iambic octosyllabics without any system except that they ended up fairly equal, sixteen to eighteen.

This later version has forty-eight lines. The ball goes forward and back fifteen times, which is better. Both characters are more sophisticated here. Dorinda displays feminine guile. The earlier ending had implied a faint death-wish on the part of Thyrsis:

> Why then should we here make delay, .
> Since we may bee as free as they?

Now Dorinda in line 40 sheds copious tears as she sings:

> I'm sick, I'm sick, and fain would dye.

She and Thyrsis affirm their preparedness to go together to 'Elizium' and a Chorus devises death by drinking an opiate in wine. The metre turns into decasyllabics and the last four lines share the same rhyme.

All the changes add wit, and musically the new version better accords with the new growth of opera. It must be a gain for the reader to find both versions printed in the same book.


# 30    'The Picture of little T.C. in a Prospect of Flowers'


Critics, for the most part, are silent on what they take 'The Picture' in the title to be, but three ladies have spoken out. At Cambridge M. C. Bradbrook and M. G. Lloyd Thomas in *Andrew Marvell* (Cambridge University Press, 1940) took it to be a painting in a frame. They noted on p.52 that the poem 'On the Portrait of Two Beautiful Young People' by Gerard Manley Hopkins was 'based on a similar theme; it too was inspired by a picture'. At Oxford, however, Helen Gardner did not agree. In her introduction to *The Metaphysical Poets* (Penguin, 1957), p.22, she wrote: 'This lovely poem would seem to have arisen from thoughts suggested by the name and family history of a friend's child. Whether Marvell actually caught sight of her in a garden we have no means of knowing.'

Miss Gardner was using the poem to illustrate what she termed 'the quintessence or soul' of a metaphysical poem — 'the vivid imagining of a moment of experience'. Many metaphysical poems 'postulate an occasion', she said. 'Marvell calls us to look at little T. C. in her garden.'

No critic has yet disagreed with the conclusion of H. M. Margoliouth in the *Modern Language Review* for October 1922 that 'little T.C.' was Theophila Cornewall, the girl baby born in September 1644 to Mrs Theophila Cornewall (née Skinner) at Thornton Curtis, Lincolnshire. This was the home of Theophila Skinner's mother, Mrs Bridget Skinner (née Coke). The family were old friends of the poet's father, the first Andrew Marvell of Hull, and it was in crossing the Humber from their home that he was drowned in January 1641 (see p.5). The poet in turn was a close friend of Cyriack Skinner (big T.C.'s brother, little Γ.C.'s uncle), a disciple and friend of John Milton and the most obvious Milton — Marvell introductory link.

Readers of the poem naturally form an impression of the age of the child. If Margoliouth was correct, they are thereby dating the poem, of course. Bradbrook and Lloyd Thomas suggest (op. cit., p.51n.) that it 'could be reasonably dated when Theophila was about eight or ten years old, i.e. 1652−54'. But in truth they had no right to that reasoning at all. It allowed no time for the painting of their 'picture', or for the months or years before Marvell happened to see the picture.

The likelihood is that this *was* little Theophila, that Marvell *did* see her with his own eyes in the garden, that she was seven or eight at the time, and that the poem was started not later than the spring of 1653.

It consists of five intricate stanzas.

I

See with what simplicity
This Nimph begins her golden daies!
In the green Grass she loves to lie,

And there with her fair Aspect tames
The Wilder flow'rs, and gives them names:                    5
But only with the Roses playes;
    And them does tell
What Colour best becomes them, and what Smell.

## II

Who can foretel for what high cause
This Darling of the Gods was born!                    10
Yet this is She whose chaster Laws
The wanton Love shall one day fear,
And, under her command severe,
See his Bow broke and Ensigns torn.
    Happy, who can                    15
Appease this virtuous Enemy of Man!

The stanza form is unique, so far as is known. Marvell seems to have carved it out of his favourite eight-line, eight-syllable iambic block; he then proceeded to show that what could be done once could be done five times.

The only irregularity is in the first line, which has seven syllables. Probably the long initial 'See' is treated as a whole foot. 'Simplicity' ends with a stressed syllable rhyming with 'lie', an option often exercised by Marvell. The meaning of 'simplicity' is 'innocence'. In 'The Garden' the sister of 'Quiet' was 'Innocence', whereas in the Latin '*Hortus*' she was 'Simplicitas'.

Though separated by many imagined years, the opening stanzas present a consistent character sketch. In stanza I the innocent little girl plays at mothering her large family of flowers; she names the wilder ones and schools them with a look, but she imparts to the favoured roses her own exquisite taste in dress and perfume. According to legend it was Eve, the mother of mankind, who named the flowers in the Garden of Eden. In stanza II, whatever God's inscrutable plans for her future life's work, she is a young woman whose exceptional virtue defeats and disarms Cupid and so ushers in a new age of chastity. In both generations she dominates her world. The child is mother to the matron.

'Darling of the Gods' in line 10 was a phrase first coined by Thomas Carew and used by him twice. He called King James I 'this Darling of the Gods and men' in his poem 'Upon the King's Sickness' (1625), line 37. And in his court masque *Coelum Britannicum* (1633), line

1034, the Chorus began their third song with this reference to 'a troope of young Lords and Noblemens sonnes' following behind:

> Whil'st thus the darlings of the Gods
> From Honour's Temple, to the Shrine
> Of Beauty, and these sweet abodes
> Of Love, we guide, . . .

If 'little T.C.' was Theophila, then Marvell was wittily resurrecting Carew's pet phrase, for 'darling' is the diminutive of 'dear' and Theophila is Greek for 'girl dear to God'.

Stanzas II and III, unlike the rest, use the last two lines to add a new thought. In lines 15–16 it is: 'Happy will that man be who succeeds in placating this chaste foe-to-all-males'. This links with the opening of III, where 'then' means 'in that case' and 'in time' means 'before it is too late'.

### III

> O then let me in time compound,
> And parly with those conquering Eyes;
> Ere they have try'd their force to wound,
> Ere, with their glancing wheels, they drive          20
> In Triumph over Hearts that strive,
> And them that yield but more despise.
>         Let me be laid,
> Where I may see thy Glories from some shade.

To 'compound' was to 'come to terms' and that meant 'capitulate' here. In line 19 'try'd their force' means 'tested their power' and 'wound' is a full rhyme to compound'. The diphthong 'ou' could be pronounced 'oo' or 'ow'. So in stanza V 'flow'rs' and 'Yours' will rhyme.

The image of the chariot wheels in lines 20–1 has a parallel in Marvell's Latin poem to Fairfax, '*Epigramma in Duos montes Amosclivum Et Bilboreum*', lines 17–18:

> Dumque triumphanti terras perlabitur Axe,
> Praeteriens aequa stringit utrumque Rota.

('While Fairfax glides over his land in triumphing chariot, in passing he glances the side of each mountain with level wheel.') There the wheel-hubs deal Mt Almscliff and Mt Bilbrough the sort of glancing blow that a classical charioteer dealt the side of the metal 'goal' as he expertly rounded it in a chariot-race. Here the actual wheels glance *over* the prostrate victims. But there is a second meaning here too. For the eyes, in a doll at any rate, are joined like wheels by an axis and women's eyes vanquish susceptible men with a glance. 'Glancing' is a pun.

In line 22 'but' means 'only'. Theophila will lay low those men who dare to fight her, but she will only despise all the more the tame ones that yield. By the time she has perfected that power, the poet, either as a condition of 'compounding' or in the ordinary course of nature (being twenty-three years her senior), will be dead. He therefore makes a last will and testament in lines 23−4:

> Let me be laid
> Where I may see thy Glories from some shade.

For, however reluctant E. M. W. Tillyard and other critics may have been to see a funeral association in these lines, there is no mistaking the verbal affinity with Feste's song in Shakespeare's *Twelfth Night* (II, iv):

> Come away, come away, Death,
> And in sad Cypress let me be laid;

That was how it began. And it ended with the same verb:

> Lay me, O where
> Sad true lover never find my grave
> To weep there.

Marvell's wit here will not let him invoke such pathos as that. But he is talking of death all the same; and a refusal to accept this must damage the poem as a work of art, for he will end it with talk of *her* death and that would be artistically tasteless, had he not already made light of his own.

Stanza IV deals with the interval between now and then.

### IV

> Mean time, whilst every verdant thing          25
> It self does at thy Beauty charm,

Reform the errours of the Spring;
Make that the Tulips may have share
Of sweetness, seeing they are fair;
And Roses of their thorns disarm:                    30
      But most procure
That Violets may a longer Age endure.

Theophila was cast as a born reformer in stanzas I and II. To go on to
reform the tulips and roses and violets (all scanned with two syllables)
would be wholly in character. It is an innocent garden activity that
can occupy her until she is old enough for suitors to arrive on the
scene.

It is a successful stanza, but highly artificial in syntax. The reflexive
in 'every verdant thing/*It self* does at thy Beauty charm' is French
idiom, not English. Its meaning is passive; 'everything is spell-bound
by her beauty'. Similarly the imperatives 'make' and 'procure' are
followed by Latin, not English, constructions — literal translations of
*ut* and the present subjunctive after *fac* and *cura*. And in line 31 'most',
a superlative adverb, while English enough, would be a good deal less
ambiguous in Latin as *maxime*.

The first word in the poem was 'See' and it is surely no accident that
there has been a 'see' in each subsequent stanza, and there is one again
in this last. The chief appeal is to our sense of sight. The girl looked a
picture.

## V

But O young beauty of the Woods,
Whom Nature courts with fruits and flow'rs,
Gather the Flow'rs, but spare the Buds;                3735
Lest *Flora* angry at thy crime,
To kill her Infants in their prime,
Do quickly make th'Example Yours;
      And, ere we see,
Nip in the blossome all our hopes and Thee.          40

Here Marvell enlarges the scope of the original 'picture' in a prospect
of spring flowers. 'Fruits' come later in the year. 'Woods' are an
extension of the scene. He enlarges the scope to make room for the
thought that the little girl risks reprisals from Flora if she picks 'Buds'
and prevents them from coming into flower; Flora will freeze the
child's 'blossome' by way of reprisal and prevent her from maturing

into 'fruit'. The buds too are 'Infants' of a sort. Infanticide breeds infanticide.

In Roman religion Flora was the goddess of fertility and flowers and the protectress of blossom. In Rome the *Ludi Florales* were an annual spring festival from 173 B.C. onwards and lasted from 28 April to 3 May.

In line 37 'prime' means 'first hour' or 'first beginning' and the 'infants' may owe something to Shakespeare's *Hamlet* (I, iii):

> The canker galls the infants of the Spring,
> Too oft before their buttons be disclosed.

In lines 39–40 the sense is: 'Lest (Flora), before we see our hopes (come to fruition), nip them all in the blossom and (nip) thee'.

It is a fact that the Theophila Cornewall, born in September 1644, had been preceded by a sister named Theophila who was born in August 1643 and only lived for two days. But Marvell was out of England then and did not return till 1647. Since the whole object of giving the next girl baby a dead sister's name was to efface a sad memory and fill the gap, it is doubtful if Marvell knew of this. He would not perhaps have playfully threatened this 'little T.C.' with death had he really known. For there is no satire in this poem; only delicate beauty and grace.

# 31   'Bermudas'

In July 1653 Marvell and his Eton College pupil joined the Oxenbridges in their house at New Windsor. As it happened, John Oxenbridge had just been put on the London Commission for the government of the Bermudas. He was well qualified, having served for two tours as a minister on the main island between 1635 and 1641. Towards the end of the second, Jane Butler had sailed out from England to marry him; she was under twenty and delicate, but abundantly brave. Now they had four children and she was beginning to suffer from dropsy.

It seems certain that Marvell wrote 'Bermudas' under the Oxenbridge roof and that their Puritan holiness and cheerfulness inspired him and fired him. The Latin epitaph that he wrote in 1658 for Jane's monument in Eton College Chapel shows how much he admired her. Some details of the poem have literary sources, but nobody's *book* gave him the tone or the spirit.

In construction his 'Bermudas' resembles his 'Eyes and Tears', only this time the octosyllabic quatrains are merged in one column. We will separate them in this chapter. The first is a prelude engagingly simple and graphic.

> Where the remote *Bermudas* ride
> In th'Oceans bosome unespy'd,
> From a small Boat, that row'd along,
> The listning Winds receiv'd this Song.

The first two lines are fluent; the next two come in two equal halves. The islands 'ride' like vessels at anchor. The Ocean is a recumbent woman. Human winds give ear to the song. The stage is peopled before any actors come in.

The two quatrains which follow deal with the emigrants' hazardous voyage from England to Bermuda and their welcome arrival; not in this 'small Boat', of course, but an ocean-going sailing-ship. The tenses are a deliberate mixture of past and present. The little company has been long enough on the island to praise God for the life there. They sing as they row 'along' parallel to the shore.

> What should we do but sing his Praise            5
> That led us through the watry Maze,
> Unto an Isle so long unknown,
> And yet far kinder than our own?

> Where he the huge Sea-Monsters wracks,
> That lift the Deep upon their Backs,            10
> He lands us on a grassy Stage;
> Safe from the Storms, and Prelat's rage.

The 1681 Folio printed a full stop after 'Backs', but the second quatrain is one sentence. As in the '*Magnificat*', God's mercy is expressed in terms of contrast. He wrecks the huge whales, but lands the men safely. 'He hath put down the mighty from their seat and hath exalted the humble and meek'. He saves the emigrants from 'the rage of Archbishop Laud', the Prelate who had put John Oxenbridge out of his Magdalen Hall fellowship, and from 'the rage of the Tempest'. For though 'Storms' has no apostrophe and 'Prelat's' has, it is quite possible that we are to read it as *Storms'* or *Storm's*. In Marvell's Latin epitaph on Jane Oxenbridge he says that she followed her John to Bermuda and 'shrank neither from the vast sea nor the terrifying storms' ('*tempestates horridas*'). She would have described the voyage in detail to the poet.

Marvell's poem follows the lines of a metrical psalm. In verse 26 of Psalm 104 we hear of the whale: 'There go the ships, and there is that Leviathan, whom thou hast made to take his pastime therein.' Thomas Carew in 1640 had versified this as:

> There the huge Whales with finny feet
> Dance underneath the Saileing fleete.

Marvell's whales likewise are plural and 'huge', and they display the same sportiveness when they 'lift the deep upon their backs', but they also demonstrate their fearful power.

The wrecking of two whales in the Bermudas was the theme of Waller's little mock-epic, 'The Battle of the Summer Islands' (1645), in which the Bermudans fought two stranded whales. The first canto was headed:

> What fruits they have, and how Heaven smiles
> Upon those late-discovered isles.

Marvell had certainly read it before coming to Eton. He borrowed Waller's phrase 'grove of pikes' in III, 54, when he wrote 'Upon the Hill and Grove at Bill-borow', lines 67–8, for Lord Fairfax:

> Through Groves of Pikes he thunder'd then,
> And Mountains rais'd of dying Men.

The name 'Bermudas' had been given to the islands by Juan Bermudez, who discovered them in 1515. They came back into the news when Sir George Summers was wrecked there in 1609 and gave them their second name, 'The Summer Islands'. But Shakespeare called them 'the still-vexed Bermoothes' in *The Tempest* in 1613. The next three quatrains leave the sea and, perhaps following Waller, paint a picture of beauty and plenty on land, thanks to God's goodness. God only appears as a pronoun; yet the result is majestic.

'He' is the subject of such vigorous verbs, and the repetition of the pronoun tells in the end.

> He gave us this eternal Spring,
> Which here enamells every thing;
> And sends the Fowls to us in care, 15
> On daily Visits through the Air.
>
> He hangs in shades the Orange bright,
> Like golden Lamps in a green Night.
> And does in the Pomgranates close,
> Jewels more rich than *Ormus* shows. 20
>
> He makes the Figs our mouths to meet;
> And throws the Melons at our feet.
> But Apples plants of such a price,
> No Tree could ever bear them twice.

Waller wrote in I, 40–3, of 'the kind spring which Inhabits there and courts them all the year', but he went on: 'Ripe fruits and blossoms on the same trees live.' Marvell's 'eternal Spring' repeats the ripe fruits of the paradisal autumn in 'The Garden'. All is ripeness in 'Bermudas'.

The whales and the fowls of the air occupy successive verses (23, 24) in the canticle '*Benedicite*': 'O ye Whales, and all that move in the Waters, bless ye the Lord'; 'O all ye Fowls of the Air, bless ye the Lord'. Marvell follows the same order, but his 'Fowls sent by God in care (for men) On daily Visits through the Air' recall the ravens feeding Elijah by the brook Cherith in I Kings, XVII 4, 6. God said: 'Thou shalt drink of the brook, and I have commanded the ravens to feed thee there . . .' 'And the ravens brought him bread and flesh in the morning, and bread and flesh in the evening; and he drank of the brook.' Elijah did not eat the ravens, and the fowls sent by God here were surely not partridges to be killed (as Kermode suggests), but carriers that came and went daily. They signalise God's Providence at work, giving the pilgrims each day their daily bread.

A passage of great beauty follows. It is a picture of abundant fruits ripe for the picking: oranges, pomegranates, figs, melons, apples. They grow within easy reach, a feast for the eye in their various colours and shapes.

The 'Orange' couplet is masterly, in or out of its context. It creates a night scene in broad daylight, a scene of dense orange groves, green and glowing. The disyllabic 'Orange' is to be taken as plural, of course.

The 'Pomgranates' couplet runs parallel. It is true that most people take the 'Jewels' to be the red pips inside the pomegranates, with 'close' meaning 'inclose' or 'enclose'. I do not. Nothing else in the poem has to be opened before it can be seen. I take 'Jewels' to be in apposition to 'Pomgranates', whose size as they hang on the trees makes them so rich. He 'does in-close the Pomgranates', the trees and the fruit. With 'in' before 'the Pomgranates' and 'close' after them, they are all the more firmly 'inclosed'. Such manipulations of the word order more naturally occurred to a poet accustomed to write strict Latin verse than modern readers can imagine.

'Ormus', the modern Hormuz on the Persian Gulf, was a byword for wealth. Satan's throne in Milton's *Paradise Lost*, II, 1−2, was 'of Royal State, which far outshone the wealth of Ormus or of Ind'.

The 'Apples' in line 23 have grown into a problem. Grosart in 1872 thought them 'Pineapples'. Margoliouth in 1927 followed suit. I maintain that the 'Apples' are apples, for the reasons that follow.

First, no 'tree' ever bore pineapples once, let alone twice. The fruit had its name from its likeness outside to a pine-cone, but it grows close to the ground. Second, when Waller brought the pineapple into 'The Battle of the Summer Islands', Canto I, 34, he called it a 'pine', not an 'apple'.

> With candied plantains, and the juicy pine,
> On choicest melons, and sweet grapes, they dine.

And Waller was Marvell's exemplar. Third, the 'But' that begins line 23 contrasts apples with figs and melons. God 'throws' the melons at the colonists' feet as an act of largesse with carefree and lordly abandon, 'but' He carefully 'plants' the apples. It was different in Waller's Canto I, 20, with figs: they grew wild. 'Figs there unplanted through the fields do grow.' Marvell is therefore contrasting well-planted apple orchards with the stray profusion of melons and figs. In so doing, he classes the apples with the pomegranates and oranges as a third well-husbanded tree fruit. All three grew in orchards of their own.

His poetic hyperbole mounts in degrees of comparison: good, better, best; rich, richer, richest. The ripe fruit on the orange trees are 'Like golden Lamps'; the ripe pomegranates on their trees seem 'Jewels' unequalled in value in Ormus; the ripe apples on their trees are so exceedingly precious that 'no Tree *could ever* bear them twice' — no tree would be able to, ever.

The most precious apples in Greek mythology were the golden apples in the garden of the Hesperides; Heracles had to carry them off as his Eleventh Labour. This garden is named in the catalogue in Waller's Canto I, 4–12, which Marvell has to some extent copied:

> Bermudas, walled with rocks, who does not know?
> That happy island where huge lemons grow,
> And orange trees, which golden fruit do bear,
> The Hesperian garden boasts of none so fair;
> Where shining pearl, coral, and many a pound,
> On the rich shore, of ambergris is found.
> The lofty cedar, which to heaven aspires,
> The prince of Trees! is fuel for their fires.

In Marvell's next quatrain he too juxtaposes ambergris and cedar, but reverses the order. It suits him to finish first with the land and then return shorewards.

> With Cedars, chosen by his hand,                    25
> From *Lebanon*, he stores the Land.
> And makes the hollow Seas, that roar,
> Proclaime the Ambergris on shoar.

Psalm 104, verse 16, has the cedars: 'The trees of the Lord also are full of sap: even the cedars of Lebanon which he hath planted.' Carew versified it thus:

> On Lebanon his Cedars stand,
> Trees full of sapp, works of his hand.

The metaphor in lines 27–8 is of a London herald of arms or a local town-crier. As he with hollow mouth roars out his proclamation, so the roar of the seas tells the islanders that there is ambergris on shore for the having. The sea 'proclaims' this at God's bidding: the sea is God's mouthpiece. Ambergris had a high market value as perfume.

The last two quatrains of Marvell's psalm are emphatically Puritan:

> He cast (of which we rather boast)
> The Gospels Pearl upon our Coast.                    30

And in these Rocks for us did frame
A Temple, where to sound his Name.

Oh let our Voice his Praise exalt,
Till it arrive at Heavens Vault:
Which thence (perhaps) rebounding, may          35
Eccho beyond the *Mexique Bay*.

The 'Pearl' metaphor completes the line of thought begun in the gold of the oranges and jewels of the pomegranates, and inestimable price of the apples; the Puritans valued their Bibles more than anything else. A natural arena of rocks was all that they wanted in the way of a church. Their 'Song' in the boat ends *fortissimo*; whatever the tune, they are singing it for the eighth and last time, like any other metrical psalm.

The final quatrain shows how their uniform rowing helped their unison song:

Thus sung they, in the *English* boat,
An holy and a chearful Note,
And all the way, to guide their Chime,
With falling Oars they kept the time.          40

For the downward beat of a conductor's baton they substituted the downward drop of their synchronised oars. The rhyme would assist the process, but it is noticeable that an unusual number of the caesuras in this poem halve the line exactly; this helps to keep the iambic rhythm well marked.

Line 39 copies 'Upon Appleton House', line 541, 'And all the way, to keep it clean,' when the woodpecker was scouring the bark of the tree for woodmoths. There were very few months between the composition of the two poems, unless I am greatly mistaken.

Dramatically, Marvell was right to keep 'Bermudas' in his one column, for the tone of the song never changes and there is no interval of time anywhere; not even after the prologue or before the epilogue. But, musically, it must be heard and read as a series of quatrains.

# 32  'The Coronet'

This is the most self-revealing of Marvell's religious poems and bears the probable stamp of the Oxenbridge years, 1653–54. Though rightly printed continuously in the 1681 Folio and since, it begins with two matching octaves, and it ends with a slow section of ten matching lines. We will call these A, B and C.

### A

When for the Thorns with which I long, too long,
    With many a piercing wound,
    My Saviours head have crown'd,
I seek with Garlands to redress that Wrong:
    Through every Garden, every Mead,                    5
I gather flow'rs (my fruits are only flow'rs)
    Dismantling all the fragrant Towers
That once adorn'd my Shepherdesses head.

The language of lines 1–3 recalls Christ's crucifixion. The unworthy poet has added new crowns of thorns to His tortured head. The three stressed adverbs 'long, too long' convey intense woe and regret. With the 'flowers', however, allegory steps in. The 'flowers' are the phrases and words, the rhymes and allusions and inventions, that go to the making of a poem. In that sense his achievements, his 'fruits', are 'only flowers'.

His 'Shepherdess' in line 8 represents the heroines of pre-Appleton love poems, whose composition he is now regretting. There was Clora in 'The Gallery', for instance; his favourite picture of her was as a 'Shepherdess',

        Transplanting Flow'rs from the green Hill,
        To crown her Head, and Bosome fill.

Her hair in fact hung loosely, but equally she might have stuck flowers in the 'Tower' or high head-dress that came into and went out of fashion more than once in Marvell's lifetime. He uses it here in opposition to the coronet or garland that he means to weave now for the head of Christ, to 're-dress' it and so make 'redress' for the wrong.

From now on he will write sacred poems, not secular. This one is his first attempt, and the preliminary need was to gather every sort of material. This he has done. He has picked 'garden flowers' and 'wild flowers' for miles around and he has unpicked his old love poems.

'And now' in the second octave an ironic situation develops:

B

And now when I have summ'd up all my store,
    Thinking (so I my self deceive)        10
    So rich a Chaplet thence to weave
As never yet the king of Glory wore:
    Alas I find the Serpent old
    That, twining in his speckled breast,
    About the flow'rs disguis'd does fold,        15
    With wreaths of Fame and Interest.

The irony lies in the fact that, having repented of the old secular love-lyrics and put his hands to a sacred poem, he is conscious of being even further from grace. Why does he want to write the best sacred poem ever written and with it crown Christ? He wants to because, being worldly, he seeks 'Fame and Interest': 'Fame' among men as a poet; 'Interest' with patrons in hope of worldly advancement. And these are the Devil's temptations, taxing him in every line that he writes.

'The Serpent old' in line 13 is a reminiscence of Revelation, XII 7—9: 'And there was war in heaven: Michael and his angels fought against the dragon; and the dragon fought and his angels . . . And the great dragon was cast out, that old serpent, called the Devil, and Satan, which deceiveth the whole world.' This was the basis in *The Faerie Queene*, I, xi, of the Red Cross Knight's battle with the Dragon, which Spenser headed: 'The Knight with that old Dragon fights Two days incessantly'.

And it was from stanza 15 of this battle that Marvell took 'his speckled breast'; from the lines where the old Dragon assailed the Knight:

    So dreadfully he towards him did pass,
    Forelifting up aloft his speckled breast,
    And often bounding on the bruised grass.

His 'king of Glory' Marvell took from Psalm 24, where it comes five times in the verses that end: 'Who is the King of glory? Even the Lord of hosts, he is the King of glory.'

In line 13 'Alas' reinforces the penitential tone of the poem. In line 14 'twining in' needs a hyphen, for it adds up to a transitive verb; it is the same with 'receiving in' which comes in 'On a Drop of Dew', line 30, 'So receiving in the day'. Marvell's adverbs are sometimes placed in prepositional order if that helps the rhythm.

When I wrote that A and B 'matched', it was with the syntax in mind. Each section is one sentence. Each begins 'when', and each 'when' clause takes four lines. In each section the main clause comes next, and after it a relative clause starting 'That'.

Taking the sixteen lines together, one can see that the serpent was insinuating itself from the outset, in the pliant and surreptitious progression of movement. Eleven words separate 'have crown'd' from the subject 'I'. Nineteen words come between 'When' and 'seek'. The parentheses in lines 6 and 10 are self-contained sentences, interrupting the flow as well as providing a rhyme. The rhyming pattern itself is devious. The first three quatrains are uniform; the fourth changes, and it is all change after that. On the other hand, the unpatterned use of decasyllabic, octosyllabic and hexasyllabic lines settles down to four successive octosyllabics in lines 13–16 and ten disciplined decasyllabics in C, which slow the pace down. To the inducements of 'Fame and Interest', the Devil adds 'mortal Glory' in line 18.

## C

Ah, foolish Man, that would'st debase with them,
And mortal Glory, Heavens Diadem!
But thou who only could'st the Serpent tame,
Either his slipp'ry knots at once untie,                          20
And disintangle all his winding Snare:
Or shatter too with him my curious frame:
And let these wither, so that he may die,
Though set with Skill and chosen out with Care.
That they, while Thou on both their Spoils dost tread,    25
May crown thy Feet, that could not crown thy Head.

The first couplet, strikingly emphatic, has moments where the kneeling Christian in Marvell's day would knock the breast in self-abasement. The verb is second person singular, not first. It is as though the damning words were being put into the reader's own mouth in judgement.

The six lines that follow resemble the sestet of a sonnet. The poet beseeches Christ, who tamed the serpent in Genesis III, either to rid the coronet of the serpent, or shatter both in order that the serpent may die. With His all-powerful hands Christ is to deal with the poet's handiwork; to untie the serpent's knots; to unwind his total length, shaped into a circular snare by the coronet's wired pattern; to shatter the coronet.

The verb 'shatter' began as a Middle English form of 'scatter', and Milton had already used it in 'Lycidas', line 5, to similar effect:

> Yet once more, O ye Laurels, and once more,
> Ye Myrtles brown, with Ivy never-sear,
> I com to pluck your Berries harsh and crude,
> And with forc'd fingers rude
> Shatter your leaves before the mellowing year.

As for 'my curious frame', that is 'my own intricate body' and it is also 'my coronet', 'my wreath', 'my Chaplet', 'my Garland', meaning 'my completed poem'; allegory and all. Sir Philip Sidney had used 'curious frame' in Sonnet 28 of *Astrophel and Stella* as a term of disdain for elaborate allegory, and Marvell was applying it to his allegory here. 'Curious' meant 'painstakingly elaborate' (Latin *curiosus*), and line 24 embroiders that notion; 'Though set with Skill and chosen out with Care' refers to the poet's selection and arrangement of the abundant material, the 'flowers' and 'store' of lines 5—9.

Christ's '*Feet*' do not enter in until we arrive at the closing couplet. But before we consider that, we must deal with a disagreement over the syntax. Leishman was sure that 'they' in line 25 referred only to the flowers, while allowing that 'both their Spoils' meant flowers and serpent. He held that Marvell had mismanaged his syntax and in *The Art of Marvell's Poetry* (Hutchinson, 1966), p.196, half-diffidently, he proposed this amendment:

> And let them wither, so that he may die,
> These flow'rs, though set with Skill and cull'd with Care,
> That they, while Thou on him and them dost tread,
> May crown thy Feet, that could not crown thy Head.

It must, however, be wiser to put one's trust in the poet and, where there is no clear misprint, to make the best of his syntax. In line 25 no wedge should be driven in between 'they' and 'their': 'they' also are coronet and serpent; 'they' include 'these' and 'he' in line 23, 'frame' and 'him' in line 22. The syntax works perfectly well.

One is a little surprised by the word 'their' in 'both their Spoils'. Would not the withered flowers and the lifeless serpent be Christ's spoils, 'His' spoils? But Tudors and Stuarts in their generations would have said No. Witness Luke, XI 21–2, in the Authorised Version (incorporating Tyndale): 'When a strong man armed keepeth his palace, his goods are in peace. But when a stronger than he shall come upon him, and overcome him, he taketh from him all his armour wherein he trusted, and divideth his spoils.' The spoils and the armour and the dead body were regarded as belonging to the vanquished, though at the victor's disposal.

Marvell was adept at holding back some novelty to brighten his ending. Christ's feet now tread on the shattered coronet and the intertwined serpent in triumph. So in Romans, XVI 20, St Paul assured his brethren: 'And the God of peace shall tread Satan under your feet.' That is the proper place for the serpent condemned to go on its belly all its days. And for the broken and contrite poet it is sufficient reward that, regardless of 'Fame and Interest' and 'mortal Glory', this allegorical coronet should so crown Christ's feet; flowers, serpent and all.

Once more Marvell has ended a poem where he began. In devising a poem called 'The Coronet', his instinctive artistry made him describe a full circle.

# 33 'On a Drop of Dew' (and '*Ros*' translated)

Though printed like its Latin partner in a monolithic column, this elaborate lyric has five distinct parts. A and B develop the title and are eight and ten lines long. C and D, eight and ten lines long likewise, parallel the career of the dewdrop with that of the human soul. E has only four lines: two on the descent of a drop of manna, two on its ascent and the dewdrop's ascent as well. Manna was, after all, a kind of dew.

The Latin poem '*Ros*' (dew) makes the same journey, but in less symmetrical stages of eight, fourteen, ten, ten and four lines. Its metre is the elegiac couplet.

Since this is the only poem that Marvell wrote completely in English and Latin, we have translated the Latin below. And since there is no means of proving that he wrote either of them first, we have alternated the order of precedence. That has the advantage of keeping the eighteen lines on the dewdrop together, and the eighteen lines on the soul together as well.

## A

You see how a small pearl of eastern dew descends and slants into the roses, a rose-red breast having been its own source. The blooms stand, backward-leaning in anxious supplication, and strive to entice it with their petals. But the dewdrop, intent on the lofty outlines of its native sphere, has no eyes for the garish portals of its new hostelry. Enclosed in the bright orb of its coil, it copies the waters of heaven's orb as much as it can.

> See how the Orient Dew,
> Shed from the Bosom of the Morn
>    Into the blowing Roses,
> Yet careless of its Mansion new,
> For the clear Region where 'twas born,      5
>    Round in its self incloses:
>    And in its little Globes Extent,
> Frames as it can its native Element.

## B

> How it the purple flow'r does slight,
>    Scarce touching where it lyes,      10
>   But gazing back upon the Skies,
>    Shines with a mournful Light;
>     Like its own Tear,
> Because so long divided from the Sphear.
>    Restless it roules and unsecure,      15

Trembling lest it grow impure:
Till the warm Sun pitty it's Pain,
And to the Skies exhale it back again.

Lo, how it scorns the less well-bred, over-scented, crimson rose and with chaste foot barely dents the soft bed, but with prolonged gazes looks up at the faraway sky and hangs on it lovingly with mournful light, sad at heart. Changed by its grief into liquid grief, it wilts like a tear shed on rosy cheeks. How scared it is! How it trembles with every movement of its bed, quite unable to rest! Every time a gentle breeze stirs the air, it takes flight. As dread assails an untried girl walking home without an escort at night, so the dewdrop is panicked into wild commotion, out of maidenly modesty fearing all; till such time as with merciful ray the sun turn the wanderer to vapour and draw it back up into his fertilising radiance.

In the poem's line 4 'Yet' means 'but' and 'Mansion' has its original sense of 'resting-place on a journey' and so a 'hospice'. 'For' means 'because of' in line 5. The punctuation of lines 1−6 adopted here is from Cooke's 1726 edition. In the difficult line 6 'incloses' must be intransitive and 'round' an adverb, as it will be in line 29; both times it means 'all about', the phrase used later in line 36.

There will be no other line in this poem as short as 'Like its own Tear'. But in the stanza form that Marvell invented for 'The Picture of little T.C.' that is the shape of every seventh line ('Let me be laid', 'Happy, who can', etc.), and in the eighth lines there are the same decasyllabics that we have here. The phrase 'its own Tear' came from Crashaw. He used it facetiously in 'Wishes. To his (supposed) mistress', at the end of *Delights of the Muses* (1646). But he used it seriously in 'The Tear', the second poem in *Steps to the Temple* (1646), and that time 'Pearl', 'dew', 'Dawn' and 'Rosebud' were all in attendance:

Each Drop leaving a place so deare,
Weeps for itself, is its own Teare.
Such a Pearle as this is,
(Slipt from Aurora's dewy Brest)
The Rosebud's sweet lip kisses.

These were the penitential tears of St Mary Magdalene, of which Marvell wrote in his 'Eyes and Tears'.

It is important to realise that in lines 17—18 the dewdrop does not return to the skies at this stage. Just as in '*Ros*' the Latin '*Donec*' is followed by the conjunctives '*vaporet*' and '*trahat*', so here 'Till' is followed by the conjunctives 'pitty' and 'exhale'; they do not mean the same thing as 'pities' and 'exhales'. The opening lines of Milton's *Paradise Lost* will reinforce this grammatical point; we have italicised the words that look forward to a future *Paradise Regained*.

> Of Man's first disobedience, and the fruit
> Of that forbidden tree, whose mortal taste
> Brought death into the World and all our Woe,
> With loss of Eden, *till one greater Man*
> *Restore us and regain the blissful seat,*
> Sing, Heavenly Muse, . . .

### C

Even so is it with the soul, if the eye could only see it in the human flower, where it spends a long period waiting in exile. It too, thinking of its native heaven and the banquets there, overturns the goblets and crimson couches here. Tyrian rugs and Sabaean warmth hold no attractions for this drop of a sacred river-source, this spark of everlasting day. Retreating entire within the citadel of its own light, it coils up into short rings like a snake. In the workings of its mind it follows the vaulted arch of the great gods, and in its small orb models the starry globe.

> So the Soul, that Drop, that Ray
> Of the clear Fountain of Eternal Day,                        20
> Could it within the humane flow'r be seen,
>    Remembring still its former height,
>    Shuns the sweet leaves and blossoms green;
>    And, recollecting its own Light,
> Does, in its pure and circling thoughts, express          25
> The greater Heaven in an Heaven less.

### D

> In how coy a Figure wound,
> Every way it turns away:

So the World excluding round,
Yet receiving in the Day. 30
Dark beneath, but bright above:
Here disdaining, there in Love.
How loose and easie hence to go:
How girt and ready to ascend.
Moving but on a point below, 35
It all about does upwards bend.

Shrunk into the small limit of its averted shape, how well at every
point it encloses the underside confronting the world! But its
ornamented upper half drinks the rays of heaven into its circular
mirror and, all open, shines in the daylight shed around. In the half
which beholds the gods above, it glows; in its lower half it is rather
dark. Disdaining all else, it burns with love for the sky. With
nimble motion imploring to be taken from this world, it leaps up,
its loins girded about, free and unencumbered for the heavenward
passage. The whole of its path stretches out to a charted course
through the air. Treading on a single point, it is poised for a swift
journey from here.

'Drop' in line 19 connects the soul with the 'Drop of Dew' in the
title. But the big difference between the pair is masked, namely that
the soul has been on earth for several years already and the dew for a
mere matter of hours. In line 22 'still' has its seventeenth-century
meaning of 'always'.
In the Latin C 'the human flower' is explicitly another wide-open
red rose, entertaining another kind of drop. The redness is omitted
from the English C, along with the distracting coiled serpentine rings
that grew out of 'The Coronet' and helped to give the soul the
semblance of an orb. But the 'blossoms green' of line 23 do surely
betoken red rose buds sheathed in an as yet unbroken calyx; in
'Young Love' the girl's 'blossoms' were said to be 'too green Yet for
Lust, but not for Love'. The 'sweet leaves' that go with them are the
scented petals of the flower. It makes a melodious line:

Shuns the sweet leaves and blossoms green.

What the ascetic soul shuns in the Latin is comfort and luxury,
'Sabaean warmth' and red 'Tyrian rugs' (the latter is a phrase straight
from Horace, applied here to the inside of the rose). What it shuns in

the English is sensuous pleasure. In 'The Garden' that was the Body's delight and there were separate delights of the Mind and the Soul. Here the Soul is *Mens* in the Latin, and in both versions it is a Soul with a Mind. So its circular shape in line 25 has correspondingly 'circular thoughts'. Is it, then, too fanciful to see one 'circling thought' in lines 1–6, beginning 'See how the Orient Dew' and ending a voyage of circumnavigation in that clause's completion by 'Round in its self incloses', and a correspondingly 'circling thought' in lines 19–26, again all one long rounded sentence?

The English part D of the poem begins with a dramatic change of metre. In A and B all the lines were iambic except line 16, 'Trembling lest it grow impure', which was a trochaic heptasyllabic, the first to appear. C began with a second trochaic, 'So the Soul, that Drop, that Ray', but seven iambic lines followed. Now D begins with a run of six trochaic heptasyllabics and the critic naturally wants to know why.

It is a lively and vibrant metre. Shakespeare used it all through 'The Phoenix and the Turtle'. The boy Milton used it for his school version of Psalm 136, 'Let us with a gladsome mind', with its perpetual refrain 'For his mercies aye endure, Ever faithful, ever sure'. Herrick in his vicarage used it for several of the poems in *Hesperides* (1648), 'If I kisse Anthea's breast', 'When a Daffadil I see', 'What I fancy, I approve', etc. It is the metre Marvell used for 'Daphnis and Chloe', a witty treatment of inconstant love. He made 'Created Pleasure' use it to tempt the 'Resolved Soul', whose replies came in sturdy iambics. The young man used it to allure the girl-child in 'Young Love'. The old man luxuriated in it in the translation from Seneca which began:

> Climb at *Court* for me that will
> Tott'ring Favour's Pinacle;
> All I seek is to lye still.

Such worldliness might make the metre appear out of place in the semi-religious 'On a Drop of Dew'. But one may hazard an explanation.

In Marvell's scheme of things, what connects the soul and the dewdrop is more than a common origin in the skies and a common desire to return there; more too than a common spherical shape and the shared pronoun 'it'. Behind that impersonal pronoun there lives a sentient human being with whom the reader can identify; in each case, a girl. In both the English and Latin, girlhood is common to the dewdrop and the soul. And it is at the point when the soul's behaviour becomes most feminine and frustrating to men that the metre waxes trochaic.

For though 'Figure' in line 27 is literally a geometrical figure, a sphere, the ball into which a skein of wool has been 'wound', metaphorically it is (or she is) a maiden who, being nubile, is 'coy'; who 'every way turns away', thereby shutting out ('so excluding') 'the World' around, while aggravatingly letting 'the Day' into her sanctum; 'disdaining' all suitors 'here' on earth, because she is 'in Love' with Heaven 'there'. Once that courtship metaphor is exhausted in line 32, the metre reverts to iambic octosyllabics, an easy transition to make. The soul-girl lives on in lines 33–6, but she is on tiptoe for the return flight to Heaven.

Looking back now, we can see that the dewdrop-girl is younger still, more passive, more vulnerable. This is the first time she has had to spend a night by herself away from home; at least, it is bedtime in the Latin, though not in the English. She is an aristocrat, class-conscious, homesick, tearful, restless, afraid of contamination, altogether in 'Pain'. The Latin similes of two other girls, one with a tear on her rosy cheek, one walking home at night alone in dark terror, have been jettisoned or, if '*Ros*' was written later, have not yet been thought of; the dewdrop is the only girl in the English and artistically that is a gain.

Parallels, as Marvell said in 'The Definition of Love', 'Though infinite, can never meet'. To achieve a satisfying end to this poem, he introduces a third party in the shape of Manna from Heaven; an apt idea, for in Exodus the Manna arrived with the morning dew.

And when the dew that lay was gone up, behold, upon the face of the wilderness there lay a small round thing, as small as the hoar frost on the ground. And when the children of Israel saw it, they said one to another It is *Manna* [Hebrew for *What is it?*]: for they wist not what it was. And Moses said unto them, This is the bread which the Lord hath given you to eat . . . And they gathered it every morning, every man according to his eating: and when the sun waxed hot, it melted. (XVI 14, 15, 21)

The Latin and English endings make an interesting contrast.

E

> Haud aliter Mensis exundans Manna beatis
> Deserto jacuit Stilla gelata solo;
> Stilla gelata solo, sed Solibus hausta benignis,
> Ad sua qua cecidit purior Astra redit.

In just the same way the Manna overflowed from the dinner-tables of the blessed and lay, a frozen drop, on the soil of the wilderness. A frozen drop, on the soil it lay; but now, drawn up by benign Suns, it returns to its Stars, purer than it was when it fell.

> Such did the Manna's sacred Dew destil;
> White, and intire, though congeal'd and chill.
> Congeal'd on Earth: but does, dissolving, run
> Into the Glories of th' Almighty Sun.                    40

In line 38 'intire' is trisyllabic. 'Such' in line 37 is an accusative adjective, agreeing with the soul-drop, however awkward that may seem, and 'destil' is a derivative of the intransitive Latin *destillare* or *distillare*, to trickle down in drops, which Marvell also used transitively, 'to precipitate in drops'. So in 'Damon the Mower', Damon said:

> On me the Morn her dew distills
> Before her darling Daffadils.

The word 'destil' picks up *stilla* (drop) in the repeated '*Stilla gelata solo*', a phrase whose music the English fails to match; 'Congeal'd' is too prosaic to bear repetition. The pun in the two Latin neighbours, '*solo*' and '*Solibus*', corresponds to the pun in line 40 on 'Sun', plainly a Christian reference to the glory of the Almighty Son of God. However, 'glories' is not found here in '*Ros*', but rather harks back to '*jubar genitale*', the 'fertilising radiance' of the sun at the end of B. It seems probable that in E the Latin version came first.

One of the secrets of the English poem's harebell lightness and elasticity is the repeated short 'i' vowel sound. Over a third of the unstressed syllables and almost a fifth of the total syllable count contain this short 'i'. The word 'it' comes nine times and the word 'its' comes nine more; 'in' occurs seven times on its own and as prefix or suffix five more, while the suffix 'ing' is used twelve times. There are twelve present participles in 'Ros'. Now it is well known that Latin poets used them far more than English poets have done (in 'To his Coy Mistress' there are none); so this also points to the Latin version's having been composed first and having influenced the English. Paradoxically, some of the loveliest English lines here turn out to be ones with no short 'i' in them at all! Such are lines 2, 5, 12, 19, 23, 31.

An unobtrusive feature of the English poem is the constant alternation between Heaven and Earth, 'here' and 'there'. A dozen times the sense passes from here up to there, a dozen times from there back to here. It is as though Marvell had taken his cue from Shakespeare's famous account of the poet at work:

> The Poet's eye, in a fine frenzy rolling,
> Doth glance from Heav'n to Earth, from Earth to Heav'n.

# 34 'A Dialogue between the Soul and the Body'

Critics neglected this poem until Bradbrook and Lloyd Thomas gave it two pages in *Andrew Marvell* (Cambridge University Press, 1940). It burst out into sudden blaze in 1953 when F. R. Leavis of Cambridge quarrelled with F. W. Bateson of Oxford over it. Bateson had written it down as a semi-grotesque, near-farcical product of the late 1640s when the aristocratic fashion for emblems and allegory was tottering to ruin with the Court. Leavis would have none of this. 'The poem is among Marvell's supreme things', he wrote in *Scrutiny*, 'profoundly original and a proof of genius.' He took its theme to be the difficulty of distinguishing between the Body and the Soul. In a weak rejoinder Bateson did not fasten on the doubtfulness of that. (Michael Wilding, *Marvell* (Macmillan, 1969), pp.165–81).

In 1957 Helen Gardner put the 'Dialogue' among the fourteen Marvell pieces printed in her anthology *The Metaphysical Poets* (Penguin) and since then it has received much attention. As no two critics, however, agree on its meaning, we will take the four speeches one by one and try to recover their seventeenth-century sense.

## Soul

O who shall, from this Dungeon, raise
A Soul inslav'd so many wayes?
With bolts of Bones, that fetter'd stands
In Feet; and manacled in Hands.
Here blinded with an Eye; and there                    5
Deaf with the drumming of an Ear.
A Soul hung up, as 'twere, in Chains
Of Nerves, and Arteries, and Veins.
Tortur'd, besides each other part,
In a vain Head, and double Heart.                     10

The Soul's 'inslav'd' in line 2 means not only 'constrained to labour
for its captor', but also 'deprived of freedom to move'. The poet was
the Lady's 'slave' in 'The Fair Singer' because her art wreathed
'fetters' of the air that he breathed. He was 'inslaved' by his feet there:
this Soul is 'inslav'd so many wayes'. Housed like a ghost in the
standing Body, all the bones are clamped on it like 'bolts' on a
prisoner. The Body's hands and feet, for instance, manacle and fetter
the Soul. The Body's eyes are a blinding obstruction to the Soul. The
impact of external sounds on the Body's eardrum or tympanum
deafens the Soul. Suspended within the Body's complex neuro-
vascular system, the Soul is like a dead felon's corpse hanging on a
gibbet and held together by a network of chains.

Dialogues between Soul and Body were all based on the words of
St Paul in Galatians, V 16– 17: 'Walk in the Spirit, and ye shall not
fulfil the lust of the flesh. For the flesh lusteth against the Spirit, and
the Spirit against the flesh; and these are contrary the one to the other.'
Lines 9– 10 here reflect 'the lust of the flesh'. The pure Soul-prisoner
is tortured by the head's vanity and the duplicity of the heart, not to
mention ('besides') the vices associated with 'each other part' of the
Body. The heart is 'double' medically also in respect of its two
ventricles. Perhaps the head is medically empty and vain.

St Paul also wrote, in Romans, VII 24: 'O wretched man that I am!
Who shall deliver me from the body of this death?' And the eighth
plate in Book V of Francis Quarles's *Emblemes* (1635) did actually
depict a sitting skeleton within which a kneeling human soul was
asking this very question in Latin: '*Quis me liberabit de corpore mortis
huius?*' But Quarles derived his plates from a slightly earlier book, *Pia
Desideria* (Antwerp, 1624), by Hermann Hugo in Latin. One cannot

tell if Marvell knew both books, but K. S. Datta has argued (in *Renaissance Quarterly*, Autumn 1969) that his first stanza is based on Hugo's Latin. If so, it is only a starting-point. Marvell at once converts the question 'Who shall deliver me from the body of this death?' or 'who shall, from this Dungeon, raise /A Soul inslav'd so many wayes?' to a very different question that the Body now asks.

### Body

> O who shall me deliver whole,
> From bonds of this Tyrannic Soul?
> Which, stretcht upright, impales me so,
> That mine own Precipice I go;
> And warms and moves this needless Frame:    15
> (A Fever could but do the same.)
> And, wanting where its spight to try,
> Has made me live to let me dye.
> A Body that could never rest,
> Since this ill Spirit it possest.    20

This, like the first stanza, is one sentence; and it apes the Soul's speech in several ways. It answers it also. First, it answers 'inslav'd': for 'deliver' means 'set free' and 'bonds' are not just physical prison restraints, but the condition of slavery or serfdom; so that 'Tyrannic' means 'slave-driving', and the Soul is more 'inslaving' than 'inslav'd'. Secondly, it answers 'tortur'd'; for it likens the shape of the Soul to a 'pale' or thin pointed stake driven into a living body by a torturer and left there. The Soul is therefore itself an instrument of torture to the Body. Stretched upright in the Body, it forces the Body into an unnaturally stiff, unbending posture which it has to maintain. The body is a walking precipice, wherever it goes, and always in danger of falling to destruction.

Marvell repeated this image in *The Rehearsal Transpros'd* (1672), when he wrote of Samuel Parker's vain head and dangerous conceit in the Archbishop's household as the new Chaplain: 'His head swell'd like any Bladder with wind and vapour. But after he was stretch'd to such a height in his own fancy, that he could not look down from top to toe but his Eyes dazled at the Precipice of his Stature; there fell out, or in, another natural chance which push'd him headlong.' (ed. D. I. B. Smith, p.30).

In line 15 the Body's frame is 'needless' in the limited sense of 'not needing' the warmth and motion of the Soul, because it has warmth and motion already. So in *As You Like It*, II, i, the wounded deer wept into 'the needless stream', augmenting it with tears, and Jaques pointed the moral:

> Poor deer, quoth he, thou mak'st a testament
> As worldings do, giving the sum of more
> To that which had too much.

Such intermittent warmth as it did need, the Body could have had from a mere fever. Of motion it needed very little. The Soul gave it too much.

In line 17, 'wanting where its spight to try' means lacking an outlet for its spite'. The Soul is thus a malevolent devil that has inflicted itself on this Body. It is an evil ('ill') spirit 'possessing' the Body.

The whole speech strikes the reader as ungrateful and churlish. At the halfway mark one's sympathies are with the Soul. And throughout the next speech they stay there.

### Soul

> What Magick could me thus confine
> Within anothers Grief to pine?
> Where whatsoever it complain,
> I feel, that cannot feel, the pain.
> And all my Care its self employes,                    25
> That to preserve, which me destroys:
> Constrain'd not only to indure
> Diseases, but, whats worse, the Cure:
> And ready oft the Port to gain,
> Am Shipwrackt into Health again.                      30

The Soul thinks of 'Magick' as a result of being called an 'ill Spirit' *possessing* the Body. The connection between demoniac possession and magic was that magicians and witches were prone to torment their familiar spirits by confining them in trees. Sycorax did this to Ariel. 'She did confine thee', Prospero told him in *The Tempest*, I, ii, 'into a cloven pine, within which rift/Imprisoned thou didst painfully remain /A dozen years.' The Soul's case is worse, for its grief is imprisoned within the grief of another, the Body. 'And there', lines 23–4 continue, 'whatever ails the Body, I feel the pain.' The use of 'complaint' for 'ailment' is still current, but Marvell's use of 'complain' for 'ail' has disappeared. It was still good English in 1731 when Pope wrote in his poem 'On his Death':

> Should some neighbour feel a pain
> Just in the parts where I complain.

In line 28 the ailments become 'Diseases'; by their 'Cure' is meant (1) their treatment with physic (proverbially 'worse than the disease') and (2) their restoration to health.

In lines 29–30 the Soul's predicament is neatly presented in a sea-voyage image. Every Body at sea desires to avoid shipwreck and come safe to port, just as every sick body hopes to get well. But the Soul's port is heaven, and that can only be reached through the death of the Body. It 'destroys' (l.26) and 'shipwrecks' the Soul if the Body is cured and gets well. And this has often happened, to the distress of the Soul.

Aping the Soul's language again, the Body begins the fourth and last speech by capping 'Magick' with 'Physick', in pursuance of the element of treatment in 'Cure'. The first ten lines again form one sentence. The intervening full stops are artificial.

> *Body*
>
> But Physick yet could never reach
> The Maladies Thou me dost teach;
> Whom first the Cramp of Hope dost Tear:
> And then the Palsie Shakes of Fear.
> The Pestilence of Love does heat:          35
> Or Hatred's hidden Ulcer eat.
> Joy's chearful Madness does perplex: ˎ
> Or Sorrow's other Madness vex.
> Which Knowledge forces me to know;
> And Memory will not foregoe.          40
> What but a Soul could have the wit
> To build me up for Sin so fit?
> So Architects do square and hew,
> Green Trees that in the Forest grew.

The Soul's last speech had been a lament at the number of times that physick had reached the Body's diseases and cured them. 'But', says the Body, 'no Physick was ever yet able to reach "The Maladies Thou me dost teach"'. This is the most dramatic line in the poem. It alone employs the second person. Elsewhere each speaker has stood full-face and four-square to the reader; here the Body turns sideways and points an accusing finger at the Soul. The word order and iambic rhythm are inverted to bring together the twin-stressed 'Thóu mé'.

In lines 32—3 'the Maladies' become 'my Maladies', and the antecedent of 'Whom' is 'me'. The same 'Whom' is understood at the start of lines 35 and 37. The Body's speeches rely on simple relative clauses. In lines 33—40 Marvell does without caesuras and balances line with line, not half-line with half-line. The change adds momentum. The argument may be paraphrased thus: 'When you feel hope, I am racked with cramp; when you fear, palsy shakes me. If you love, I am fevered with the plague; if you hate, I am consumed with internal ulcers. If you joy, I am madly elated; if you sorrow, I am madly depressed. It is your knowledge that makes me know this, and your memory that will not let me forget.'

Though it cannot feel physical pain, the Soul does feel strong emotions. Their seat is its heart. Knowledge and memory reside in its head. Whereas in lines 27—30 the Soul had complained of the Body's ills being cured, the Body complains now of not being cured of maladies caused by the Soul's head and heart. Not too much should be read into 'teach' in line 32; the word is rather dragged in as a rhyme. What matters is that the Body suffers from the Soul's mastery and suffers acutely, irremediably. One's sympathies are now with the Body.

At the end of line 40 the dialogue loses its shape. In a poem of ten-line stanzas it should now be the Soul's turn to speak, but the Body goes on for four lines, and they end the poem. Did the printers of the 1681 Folio make a mistake?

The eighteenth-century owner of T2 (Thompson's second note-book) crossed out these four lines and wrote below them '*Desunt multa*' ('Much is missing'). He found no other fault in the poem and he made no addition. He simply distrusted the shape at the end. J. B. Leishman fully agreed. 'The poem as we have it is almost certainly incomplete,' he wrote in *The Art of Marvell's Poetry* (Hutchinson, 1966), p.216. 'It looks as though the debate had originally continued through several more ten-line stanzas, and as though the last four lines of the present fourth had somehow survived from one of these.' That appears to allow for a poem two or three times as long. Professor Kermode a year later suggested in *The Selected Poetry of Marvell*

(Signet Classics, 1967), p.66, that 'the four extra lines may have survived from a third rejoinder to the Soul'. That would add sixteen lines only.

I take the contrary view, that the 1681 Folio carried Marvell's fair copy in its entirety, in accordance with its printed certificate 'To The Reader'. The poem was not picked from the worm-holes of long-vanished days or raked from the dust of oblivion. Marvell had remembered it in writing *The Rehearsal Transpros'd* in 1672. Why should not he lengthen his last stanza? He was no slave to uniformity elsewhere. If the extra lines could not have been spoken by the Body or if they had no logical or artistic connection with the previous ten, the case would be different. But they *are* spoken by the Body and they *do* so connect. Indeed, without them the speech would be odd in another way. For the first three speeches begin with a question and this one could perfectly well have begun:

> What Physick yet could ever reach
> The Maladies Thou me dost teach?

But, instead, the Body makes a ten-line statement and then asks its question and then adds its final couplet:

> What but a Soul could have the wit
> To build me up for Sin so fit?
> So Architects do square and hew,
> Green Trees that in the Forest grew.

There are three distinct ways in which these lines do connect with the preceding forty. (1) Though Marvell had not used the word 'Sin' hitherto, it was the sins of the Body that irked the pure Soul in lines 9–10; the vanity of the head and duplicity of the heart, and the unnamed sins of 'each other part'. The Body did not answer that charge at the time, but now it asserts that all sin stems from the Soul's head and heart; from the head's knowledge and memory, and from the conflicting emotions of the heart. It could not have saddled the Soul with 'the Works of the Flesh' in Galatians, V 19–21, and that is why they were unnamed. (2) The late entry of the Soul's knowledge and memory in lines 39–40 is skilfully arranged to lead on to the Soul's 'wit' in line 41. For the word 'wit' means 'brain-power' and includes all the powers of imagination and intellect, knowledge and memory in the head; and that wit is also the wit which an architect-carpenter needed to design and build a great timber-framed house. (3) The 'build me up' metaphor had its first airing in lines 13–14, where the Body was 'stretcht upright' by the Soul until it seemed its 'own Precipice'. And then in line 15 it was a 'Frame'. That meant no more than the skeletal system. And the skeletal system is what it means here:

> What but a Soul could have the wit
> To build me up for Sin so fit?

One thinks only of bone-spread and brawn when one says that a man is 'well-built'. But the 'Architects' in the next line extend this first thought into the frame or carcase of a tall timber house, and then one sees that 'for Sin so fit' means 'so fit for Sin to reside in'.

The past tense of 'grew' proves that the trees have been felled already. The carpenters proceed now to 'hew' them, that is, trim the trunks and reduce them in size. They then 'square' them into rectangular building-members with axe and saw, using rule and line for precision.

Since the forty-four lines, then, are in my view the whole poem, it should be possible to grasp their whole meaning. The Soul and Body throughout are 'contrary the one to the other' and to that extent are scriptural. This Soul is nothing romantic or exotic; no drop of dew or silver bird or armed warrior. It stands up, but is a simulacrum, a thin-shouldered ghost, immaterial and boneless. It has emotions, and reason, and is immortal. It came from Heaven to be incarnate. It wants to go back there. In the meantime its hope and fear, love or hate, joy or sorrow, depend on the chances of the Body dying.

The Body stands up for itself. It too was in scripture immortal at first. Knowledge and Sin made it mortal. It now blames both of these on the Soul. The Body wants quiet and innocence, the 'sisters dear' of 'The Garden'. Its hopes of recovering them depend on 'being delivered whole'. It sees itself at present as a natural animal unnaturally distorted by the Soul. It admires forest trees, green and growing. It compares their fate at the hands of the builders with its own fate at the hands of the Soul.

Marvell's triumph is in making out such a strong philosophical case for the Body against the Soul. Only thus could the dialogue balance and the debate achieve drama.

# 35 'Clorinda and Damon'

*C.*   *Damon* come drive thy flocks this way.
*D.*   No: 'tis too late they went astray.
*C.*   I have a grassy Scutcheon spy'd,
        Where *Flora* blazons all her pride.
        The Grass I aim to feast thy Sheep:                    5
        The Flow'rs I for thy Temples keep.
*D.*   Grass withers; and the Flow'rs too fade.
*C.*   Seize the short Joyes then, ere they vade.
        Seest thou that unfrequented Cave?
*D.*   That den?   *C.* Loves Shrine.   *D.* But Virtue's Grave.   10
*C.*   In whose cool bosome we may lye
        Safe from the Sun.   *D.* not Heaven's Eye.
*C.*   Near this, a Fountaines liquid Bell
        Tinkles within the concave Shell.
*D.*   Might a Soul bath there and be clean,                    15
        Or slake its Drought?   *C.* What is't you mean?
*D.*   These once had been enticing things,
        *Clorinda*, Pastures, Caves and Springs.
*C.*   And what late change?   *D.* The other day
        *Pan* met me.   *C.* What did great *Pan* say?           20
*D.*   Words that transcend poor Shepherds skill,
        But He ere since my Songs does fill:
        And his Name swells my slender Oate.
*C.*   Sweet must *Pan* sound in *Damons* Note.
*D.*   *Clorinda's* voice might make it sweet.                  25
*C.*   Who would not in *Pan's* Praises meet?

### Chorus

> *Of* Pan *the flowry Pastures sing,*
> *Caves eccho, and the Fountains ring.*
> *Sing then while he doth us inspire;*
> *For all the World is our* Pan's *Quire.*          30

This pleasant pastoral links Marvell to Spenser in three respects.
1. The phrase 'Flora's pride' is used in *The Faerie Queene*, II, xii, 50,

where 'faire grassy ground' is 'beautifide With all the ornaments of Floraes pride' (i.e. flower beds).

2. In stanzas 74–5 of the same book and canto a singer compares the swift passing of a maiden's beauty with a virgin rose's decay, and points the moral.

> So passeth, in the passing of a day,
> Of mortall life the leafe, the bud, the flowre,
> Ne more doth flourish after first decay.
> Gather therefore the Rose, whilest yet is prime,
> For soone comes age, that will her pride deflowre:
> Gather the Rose of love, whilest yet is time.

Clorinda urges the same thing more briefly in 'Seize the short Joyes then, ere they vade.' Shakespeare had used 'vade' in sonnet 54 as a variant of 'fade'.

3. *The Shepheardes Calender* has 'great Pan' presiding over a pastoral Last Judgement in line 54 of the eclogue on May: 'When great Pan account of shepeherds shall aske.' On that line in 1579 E. K.'s long gloss began: 'Great Pan is Christ, the very God of all shepheards, which calleth himselfe the greate and good shepherd. The name is most rightly (me thinkes) applyed to him, for Pan signifieth all or omnipotent, which is onely the Lord Jesus.'

In passing, one may note that Milton turned Spenser's 'great Pan' into 'mighty Pan' in the 'Nativity Ode', the poem from which Marvell drew inspiration more often that from any except 'Lycidas'. Milton wrote:

> The Shepherds on the Lawn,
> Or e're the point of dawn,
>   Sate simply chatting in a rustick row;
> Full little thought they than,
> That the mighty *Pan*
>   Was kindly come to live with them below.

Two respects in which 'Clorinda and Damon' improves on Elizabethan pastoral are characterisation and wit. Clorinda is highly intelligent. This comes out in her refined use of metaphor and her swift adaptation to the new Damon. In lines 3–6 she makes 'Flora's pride' a matter of ancestry as well as wild flowers; the coloured flowers 'blazon' or tincture her 'scutcheon' or shield of arms in a 'field vert', in the language of heraldry. Yet field and flowers have each a function; the one for the sheep, the other for garlands in the dalliance of love. In lines 13–14 the metaphor is cleverer still. The water of a spring or 'fountain', bubbling up musically in a concave bed or 'shell', sounds like a small bell 'tinkling', and this fancy is repeated in line 28 when 'Fountains *ring*'. It is Clorinda who turns 'Pan' into 'great Pan' and she swiftly makes common cause with the swain who had resolved to reject her. They worship together: he for Pan only, she for Pan in him.

In Damon Marvell portrays a changed man. Two-thirds of the poem are over before one learns the reason for the change: Damon has come face to face with Pan and undergone a religious conversion. The irony underlying his answers then becomes clear. No, he will not drive his sheep her way: it is too recently that they erred and strayed like lost sinners. Grass and flowers have no ultimate value: 'the grass withereth, the flower fadeth, but the word of the Lord endureth for ever'. (Isaiah, XL 8). The empty cave is an invitation to sin, which God, who sees everything, will see and will punish. Whatever pleasure spring water offers to the body, it can do nothing for the soul.

> These once had been enticing things,
> *Clorinda*, Pastures, Caves and Springs.

Clorinda is in the vocative case. The three nominative nouns that follow sum up lines 3–14; 'they would once have been enticing, but not now and not any more'.

In the last ten lines Damon displays an unconscious humility and an infectious joy. He cannot quote Pan's actual words. What Pan said was beyond the vocabulary of a poor shepherd (we take 'Shepherds' to be genitive singular). But it has changed Damon's whole being. 'He ere since my Songs does fill'. In no time Clorinda and he are singing of Pan.

In their song Damon discards his religious objections to grass and flowers, caves and fountains. The objections stemmed from their offer by a carnal Clorinda as 'enticing things'. Now pastures, caves and springs (the same trio as in line 18) are represented as regular worshippers of Pan. Clorinda and Damon invite them to join in.

> Sing then while he doth us inspire;
> For all the World is our *Pan's* Quire.

That is in the spirit, though not the idiom, of George Herbert's hymn:

> Let all the World in every corner sing
> My God and King.

# 36   Two Songs at the Marriage of the Lord Fauconberg and the Lady Mary Cromwell

This wedding took place on Thursday, 19 November 1657 at Hampton Court. Viscount Fauconberg was a widower thirty years old. Mary Cromwell was a spinster aged twenty-one, Oliver's seventh child and third daughter.

Mary's younger sister Frances had been married only eight days before at Whitehall to Robert Riche, son and heir of Lord Riche and grandson of the Earl of Warwick. She had long been half-promised to William Dutton, but, while he was a teenager maturing in France with Marvell as tutor, she fell in love with the nineteen-year-old Robert and gave herself to him months before Cromwell and Warwick had negotiated a marriage between them.

Under the conditions of the Second Protectorate, settled five months before, 'His Highness the Lord Protector' took sovereign rank with the crowned heads of Europe, and his family with him. Marvell's First Song recognised that and made clever use of a classical parallel. In Greek mythology the great god Zeus had two daughters, Aphrodite and Artemis, who took to themselves mortal lovers, Anchises and Endymion. In Roman mythology Zeus became Jove, Aphrodite Venus, and Artemis Diana or Cynthia or Phoebe, three different names for the moon goddess. Cromwell could therefore be Jove, and Frances Venus, and Riche Anchises, while Mary could be Cynthia and Fauconberg Endymion. It was all very masque-like.

Better still, it was all very pastoral. Though Anchises was a prince of Troy, Theocritus in the First Idyll made him a shepherd, or more precisely a neatherd, on Mount Ida; there the all-seeing eye of Aphrodite espied him and loved him and they had the baby Aeneas born to them. Endymion was always pure shepherd. His mythical romance with the Moon had been further romanticised by Drayton in *The Man in the Moon* (1593). There the shepherd Rowland told the tale of Endymion and Phoebe in 538 lines. Endymion the Carian shepherd kept his sheep on the heights of Mount Latmos, to be as near as he could to the Moon. She descended to him once every month before finally sweeping him off to be her Man in the Moon.

Marvell's first song takes Drayton's romantic Endymion and makes him court Cynthia the Moon, with a Chorus to introduce him, encourage him half-way through, and congratulate him and Cynthia and Jove at the end. The song lasts for fifty-eight lines.

### FIRST SONG

#### Chorus

Th'*Astrologers* own Eyes are set,
And even Wolves the Sheep forget;
Only *this Shepheard*, late and soon,
Upon this Hill outwakes the *Moon*.
Heark how he sings, with sad delight,          5
Thorough the clear and silent Night.

#### Endymion

*Cynthia, O Cynthia*, turn thine Ear,
Nor scorn *Endymions* plaints to hear.
As we our Flocks, so you command
The fleecy Clouds with silver wand.          10

#### Cynthia

If thou a *Mortal*, rather sleep;
Or if a *Shepheard*, watch thy Sheep.

#### Endymion

The *Shepheard*, since he saw thine Eyes,
And *Sheep* are both thy *Sacrifice*.
Nor merits he a *Mortal's* name,          15
That burns with an *immortal Flame*.

### Cynthia

I have enough for me to do,
Ruling the Waves that Ebb and flow.

### Endymion

Since thou disdain'st not then to share
On Sublunary things thy care;                                    20
Rather restrain these double Seas,
Mine Eyes uncessant deluges.

### Cynthia

My wakeful Lamp all night must move,
Securing their Repose above.

### Endymion

If therefore thy resplendent Ray                                 25
Can make a Night more bright then Day;
Shine thorough this obscurer Brest,
With shades of deep Despair opprest.

### Chorus

Courage, *Endymion*, boldly Woo,
*Anchises* was a *Shepheard* too;                                30
Yet is *her younger Sister* laid
Sporting with him in *Ida's shade*:
      And *Cynthia*, though the strongest,
Seeks but the honour to have held out longest.

### Endymion

Here unto *Latmos Top* I climbe:                                 35
How far below thine *Orbe* sublime?
O why, as well as Eyes to see,
Have I not Armes that reach to thee?

### Cynthia

'Tis needless then that I refuse,
Would you but your own Reason use.                               40

### Endymion

Though I so high may not pretend,
It is the same so you descend.

### Cynthia

*These Stars* would say I do them wrong,
Rivals each one for thee too strong.

### Endymion

*The Stars* are fix'd unto their *Sphere*,                    45
And cannot, though they would, come near.
Less Loves set of each others praise,
While *Stars* Eclypse by mixing Rayes.

### Cynthia

That Cave is dark.

### Endymion

                    Then none can spy:
Or shine Thou there and 'tis the Sky.                    50

### Chorus

Joy to *Endymion*,
For he has *Cynthia's* favour won.
And *Jove* himself approves
With his. serenest influence their Loves.
For he did never love to pair                    55
His Progeny above the Air;
But to be honest, valiant, wise,
Makes *Mortals* matches fit for *Deityes*.

Clearly the song is devised for presentation as drama. The Chorus
stand and sing to an instrumental accompaniment at ground level,
with Endymion on the slope of his hill and Cynthia above in the
gallery. He climbs slightly higher at line 35. She descends to him at
line 48 and points to the mouth of a cave lower still, 'That Cave is
dark'. They enter it together at line 50, so simulating the customary

retirement of bride and groom from the wedding feast to the bridal chamber.

The second song, by contrast, is unaffectedly plebeian. The shepherds Hobbinol and Tomalin and the shepherdess Phillis are young and energetically excited. The metre for the first twenty-eight lines is heptasyllabic trochaic, a sure sign of levity in Marvell. These introductory lines may well have been acted and spoken, not sung. The twenty lines of the Chorus, on the other hand, are iambic and eloquent and sincerely well-wishing. 'All' should mean 'all three', but surely more than three voices were needed. The guests may well have joined in.

## SECOND SONG

### Hobbinol

*Phillis, Tomalin,* away:
Never such a merry day.
For the *Northern Shepheards Son*
Has *Menalca's daughter* won.

### Phillis

Stay till I some flow'rs ha' ty'd          5
In a Garland for the Bride.

### Tomalin

If thou would'st a Garland bring,
*Phillis* you may wait the Spring:
They ha' chosen such an hour
When *She* is the only flow'r.          10

### Phillis

Let's not then at least be seen
Without each a Sprig of Green.

### Hobbinol

Fear not; at *Menalca's Hall*
There is Bayes enough for all.
He when Young as we did graze,          15
But when Old he planted Bayes.

### Tomalin

Here *She* comes; but with a Look
Far more catching then my Hook.
'Twas those Eyes, I now dare swear,
Led our Lambs we knew not where.                    20

### Hobbinol

Not our Lambs own Fleeces are
Curl'd so lovely as her Hair:
Nor our Sheep new Wash'd can be
Half so white or sweet as *She*.

### Phillis

*He* so looks as fit to keep                        25
Somewhat else then silly *Sheep*.

### Hobbinol

Come, lets in some Carol new
Pay to Love and Them their due.

### All

Joy to that *happy Pair*,
Whose Hopes united banish our Despair.              30
What *Shepheard* could for Love pretend,
Whil'st all the *Nymphs* on *Damon's* choice attend?
What *Shepherdess* could hope to wed
Before *Marina's* turn were sped?
Now lesser Beauties may take place,                 35
And meaner Virtues come in play;
While they,
Looking from high,
Shall grace
Our Flocks and us with a propitious Eye.            40
But what is most, the gentle Swain
No more shall need of Love complain;
But Virtue shall be Beauties hire,
And those be equal that have equal Fire.
*Marina* yields. Who dares be coy?                  45

Or who despair, now *Damon* does enjoy?
Joy to that happy Pair,
Whose Hopes united banish our Despair.

The couplet with which 'All' begin and end sums up the sense of
the lines in between. The normal courtship of shepherd—swains
(virtues) and shepherdess—nymphs (beauties) had to wait for Damon
to take his pick and for Marina to take hers. Normal courtship can
now be resumed. And it will go better than ever, for Marina's sturdy
example has banished feminine coyness and from Damon's example
the men can take heart. The sheep too will be all the better for the
godlike goodwill of Marina and Damon above.

It is natural to wonder how long a time Marvell had to write these
'Two Songs', how long before the composer of the music required
them and the singers were rehearsed. Since the beginning of
September the poet had been working for Thurloe as Latin Secretary
to the new Privy Council. One suspects that he deserves extra credit
for writing these poems unwontedly fast.

# 37  'An Epitaph upon———'

Enough: and leave the rest to Fame.
'Tis to commend her but to name.
Courtship, which living she declin'd,
When dead to offer were unkind.
Where never any could speak ill,                    5
Who would officious Praises spill?
Nor can the truest Wit or Friend,
Without Detracting, her commend.
To say she liv'd a *Virgin* chast,
In this Age loose and all unlac't;                  10
Nor was, when Vice is so allow'd,
Of *Virtue* or asham'd, or proud;
That her Soul was on *Heav'n* so bent
No Minute but it came and went;
That ready her last Debt to pay                     15

> She summ'd her Life up ev'ry day;
> Modest as Morn; as Mid-day bright;
> Gentle as Ev'ning; cool as Night;
> 'Tis true: but all so weakly said;
> 'Twere more Significant, *She's Dead.*  20

This poem was printed on pp.71–2 of the 1681 Folio at the end of eight funeral pages. The Latin elegy on Jane Oxenbridge (1658) came first; then the Latin elegy on John Trott (1664); then the letter of condolence to Sir John Trott and the Latin epitaph on Edmund Trott (1667) which had been enclosed; then an undated English prose epitaph on an unnamed married man; then this undated poem on an unnamed maiden lady. All were printed from copies that Marvell had kept.

It is a pity that his manuscript of this poem left a blank for the name. As so often with Marvell, his title was an integral part of the poem. 'Enough' means 'Stop here, at the name in the title'. 'Let Fame say the rest'. 'Merely to name her is commendation enough.' The personified Fame is the trumpeter sounding the dead person's praise. In line 64 of 'Upon the Hill and Grove at Bill-borow' there were likewise 'those Acts that swell'd the Cheek of Fame' in Fairfax's life-time.

The next three couplets give three more reasons for reticence. (1) To those men who courted her in her lifetime, she always said no; it would be unkind to pay courtly compliments to her after her death. (2) Acknowledged perfection in anyone inhibits duteous outpouring of praise. (3) The best scholar or most loyal friend praising her cannot fail to be inadequate and fall short of the truth.

Lines 9–20 are framed as one sentence. 'To say' in line 9 is the subject of 'is true' in line 19; the change to ' 'Tis true' merely copies *c'est vrai* in French. The lines in between carry four noun clauses, direct objects of 'say', with the conjunction 'that' either stated or understood: '(that) she lived . . . and (that she) was not ashamed or proud . . . that her Soul was bent on Heaven . . . that she summed her life up every day.'

There are two indications that the poem was written after 1667. (1) The eight pages in the Folio seem to be in chronological order; the first six certainly are. (2) In the 1667 Edmund Trott Elegy the Latin in lines 18–21 translates: 'He sailed past the Island of Circe and the Rocks of the Sirens and in this shipwreck of the Age and its Morals he alone succeeded in losing nothing and gaining a great deal.' The year 1667 saw the Dutch fleet in the Medway and Thames, and

Court morals were then at a new low level. That autumn Marvell fiercely satirised the Age in 'The last Instructions to a Painter'. Here in this poem's lines 10–11 he writes of the lady's unblemished virtue 'In this Age loose and all unlac't . . . when Vice is so allowed.' He went on thinking that way of the Age of Charles II. There was no recovery.

The heavily compressed lines 13–14 mean to say: 'That her Soul was so set on Heaven that there was no minute when it was not half in and half out of her Body'. This seems a state of contemplation and ecstasy rather than prayer. There were the ecstasies of lovers: Troilus sighing his soul at night towards the Grecian tents where Cressid lay; John Donne and Anne More's souls 'interinanimating' in 'The Ecstasy'; the Coy Mistress's soul transpiring 'at every pore'. There were also the Souls leaving Bodies on practice flights in their eagerness to be back in Heaven. In 'The Garden', lines 49–56, the poet's Soul was given to 'casting the Body's vest aside'; like a silver bird it would then perch on a tree 'till prepared for longer flight'. The Soul in 'On a Drop of Dew' was pictured as 'girt and ready to ascend'; 'Moving but on a point below, /It all about does upwards bend'. This lady had a soul in that admirable state of alacrity.

Lines 15–16 exploit two separate ideas. There is the accountancy metaphor first; every day might be her last and in her evening prayers she therefore examined herself and made ready to go, as a scrupulous housewife at the end of each day 'summed up' (added up) her housekeeping debits on paper. There is also her life and character as seen by others. That was 'summed up' (epitomised) in the behaviour of an ideal day. She had the four natural feminine virtues which I italicise here:

> *Modest* as Morn; as Mid-day *bright*;
> *Gentle* as Ev'ning; *cool* as Night.

These moving lines are the climax of the poem. They appeal by their balanced restraint. Her four virtues are the virtues of Marvell's own verse here.

Lines 19–20 conclude: 'To say each of these things is true, but all this is so weakly said; it would be more telling simply to say "*She is dead*".' As telling, that is, as simply to utter her name.

Was this a real epitaph? Was it ever actually inscribed? Marvell's other epitaphs indicate a knowledge of intended location. The Latin one for Eton College Chapel began: 'Near this marble lie the remains of Jane Oxenbridge . . . wife of John Oxenbridge, Fellow of this College.' The Latin one on John Trott of Laverstoke began: 'To our dearest son John Trott . . . we, his father and mother, have set up this memorial tablet. Come, Marble, and pronounce his epitaph.' The unnamed English epitaph began: 'Here under rests the body of——, who in his lifetime etc.' It seems likely then that this unnamed verse epitaph did serve as a memorial inscription; but one doubts if it was ever intended to be the only inscription there.

Did it express personal grief? Bradbrook and Lloyd Thomas in *Andrew Marvell* (Cambridge University Press, 1940), p.82, had no doubt that it did. 'The keenness of grief rejecting comment and the control almost unconsciously cutting it short concur in that measured brevity which both demand. The need to write at length defeated him.' This may be so. Marvell refused to be sentimental about anything. He certainly did not think death daunting or dreadful. He was at pains to put that point of view in his letter of condolence to Sir John Trott on losing the last of his four sons. 'He that gave his own Son, may he not take ours? 'Tis pride that makes a Rebel.'

But he had already written on the page before that: 'I know the contagion of grief, and infection of Tears . . . And I myself could sooner imitate those innocent relentings of Nature, so that they spring from tenderness only and humanity, not from an implacable sorrow . . . But the dissoluteness of grief, the prodigality of sorrow is neither to be indulg'd in a man's self nor comply'd with in others.' That was well said.


# 38   Seneca Translated


The younger Seneca tutored Nero as a boy and was the uncle of the great poet Lucan. Though Seneca's nine Latin tragedies had been pale imitations of the earlier Greek, they were rated highly in England by the Tudors and Stuarts. The Second Chorus of his *Thyestes*, lines 339–403, dilates on 'The Lot of Kings' and ends with these lines:

> Stet, quicunque volet, potens
> aulae culmine lubrico:
> me dulcis saturet quies;

obscuro positus loco,
leni perfruar otio;
nullis notaque litibus
aetas per tacitum fluat.
Sic cum transierint mei
nullo cum strepitu dies,
plebeius moriar senex.
Illi mors gravis incubat
qui, notus nimis omnibus,
ignotus moritur sibi.

Let anyone who shall so wish stand in power on the slippery top of a palace: but let sweet repose satisfy me. Planted in some obscure place, let me enjoy calm leisure. Let my age flow smoothly on, a stranger to law suits; and when my days have thus passed without clatter, let me die (*or* I shall die) unaristocratic but old. On that man death lies heavy who, known only too well to the world, dies still unknown to himself.

In the reign of Henry VIII, Sir Thomas Wyatt translated these Latin lines into verses which he entitled 'Of the Mean and Sure Estate'. He made no acknowledgement to Seneca. Some must have thought it an original poem.

Stand, whoso list, upon the slipper wheel
    Of high estate; and let me here rejoice,
And use my life in quietness each dele.
    Unknown in Court that hath the wanton toys:
In hidden place my time shall slowly pass,
    And when my years be past withouten noise,
Let me die old after the common trace;
    For gripes of death doth he too hardly pass,
That knowen is to all, but to himself, alas,
He dieth unknown, daised with dreadful face.

Marvell's version is lighter and brighter than this. He wrote it in heptasyllabic trochaics and they make a more suitable match for Seneca's airy glyconics. He set out his fourteen lines as one continuous poem, but they really consist of four parts as follows:

Climb at *Court* for me that will
Tott'ring Favour's Pinacle;
All I seek is to lye still.

Settled in some secret Nest
In calm Leisure let me rest;                                    5
And far off the publick Stage
Pass away my silent Age.

Thus when without noise, unknown,
I have liv'd out all my span,
I shall dye, without a groan,                                    10
An old honest Country man.

Who expos'd to others Eyes
Into his own Heart ne'r pry's,
Death to him's a Strange surprise.

The word 'Pinacle' may be an imperfect rhyme, but it translates
*Culmen* well and has its Biblical association with the Temptation of
Jesus. In St Matthew IV 5, and St Luke IV 9, the Devil placed Him on
'a pinnacle of the Temple' in Jerusalem. The correcting hand in T2
changed 'Tott'ring', to 'Giddy' and 'Pinacle' to 'slipp'ry hill'. E. S.
Donno adopted the T2 reading in her *Andrew Marvell* (Penguin,
1972), p.137. I have not. Only the rhyme would be improved.

It was characteristic of Marvell to import metaphor. His 'Nest' and
his 'Stage' were metaphors that came readily to his mind and they
typify country and town. Equally characteristic was the personification of leisure and age. Indeed, his first seven lines reproduce
the start of his poem 'The Garden' in essence.

His final triplet owes its magnificent end to the thought added by
Wyatt to Seneca. The Latin merely contrasted '*notus omnibus*',
'known to all', with '*ignotus sibi*', 'unknown to himself'. Wyatt read
into the latter the shock of a death that was part of the state of
unknowing and he finished 'dazed with dreadful face'. Marvell's
ending adopts that, more tenderly but more dramatically:

Death to him's a Strange surprise.

Two thoughts should come to mind if there is any attempt to date
this poem exactly. When Marvell was fifty, he bought a cottage in

Highgate, five miles from his busy Westminster. On Saturday, 3 May 1673 he wrote to his fellow MP Sir Edward Harley: 'I intend by the end of next week to betake myself some five miles off to injoy the spring and my privacy.' That was the 'country' for him. Furthermore, and this is the second thought, as the 1660s wore on and the 1670s started, the political divisions of England polarised into the obsequious and well-rewarded Court Party and the sturdy, unrewarded Country Party to which Harley and Marvell belonged and from which the Whig Party was soon to arise. With some feeling Marvell can begin 'Climb at Court for me that will'; 'for me' in the sense of 'as far as I am concerned'. With some feeling he can picture himself in line 11 as 'An old honest Country man', above bribes and, despite the loose Age, uncorrupted. But he *has pried* into his own heart and he *has* acquired a rigorous and wry *self-knowledge*.

Copies of his translation appear in the Bodleian MS Rawlinson poet. 90 and 196 and in the British Museum Additional MS. 29921. I regard it as a fairly late lyric. Hence its position in this book.

# 39   'On Mr Milton's *Paradise lost*'

Thus Marvell's title was printed in the 1681 Folio of his *Miscellaneous Poems*. Thus *Paradise lost* was spelt on the nine different title pages of Milton's first edition in 1667–9. In the second edition of 1674 the spelling became *Paradise Lost* and Marvell's poem was headed *On Paradise Lost*. That was its first appearance in print and only the initials A. M. gave a clue to the identity of the author. It next appeared in the third edition of 1678.

> When I beheld the Poet blind, yet bold,
> In slender Book his vast Design unfold,
> *Messiah* Crown'd, *Gods* Reconcil'd Decree,
> Rebelling *Angels*, the Forbidden Tree,
> Heav'n, Hell, Earth, Chaos, All; the Argument          5
> Held me a while misdoubting his Intent,
> That he would ruine (for I saw him strong)
> The sacred Truths to Fable and old Song,
> (So *Sampson* groap'd the Temples Posts in spight)

The World o'rewhelming to revenge his Sight. 10
    Yet as I read, soon growing less severe,
I lik'd his Project, the success did fear;
Through that wide Field how he his way should find
O're which lame Faith leads Understanding blind;
Lest he perplext the things he would explain, 15
And what was easie he should render vain.
    Or if a Work so infinite he spann'd,
Jealous I was that some less skilful hand
(Such as disquiet always what is well,
And by ill imitating would excell) 20
Might hence presume the whole Creations day
To change in Scenes, and show it in a Play.
    Pardon me, *mighty Poet*, nor despise
My causeless, yet not impious, surmise.
But I am now convinc'd, and none will dare 25
Within thy Labours to pretend a Share.
Thou hast not miss'd one thought that could be fit,
And all that was improper dost omit:
So that no room is here for Writers left,
But to detect their Ignorance or Theft. 30
    That Majesty which through thy Work doth Reign
Draws the Devout, deterring the Profane.
And things divine thou treatst of in such state
As them preserves, and Thee inviolate.
At once delight and horrour on us seize, 35
Thou singst with so much gravity and ease;
And above humane flight dost soar aloft,
With Plume so strong, so equal, and so soft.
The *Bird* nam'd from that *Paradise* you sing
So never Flags, but alwaies keeps on Wing. 40
    Where couldst thou Words of such a compass find?
Whence furnish such a vast expense of Mind?
Just Heav'n Thee, like *Tiresias*, to requite,
Rewards with *Prophesie* thy loss of Sight.
    Well mightst thou scorn thy Readers to allure 45
With tinkling Rhime, of thy own Sense secure;
While the *Town-Bayes* writes all the while and spells,
And like a Pack-Horse tires without his Bells.
Their Fancies like our bushy Points appear,
The Poets tag them; we for fashion wear. 50

I too transported by the *Mode* offend,
And while I meant to *Praise* thee, must Commend.
Thy verse created like thy *Theme* sublime,
In Number, Weight, and Measure, needs not *Rhime*.

This tribute of Marvell's is based on the reading of a first edition copy of *Paradise Lost* not earlier than the fifth issue, printed late in 1668. It was only then that two prose additions of Milton's were inserted between title page and text as aids to the 'Courteous Reader'. These were THE ARGUMENT, a book-by-book synopsis which totalled 2500 words, and THE VERSE, a 250-word note justifying the absence of rhyme. It was this note that gave Marvell his concluding lines 45–54, and this 'Argument' that gave him his initial 'misdoubts' in lines 5–10. The 'slender Book' of line 2 was thus a quarto of 356 unnumbered pages in one of the fifth to ninth issues; fatter by fourteen pages than any of the first to the fourth, but still 'slender'.

What Milton's note called 'the jingling sound of like endings', Marvell's line 46 calls 'tinkling Rhime'; with a pedestrian poet, he says, it has the encouraging effect of bells on a pack-horse. Where Milton's note spoke of the use of rhyme by 'some famous modern Poets, carried away by Custom, but much to their own vexation, hindrance, and constraint to express many things otherwise, and for the most part worse then else they would have exprest them', Marvell accepts with a smile that all this is true of himself. (Does that make him a 'famous modern Poet'?) In lines 51–2 he takes 'carried away by Custom' and turns it into 'transported by the Mode' and he pleads guilty to the constraint to express '*Praise*' otherwise, by the worse word 'Commend', for the sake of a rhyme with 'offend'. The non-rhyming Milton he compliments in line 46 as 'of thy own Sense secure'.

The less obvious jest in lines 45–54 is the satire on Dryden. He is 'the Town-Bayes'. Because he was the new Poet Laureate, he had been introduced as 'Mr Bayes' into Buckingham's play *The Rehearsal*, which was staged in December 1671 and published in July 1672. The portrait showed an unoriginal writer turning other men's prose into verse or other men's verse into prose and called this 'transversing' and 'transprosing'. Dryden had created a fashion by writing rhyming tragedies for the stage and he soon sought to rhyme *Paradise Lost*. In the 'Minutes on the Life of Mr John Milton' which Aubrey jotted down in 1681, it is stated that Dryden 'went to him to have leave to putt his Paradise-lost into a Drama in Rhyme: Mr. Milton received

him civilly and told him he would give him leave to tagge his Verses';
that is, 'tag his Lines'. It was not an original expression for rhyming;
Marvell himself had used it in 1672. Pairs of laces were 'tagged' with
metal points by the makers, and rhyming could give the same finish to
a pair of verse lines. Marvell's 'bushy Points' in line 49 were more
elaborate laces with tasselled ends which hung below the tying of a
fashionable man's collar or where the doublet was fastened to a man's
hose; he says *our* because he is speaking for contemporary men.

According to Dryden it took him a whole month to work *Paradise
Lost* into a rhyming opera in five acts. Its printing was licensed on 17
April 1674, but it was not in fact printed for another three years and it
was never set to music or staged. Marvell's lines 18–22 and 25–6
reveal a certainty that the Dryden version had been still-born. Since
his poem was printed by 6 July 1674, one concludes that he finished it
in late May or early June.

He and Milton were then in close touch again after a long
interruption. In *The Rehearsal Transpros'd: The Second Part* (ed.
Smith, Oxford University Press, 1971, p.311) Marvell tells his
antagonist, Archdeacon Parker:

> You do three times at least in your *Reproof* . . . run upon an
> Author *J. M.* which does not a little offend me. For why should any
> other mans reputation suffer in a contest betwixt you and me? But
> it is because you resolved to suspect that he had a hand in my
> former book, wherein, whether you deceive your self or no, you
> deceive others extremely. For by chance I had not seen him of two
> years before; but after I undertook writing, I did more carefully
> avoid either visiting him or sending to him, least I should any way
> involve him in my consequences.

Marvell wrote this in December 1673, having written his 'former
book', *The Rehearsal Transpros'd*, in the autumn of 1672. It was a
perilous undertaking to mock the Archbishop of Canterbury's
Chaplain and to attack the official policy of Church and State on
behalf of the oppressed Dissenters. To do it in an unlicensed,
anonymous book was almost suicidal. Fortunately the King liked
anything that gave him a good laugh and so he sheltered the author.
Indeed, Marvell was able to publish *The Second Part* openly over his
name. By the time it came out he had resumed his visits to Milton
after a three-year gap, during which the blind poet had published

*Paradise Regained* and *Samson Agonistes* in 1671 and the second edition of his *Minor Poems* in 1673.

Marvell's poem 'On *Paradise lost*' is the sort of tribute that would help to sell the book, but it is a judicious tribute. He rightly insists on Milton's triumph over the handicap of blindness. He emphasises the vastness of the design, the sublimity of the theme, the majesty of the language, its wide-ranging vocabulary, the immense scholarship involved, the skill of the versification, the sustained grandeur of the performance. 'Milton has succeeded in spanning the infinite. He has found his way through the wide field of Christian theology. He has picked his material well. He has blended gravity and ease, horror and delight.'

The 'Number, Weight, and Measure' of the last line are taken from Wisdom, XI 20: 'Thou hast arranged all things in measure and number and weight.' But the quotation is wittily adapted to the new context. For 'Weight' recalls the gravity remarked on in line 36, while 'Measure' and 'Number' both figured in Milton's note on the verse in senses not intended in the Book of Wisdom. The note began: 'The Measure is English Heroic Verse without Rime.' It went on to say that in poetry 'true musical delight' consisted 'onely in apt Numbers, fit quantity of Syllables, and the sense variously drawn out from one verse into another'.

> Thy verse created like thy *Theme* sublime,
> In Number, Weight, and Measure, needs not *Rhime*.

# 40   'To his Coy Mistress'

This masterpiece was not made in six days or even six years. Stray connections with poems published by Cowley in 1647, Herrick in 1648 and Lovelace in 1647–49 suggest a beginning in England after Marvell's return from abroad; the Cavalier tone suggests a London beginning. But there is evidence that he worked on the poem again in the 1670s and that its final perfection owed much to improvements made then.

The title would not have been novel in 1649. It is quite wrong to read a 'Marvellian detachment' into the choice of 'his' and not 'my'. John Donne made the same choice in the Elegies 'On His Mistris' and 'To his Mistris Going to Bed'. The arch-amorist Thomas Carew worked 'My Mistress' into ten titles, but worked 'His Mistress' into six more, including one 'To his jealous Mistris'. It is equally wrong to credit Marvell with any 'extension' of the meaning of 'coy'. Randolph in 1638 and Carew in 1640 had already used it of a 'sexually reluctant' female and, a whole generation earlier, Shakespeare in *Venus and Adonis*, lines 95–6, had used it of a 'sexually reluctant' male:

> O pity, gan she cry, flint-hearted boy,
> 'Tis but a kiss I beg, why art thou coy?

Of Marvell's three unequal sections, this first is the longest:

> Had we but World enough, and Time,
> This coyness Lady were no crime.
> We would sit down, and think which way
> To walk, and pass our long Loves Day.
> Thou by the *Indian Ganges* side      5
> Should'st Rubies find: I by the Tide
> Of *Humber* would complain. I would
> Love you ten years before the Flood:
> And you should if you please refuse
> Till the Conversion of the *Jews*.      10
> My vegetable Love should grow
> Vaster then Empires, and more slow.
> An hundred years should go to praise
> Thine Eyes, and on thy Forehead Gaze.
> Two hundred to adore each Breast:      15
> But thirty thousand to the rest.
> An Age at least to every part,
> And the last Age should show your Heart.
> For Lady you deserve this State;
> Nor would I love at lower rate.      20

Two distinct ten-line stanzas are discernible above, the same stanza form that Marvell used throughout 'A Dialogue between the Soul and Body'. For some reason he decided not to continue it here. What

he did continue was a deliberate interweaving of 'World' and 'Time';
they were his warp and his weft. The poem thus goes beyond the
limits of *carpe diem* or *carpe florem*. It says more than 'Gather ye
Rosebuds while ye may', though in line 37 it will say that.

'World enough' means 'a large enough extent of the terrestrial
globe'. There must be room for India and England. One is reminded
of the global imagination of Donne: 'If some King of the earth have
so large an extent of Dominion, in North, and South, as that he
hath Winter and Summer together in his Dominions, so large an
extent East and West, as that he hath day and night together in his
Dominions, much more hath God mercy and judgement together'.
Marvell's imagined horizons were equally wide.

'Time' implies 'Time enough'. There has to be room for all the
future and most of the past. Modern readers must step back into the
seventeenth century if they are to appreciate the daring degree of
hyperbole here. According to the Bible-based Stuart chronology, the
World was created in 4000 B.C. and the First Age ended with Noah's
Flood in 2344 B.C., *Anno Mundi* 1656. The Third Age began with
start of the Hebrew wanderings in 1917 B.C., the Fourth with the
Exodus from Egypt in 1487 B.C., the Fifth with the building of
Solomon's Temple in 1008 B.C., the Sixth with the burning of the
Temple in 583 B.C. and the Seventh with the Birth of Christ; '*mundi
melioris ab ortu*' ('from the start of a better world'), in Marvell's own
Latin verse phrase.

He was living in the Seventh Age of the World. For him A.D. 1649
was *Anno Mundi* 5649, some 4000 years after the Flood. Thus far, the
Ages had averaged 800 years each. The Last Age, according to
Romans XI and Revelation VII, was to coincide with the conversion
of all Israel to Christ. Many Christians in A.D. 1649 believed this
culmination to be near. Francis Potter, using methods of his own,
reckoned that the world would end on 10 November 1666. Marvell's
playful 'thirty thousand years' implicitly scouted such notions. As he
imagined it, he would have time to devote 'An Age at least to every
part' of the Lady's beauty. He would go back and begin his courtship
all over again at a point 'ten years before the Flood' (that is, in 2354
B.C.) and patiently suffer her 'coyness' for 30,600 years. They would
put their heads together and agree to tread different paths (ways) and
select different methods (ways) of passing the time, thereby exploit-
ing their lovers' dominion over the whole world.

'State' in line 19 means 'protracted ceremoniousness'. In 20 'lower
rate' means 'a less exalted estimate of your worth'. He adopts the

fashionable Cavalier stance. He has no eye for any other lady. He bows to her superior worth.

Cavalier sensibility succeeded best when laced with Cavalier wit. His aim is to provoke her to mirth. There is warmth in laughter and he hopes to thaw her that way. If he does not succeed with 'the Ganges' and 'Rubies' or 'the Conversion of the Jews', surely he will with:

> My vegetable Love should grow
> Vaster than Empires, and more slow.

The word 'vegetable' is a genuine metaphor, not a generic term, here. Metaphors are compressed similes and in 1667 Marvell used the full simile, uncompressed, in *Clarindon's House-Warming*, lines 53—6, about the Earl of Clarendon's new London house:

> They approved it thus far, and said it was fine;
> Yet his Lordship to finish it would be unable;
> Unless all abroad he divulg'd the design,
> For his House would then grow like a Vegetable.

The Earl of Clarendon ran out of funds in 1665 when his new mansion in St James's was half-built. As a Lord Chancellor brimful of patronage, he could surely have attracted all the funds he needed in 'gifts'. The fact is that 'vegetables' included trees then, and all the rest of plant life. Swift wrote of the Lilliputians in *Gulliver's Travels* (1700), chapter 6: 'Their smallest trees are about seven Foot high . . . The other vegetables are in the same proportion.' The first property of 'vegetables' was growth. Ideal love also grows. 'Thirty thousand years' and more might indeed make Marvell's 'vegetable Love . . . grow vaster than Empires', though, like some trees, slower than empires to grow.

It is interesting that Marvell had this same 'vegetable' image in mind as late as 1667, because the Bodleian Library has an earlier draft of 'To his Coy Mistress' (MS. Don. b.8, pp.283—4), which was written after 1667. It was copied fair without title or paragraphs in 1672 by Sir William Haward of Tandridge. From 1661 to 1678 he was a fellow-MP and Westminster neighbour of Marvell's. This manuscript has 36 lines, ten short of the 46 in the 1681 Folio. The second and third sections in 1681 had twelve and fourteen lines. In Haward's MS. each has eight. In fact, the Haward MS. could well be

set out in four stanzas of ten, ten, eight, eight lines. The first section is
present in full and the differences, though frequent, are slight. It reads
as follows:

> Had I but world enough, and tyme,
> This Coynesse, Madam, were noe Crime.
> I could sitt downe, and thinke, which way
> To walke, and passe our long-loves day.
> You by the Indian Ganges side                           5
> Should Rubyes seeke, I by the Tide
> Of Humber would complaine, I wou'd
> Love you ten yeares before the Floud,
> And you should, if you please, refuse,
> Till the Conversion of the Jewes.                       10
> My vegetable Love should grow
> Vaster then Empires, but more slow.
> One hundred yeares should goe to prayse
> Your Brow, and on your forehead gaze;
> Two hundred to adore your eyes,                         15
> But thirty thousand to your Thighes.
> An age att least to every part,
> And the last Age to shew your heart.
> For, Madam, you deserve this State,
> Nor can I love att lower Rate.                          20

The chief deviation is the 'eyes–Thighes' rhyme in lines 15 and 16.
It cannot be just a mistake. Marvell used a 'lies–Thighs' rhyme in 'The
Gallery' and there is an attraction in the extra 'th' of 'thirty thousand
to your Thighes'. But if 'thirty thousand to the rest' is less alliterative,
it is also less crude. And the tapering, downward inspection suggested
by 'Eyes and Forehead', then 'Breast,' then 'the rest', is better than the
more random 'Brow' and 'forehead', then 'eyes' and then 'Thighes'.
Moreover the adoration of 'each Breast' suggests an apt image of a
statuesque Madonna and a kneeling adorer.

Haward's more distant 'Madam' and his 'you' and 'your', unvaried
throughout his thirty-six lines, also proclaim a version earlier than the
Folio of 1681. So does the deliberate 'I' (twice) and the 'could' in line
3 and the 'can' in line 20; and so does the 'seeke' in line 6.

In two respects the 1681 version is technically more sophisticated.
First, the sound is cleverly varied by ringing the changes on 'you',
'your', 'thou', 'thy' and 'thine'. Second, variety is also achieved by

deploying the full tense of 'I would'. Marvell uses all three persons, singular and plural, with strict grammatical correctness: 'I would, thou shouldest, it should, we would, you should, they should'. Under French influence, seventeenth-century English grammar was stricter in the 1670s than it had been before. But common to Haward and the 1681 Folio is the conjunctive 'please' in line 9 after the conjunction 'if', a rule Marvell had always observed.

T. S. Eliot, in his 1921 essay 'Andrew Marvell' (reprinted in *Selected Essays*, Faber, 1932, pp.292–304), commended the sudden surprise which he regarded as the great virtue of the second section. Yet when a poem begins 'Had we but' (if only we had), the reader surely knows that what follows is necessarily unfulfilled; sooner or later there will be a 'But'. The virtues of the second section are really the same as the virtues of the first — sensibility, imagination and wit. There is also heightened drama and a new terseness to match the new time-scale. Professor Grierson in *Metaphysical Lyrics: Donne to Butler* (Oxford University Press), also in 1921, pronounced this section 'the very roof and crown of the metaphysical lyric, at once fantastic and passionate'. Coming from him, that was high praise. This is the 1681 version:

> But at my back I alwaies hear
> Times winged Charriot hurrying near:
> And yonder all before us lye
> Desarts of vast Eternity.
> Thy Beauty shall no more be found;                    25
> Nor, in thy marble Vault, shall sound
> My ecchoing Song: then Worms shall try
> That long preserv'd Virginity:
> And your quaint Honour turn to dust;
> And into ashes all my Lust.                           30
> The Grave's a fine and private place,
> But none I think do there embrace.

The first couplet dispels unreality at once. Time does not dawdle. Time flies. Time is an enemy with wings on his chariot. He excels in pursuit. To be overtaken by Time is to die. The three successive words 'wingèd Charriot hurrying' are all disyllabic and combine to suggest urgent progression.

In the Haward MS. a different first line gave the couplet a staccato start:

> But harke, behind meethinkes I heare
> Tymes winged Charriot hurrying neare, . . .

The 1681 version improved on this first line, but the second line was perfect already and could not be improved.

In the next couplet we *see* eternity ahead, expressed in 'World' terms of dry, barren Saharas of sand; the very opposite of the fertilising waters of the Ganges and the familar tide of the Humber, which for Marvell spelt home. The pace is slowed down and the imagined monotony marked by three stressed 'ah' sounds (in the pronunciation of the day):

> Desárts   of vást   Etár     nitý.

Herrick had written 'Sea of vast Eternitie' in his poem 'Eternitie' in 1648, but Marvell is capitalising here, as the argument proves, on the poem 'My Dyet' in Cowley's collection, *The Mistress* (1647). Its third stanza went thus:

> On a *Sigh* of Pity I a year can live,
>     One *Tear* will keep me twenty at least,
>     Fifty a gentle *Look* will give;
> An hundred years on one *kind word* I'll feast:
>     A thousand more will added be,
> If you an Inclination have for me;
> And all beyond is vast *Eternity*.

Benlowes and Davenant and Cowley (a second time) wrote 'vast Eternity' before Isaac Watts, who alone could have had it from Marvell, printed the same combination in his hymn 'Before Jehovah's awful throne' in 1719:

> Wide as the world is Thy command;
> Vast as Eternity Thy love.

With keen directness Marvell next confronts the lady with the imminence of her death (though this is as much make-believe as the first section was). The three irresistible 'shalls' toll her knell. Her beauty 'shall' vanish from view. In her marble vault (a patrician setting) his song 'shall' not sound. Worms 'shall' set about deflowering her corpse. Each prospect is a degree more galling than the one before.

The words 'dust' and 'ashes', so deftly juxtaposed, (her dust, his ashes), echo the committal words of the Burial Service: 'We commit their bodies to the ground; earth to earth, ashes to ashes, dust to dust.' This thought leads naturally on to the grave (though 'grave' contradicts 'marble vault').

> The Gráve's a fíne and prívate pláce,
> But nóne I thínk do thére embráce.

The apparent artlessness here is partly due to the colloquial tone, partly to the normality of the iambic metre, but most to the masterly workmanship; the best art never seems contrived.

Consider the sound of the first line. The four vowels in the stressed syllables go 'a, i, i, a', forming a chiasmus. The three alliterating consonants, uninverted, go 'r, v, p, r, v, p'. Balance and euphony result. Consider 'a fine and private place' next. In such words a contemporary of Marvell's might have enthused over what we call 'a stately home': an ancestral 'place' in the country or on the edge of a town; a 'fine' house (the very adjective used in *Clarindon's House-Warming* above), surrounded by 'fine' gardens and a 'fine' park; altogether as 'private' a place as any aristocratic couple could want for living and love-making. 'But no couples, I think, make love in the grave.' There is vinegar in that sardonic 'I think' and its sardonic successors, the drawled 'there' and the acid 'embrace'.

The 1672 Haward MS. lacks the last four 1681 lines. It has only these eight:

> But harke, behind meethinkes I heare
> Tymes winged Charriot hurrying neare,
> And yonder all before us lyes
> Desarts of vast Eternityes.
> Your beauty will stand neede of Salt,      25
> For in the hollow Marble Vault
> Will my Songs Eccho, Wormes must try
> Your longe preserv'd Virginity.

It would be easy to explain away the missing lines by saying that Haward forgot them, or the scribe of the copy he was using forgot them. But the 'meethinkes' of the first line above is the source of the later 'I think'. The two could not co-exist. And if Haward or his predecessor forgot these four lines, then in the third section we shall

have to argue that he 'forgot' six more; which would be odd, seeing
that his bad memory resulted in two stanzas of eight lines, after two
stanzas of ten. Haward surely never invented the 'Salt—Vault' rhyme,
any more than he did the 'eyes—Thighes'. And in his version the lady
is to die, but not Marvell. Marvell's live songs will echo in her vault.
That is a big difference.

It should be noted that a 'must' and two 'wills' occupy the places of
the three later 'shalls'. Dr John Wallis in his *Grammatica linguae
Anglicanae* (1653) distinguished clearly between 'will' and 'shall'.
Both indicated futurity, he said, but 'shall' in the first person and 'will'
in the second and third were *prophetic*, whereas 'will' in the first
person and 'shall' in the second and third either *promised* or *threatened*,
he said. This again marked a growing strictness; Charles Butler in *The
English Grammar* of 1633 had treated 'will' and 'shall' as interchange-
able. I would argue, therefore, that in the final version Marvell was
deliberately threatening his coy mistress.

The last word of the 1681 second section, 'embrace', governs the
opening thought of the final third section. In 1681 it read as follows:

> Now therefore, while the youthful hew
> Sits on thy skin like morning glew,
> And while thy willing Soul transpires          35
> At every pore with instant Fires,
> Now let us sport us while we may;
> And now, like am'rous birds of prey,
> Rather at once our Time devour,
> Than languish in his slow-chapt pow'r.          40
> Let us roll all our Strength, and all
> Our sweetness, up into one Ball:
> And tear our Pleasures with rough strife,
> Thorough the Iron gates of Life.
> Thus, though we cannot make our Sun          45
> Stand still, yet we will make him run.

The first five lines are headlong and swift. They contain no
inversion. There is a slight caesura in the first line after 'therefore', but
no caesuras in the next four. The three 'while' clauses drive the syntax
straight forward. The dramatic purpose of the new imperious
swiftness is to sweep the lady off her feet. Such dynamism is the
opposite of the poem's much-enduring, ultra-leisurely start, the
opposite too of the second section's sardonic, slow close.

Yet in the Haward MS. these five rapid lines are a mere couplet:

> Now then whil'st the youthfull Glue
> Stickes on your Cheeke, like Morning Dew, . . .

This 'glue—dew' combination is far better than the Folio's 'hew—glew', better too than the 'hew—dew' of Cooke's alteration in 1726. What makes 'glew—dew' more certain is that the corrector's hand in T2 wrote those same rhymes in. The 'glue' or 'glew' which in T2 'sits on thy skin' is youthful perspiration; in the Haward MS. it 'stickes on your Cheeke'. The Folio then goes on and adds 'Soul transpires' to 'Body perspires', with 'every pore' as the logical connection.

Here Marvell is drawing on Crashaw's poem, 'On the name of Jesus', which went through three editions in 1648, 1650 and 1672. In lines 211—15 Crashaw asks rhetorically what good the torturers did themselves in making martyrs of the faithful.

> What did Their weapons but with wider Pores
> Inlarge the flaming-breasted Lovers
> More freely to transpire
> That impatient Fire
> The Heart that hides Thee hardly covers?

Three lines earlier, Crashaw had written the short line 'Little, alas, thought They', which Marvell matched with his own 'Little, alas, they know or heed' in 'The Garden'. The two poets had every opportunity to meet many times at Cambridge, in London, and on the Continent, before Crashaw's death abroad in 1649.

After the rapid opening, the pace is slowed down to make greater emphasis possible. The caesuras return and in line 39 the natural prose order 'devour our Time at once rather (than languish)' is turned back to front; not just for the rhyme's sake, but also for the retarding effect required by the sense at this point.

> Rather at once our Time devour,
> Than languish in his slow-chapt pow'r.

The 'chaps' or 'chops' are the two jaws with which the now stationary Time munches man. So when Lepidus had been eliminated from the Triumvirate and Antony and Caesar were supreme, Shakespeare made Enorbarbus say (*Antony and Cleopatra*, III, v):

> Then, world, thou hast a pair of chaps, no more;
> And throw between them all the food thou hast,
> They'll grind the one the other.

In the Haward MS. Time's power is 'slow-Chop't' and the verb is 'linger', not 'languish'. These surely were not Haward's 'mistakes'.

The next four lines are the most intense in the poem and yet the Haward MS. does not have any of them. See with what art Marvell manipulates the stresses and varies the caesuras as he nears his new climax.

> Let us róll áll our Stréngth | and áll
> Our swéetness, úp | into óne Báll:
> And teár our Pléasures | with roúgh strífe,
> Thórough | the Íron gátes of Lífe.

'All' was a word Marvell loved to employ. Its double use for the weighty fourth and eighth syllables here provides 'Ball' with an internal and external rhyme. This is a rhyming variation that he had already worked into lines 7 and 8 (which the Haward MS. did have). The italics are mine.

> Of Humber *would* complain. I *would*
> Love you ten years before the *Flood:*

'Flood' or 'Floud', as then pronounced, was a full rhyme to 'would'.

See also how the alliterative twin-stressed 'róll áll' is given a precise counterpoise in the twin-stressed alliterative 'rúff strife' (as it sounds to the ear). The twin-stressed 'óne Báll' acts between as a fulcrum. And observe that the fourth syllable 'up', by virtue of that privileged position, has an extra force which is deliberately contrived; for the word should have succeeded 'roll'.

The eight lines of the final section in the Haward MS. were:

> Now then whil'st the youthfull Glue
> Stickes on your Cheeke, like Morning Dew,                    30
> Or like the amorous Bird of prey,
> Scorning to admitt delay,
> Lett us att once our Selves devoure,
> Not linger in Tymes slow-Chop't power,
> And synce Wee cannot make the Sun                            35
> Goe backe, nor stand, wee'l make him run.

The first and fourth lines above are trochaic heptasyllabics, a metre that Marvell favoured as a young man. In the 1681 version he ruled them out here. There must be some error in line 31, where the syntax goes astray.

The final line unquestionably derives from three Old Testament books. It was the sick Hezekiah's sun that 'went back'. In 2 Kings, XX, Isaiah told him that the Lord would let him live fifteen more years; but Hezekiah asked for 'a sign'.

And Isaiah said, 'This sign shalt thou have of the Lord, that the Lord will do the thing that he hath spoken: shall the shadow go forward ten degrees, or go back ten degrees?' And Hezekiah answered, 'It is a light thing for the shadow to go down ten degrees: nay, but let the shadow return backward ten degrees.' And Isaiah the prophet cried unto the Lord: and he brought the shadow ten degrees backward, by which it had gone down in the dial of Ahaz (9–11).

The story is recorded also in Isaiah, XXXVIII 1–8.

It was Joshua's sun that 'stood still'. In Joshua, X, we read:

Then spake Joshua to the Lord in the day when the Lord delivered up the Amorites before the children of Israel, and he said in the sight of Israel, 'Sun, stand thou still upon Gibeon: and thou, Moon, in the valley of Ajalon'. And the sun stood still, and the moon stayed, until the people had avenged themselves upon their enemies . . . So the sun stood still in the midst of heaven, and hasted not to go down about a whole day. And there was no day like that before it or after it, that the Lord hearkened unto the voice of a man: for the Lord fought for Israel (12–14).

The Joshua and Hezekiah stories are also referred to in neighbouring chapters of Ecclesiasticus, namely XLVI 4–5 and XLVIII 22–3.

It was David's sun that 'ran'. In the Psalms of David, XIX, are the verses:

The heavens declare the glory of God: and the firmament sheweth his handiwork. In them hath he set a tabernacle for the sun: which cometh forth as a bridegroom out of his chamber and rejoiceth as a giant to run his course. It goeth forth from the uttermost part of the heaven, and runneth about unto the end of it again (1, 5, 6).

The three suns were coalesced at least twice by contemporaries of Marvell; in prose by Bishop Joseph Hall, in verse by Edward Benlowes. Bishop Hall (1574–1656) wrote succinctly: 'A good man must not be like Ezechia's sun, that went backward, nor like Joshua's sun, that stood still, but David's sun, that (like a bridegroom) comes out of his chamber, and as a champion rejoiceth to run his race.' (*Meditations and Vows*, 1901, p.7). In *Theophila's Love Sacrifice* (1652), Canto V, Benlowes reversed the order and in successive stanzas wrote of David's, Joshua's and Hezekiah's suns.

## XXI

Canst thou take post-horse with the coursing sun,
And with him through the zodiac run?
How many stages be there ere the race be done?

## XXII

Then, tell how once he shot his beams down-right
From the same zenith, while for night,
Mortals stood gazing at a doubled noon-day's light.

## XXIII

Tell, how that planet did in after-days
Turn Cancer, shooting Parthian rays,
Ten whole degrees revers'd, which did the world amaze.

Evidently Marvell always saw his poem ending in the 'Sun–run' rhyme. The really vital change in his final version was not so much the elimination of Hezekiah's sun, as the insertion of 'our' before 'Sun'. This needs to be explained. But it must be explained in a way that takes full account of the new fivefold 'our'. The five grew out of 'our Selves', the only 'our' in the Haward MS. after line 4; the lovers were to indulge in amorous cannibalism, do away with time and make 'the Sun' run. It seems certain that in the 1681 finish there is an additional idea, which the six new lines are brought in to express. If pleasurable mating were the only consummation, that is fully proposed in the fifth of our fourteen lines: 'Now let us sport us while we may', i.e. while we *can*. 'Sport us' means 'mate'.

Clearly 'our Time' means 'what remains of your and my time in this world'. 'Our Strength' is 'your and my strength'. 'Our sweetness' is 'your sweetness and mine'. He is not saying 'my male strength and your feminine sweetness', though annotators are apt to say that. 'Our Pleasures' may be 'my pleasures and your pleasures', but are more probably both singular, 'my pleasure and your pleasure'; each sexual, if so. What, fifthly, is 'your and my Sun'?

But another question needs answering first: What are 'the Iron gates of Life'? The phrase has baffled the critics and led to much shoulder-shrugging. Most tend to follow F. W. Bateson, who wrote in *English Poetry: A Critical Introduction* (Longmans, Green, 1950), p.9, that Marvell was 'employing a simple image of a cannon ball crashing through the gates of a town'. Geoffrey Walton seemed to be heading for something better, when he wrote in *Metaphysical to Augustan* (Bowes & Bowes, 1955), p.132, that 'Marvell and his mistress are themselves the ball'; but then, quoting Bateson, he added that 'the cannon ball may be somewhere in the background'. J. B. Broadbent in *Poetic Love* (Chatto & Windus, 1964) called the poem 'an exquisite exercise in not making love' and went on to say that 'their strength and sweetness (which, as "lust" and "quaint honour", have already turned to ashes and dust) are rolled into a sweetmeat ball and then turned into a cannon-ball shot "thorough the iron gates of life".' This seems an exquisite exercise in not making sense.

These scholars all saw iron gates at ground level in a town wall. They all sundered 'thorough' from 'tear'.

Now Marvell used 'iron gates' elsewhere. In his Latin verses on 'The Embassy of the Lord Oliver St John to the Federated Provinces' (1651), line 10, he wrote: '*Clavibus his Jani ferrea claustra regis*' ('with these keys thou rulest the iron gates of Janus'). He was drawing on his favourite Lucan, *De Bello Civili*, lines 61−2: '*Pax missa per orbem Ferrea belligeri conpescat limina Jani*', which J. D. Duff rendered in the Loeb edition (Heinemann, 1928): 'Let Peace fly over the earth and shut fast the iron gates of Janus'.

As for 'gates of life', Lucretius used the phrase '*vitae claustra resolvere*' ('to unlock the gates of life') in his *De Rerum Natura*, I, 415, in the sense of 'to die'. And he used '*vitae claustra*' again in III, 396 and VI, 1153.

Since the lovers in Marvell's final version are not merely to 'sport themselves' while they can, but are also 'at once' to devour their time and not stay to be slowly devoured, one can infer that 'the Iron gates of Life', *ferrea claustra vitae*, are to be their exit up in the sky, their way of escape from this life. They are, of their own volition, to finish with this world and with time.

Cranmer's Easter Day collect began with this same 'gate' metaphor in reverse, viewed from the other side: 'Almighty God, who through thine only-begotten Son Jesus Christ hast overcome death, and opened unto us the gate of everlasting life . . . '

There are those who have wanted to substitute 'iron grates' for 'iron gates'. Alfred Lord Tennyson, according to his son Hallam, was one. It was therefore interesting to find that the pen of the corrector in T2 had indeed substituted 'grates' for 'gates'. Either word would render *claustra* equally well. Lovelace used the pair as rhymes in 'To Althea from Prison', and Marvell used them as rhymes in 'Upon Appleton House', lines 103–4:

> These Bars inclose that wider Den
> Of those wild Creatures, called Men.
> The Cloyster outward shuts its Gates,
> And, from us, locks on them the Grates.

It seems possible that he did consider 'Grates of Life', but I have retained the Folio reading here.

What, then, is 'your and my Sun'? The answer now proposed takes account of all Marvell's last six lines. For they are surely meant to cohere. 'Our Sun' is not 'the Sun' any more. It is the 'one Ball', into which all the couple's combined strength and sweetness are rolled up when she surrenders and he has his way with her and they are both pleasured. The two become one and they stay one. With the voracity of vultures or eagles they will devour the time that is theirs in this world and in a hectic exodus *tear* their pleasures *through* 'the iron gates of life' up in the sky. In the far heavens they will enter upon a planetary existence as a minor sun of their own. It will be no tedious existence, for they will make their sun race like David's sun in the psalm. (Observe the mischievous scamper of light monosyllables on the way to the jubilant RUN.)

The vertical flight-path of the 'one Ball' is the same that Marvell imagined the soul taking in 'On a Drop of Dew' or 'The Resolved Soul dialogue', or in 'The Garden', when it was a silver bird not yet 'prepar'd for longer flight'. His most tender expression of this bird fancy was in the Latin prose epitaph of 1658 on Jane Oxenbridge of Eton, his age-fellow and hostess there: '*Anima . . . evolavit ad Coelos, tanquam Columba ex Arca Corporis*' (Her soul winged its way out to heaven, like a dove from the ark of the body').

We can see now why Marvell, with this altered ending in mind, joined 'willing Soul' to youthful body in the new couplet:

> And while thy willing Soul transpires
> At every pore with instant Fires,

and why he took those key words from a sacred poem of Crashaw's.

The link word 'Thus' at the start of the last couplet (line 45) means 'in this form'; by escape upwards through the exit that must be there, 'in the sun-shape of the ball'. William Blake would have engraved it to perfection.

The objector who thinks that this interpretation smacks too much of twentieth century space travel should read again the poems of John Hall (1627–56), that bright young Cambridge undergraduate whose commendatory verses to Lovelace's *Lucasta* in 1649 were printed near Marvell's. John Hall's *Poems* (1647) included 'An Ode to his Tutor, Master Pawson'. In six twelve-line stanzas he proposed a joint sight-seeing flight through the sky instead of the conventional pupil-cum-tutor grand tour. After four stanzas of imaginary looking down at the earth, he urged an escape from this sphere and a far flight to the firmament itself. His fifth stanza began:

> But objects here
> Cloy in the very taste: O, *let us tear*
> *A passage through*
> *That floating vault above*; there may we know
> Some rosy brethren stray
> To a set battalia,
> And others scout
> Still round about,
> Fix'd in their courses, and uncertain too.

What my italicised words state clearly is what I think Marvell also had in mind. Had he written 'a passage' instead of 'our pleasures', his meaning would have been clear. To 'tear a passage through' is to 'hurry forcibly through': to 'tear our pleasures through' is to 'hurry our pleasures forcibly through' and only needs the addition of 'with rough strife' to round off the winged image of 'birds of prey'.

In Haward's MS. this lyric was catalogued 'Poeme amorous' and given no other title. It was W. Hilton Kelliher who found it and gave it to the world of scholarship in *Notes and Queries*, CCXV, July 1970.

He has given it to a larger world now, in photographs on p. 53 of his excellent guide catalogue to the British Library's Andrew Marvell Exhibition, August–September 1978, marking the tercentenary of the poet's death on 16 August 1678.

# Index